CHRISTIANITY
IN EVOLUTION

Christianity
in Evolution

An Exploration

JACK MAHONEY

Georgetown University Press/Washington, D.C.

Library of Congress Cataloging-in-Publication Data
Mahoney, John, 1931–
    Christianity in evolution : an exploration / Jack Mahoney.
        p. cm.
    Includes bibliographical references and index.
    ISBN 978-1-58901-769-6 (pbk. : alk. paper)
    1. Evolution--Religious aspects—Catholic Church.   I. Title.
    BX1795.E85M34 2011
    231.7′652—dc22
2010051205

♾ This book is printed on acid-free paper meeting the requirements of the American National Standard for Permanence in Paper for Printed Library Materials.

15   14   13   12   11   9 8 7 6 5 4 3 2   First printing

Printed in the United States of America

I have come that they may have life.

JOHN 10:10

Lord, teach me to be generous.

SAINT IGNATIUS LOYOLA

Contents

Introduction

I N 1988 POPE JOHN PAUL II put the following questions to the participants of a conference held in Rome to study the relationships between evolution and religion: "Does an evolutionary perspective bring any light to bear upon theological anthropology, the meaning of the human person as the *imago Dei*, the problem of Christology—and even upon the development of doctrine itself?" The pope was obviously aware that pursuing these and similar questions raised by the development of evolutionary science could stir the depths of Christian theology and required serious dialogue between theology and science. Engaging in such study, he observed, could provide a much-needed ministry to people "struggling to integrate the worlds of science and religion in their own intellectual and spiritual lives." But such dialogue with evolution, he observed disappointedly, "has on the whole been lacking among those engaged in theological research and teaching."[1]

This book, *Christianity in Evolution: An Exploration*, is one attempt to provide answers to questions such as those raised by Pope John Paul II that concern the implications of evolution for Christian beliefs. It is also the product of a feeling that I have had for a number of years that Christianity, and notably the Catholic Church, has been strangely silent about the doctrine of evolution. My disquiet has not been about the compatibility between religion and science, a topic that regularly returns to public notice and discussion and that the majority of believers in fact have no difficulty in accepting in principle. Nor has it been about the acceptability of Darwinian evolution to Christian belief, as acceptance has largely become the main attitude on the part of believers and the churches, apart from the militant attitude of the comparatively few who advocate intelligent design. My unease concerns pursuing the implications that accepting biological evolution entails for Christian beliefs and doctrines, to which,

ix

I think, remarkably little attention has been given, as distinct from what I call postevolutionary apologetics, which concentrate today on defending the existence and providence of God and the unique dignity of his human creatures. In what follows, I attempt to remedy this inattention and to identify and explore the wider doctrinal implications of what, in my opinion, ungrudging acceptance of evolution can hold for Christian believers; and I do so in what, in default of other extended studies in the field, I have inevitably had to describe as a personal exploration.

In my first chapter I lay the groundwork by considering the response of Christian bodies and thinkers to the new science of evolution as it developed, and I begin to identify the main Christian topics that I conclude are likely to be most affected by accepting this new scientific explanation of created reality. In chapter 2 I address directly Pope John Paul II's first question, whether an evolutionary perspective can throw any light upon the meaning of the human person as the *imago Dei*, created in the image of God. I pick up a central concern of the modern evolutionary study of sociobiology to account for the existence and nature of altruism, and I offer what I term a theology of altruism that finds its origin in the initiative of God who is characterized as an interpersonal, total love of mutual altruism within the persons of the Trinity. In the incarnation God became a member of the human species in order to provide the human race with a human expression in Christ, *the* image of God (Col 1:15), of the divine altruism that would counter any innate evolutionary tendency to aggressive self- or tribe interest. By his teaching and by his life and death, Jesus confirmed and advanced the ethical horizon of the human species and provided a living and dying inspiration for its members, who are individually and as a whole created to live in the image of God's own altruism.

A second purpose of the incarnation from an evolutionary point of view, which I examine in chapter 3, is to understand the death of Jesus as saving humanity, not from the original sin of Adam and the consequent fallen state of nature, as in the traditional belief, but from mortality and death, a normal feature of all evolutionary life. What I describe as the evolutionary achievement of Jesus was his confronting his own death and overcoming it, returning to life in an act of cosmic significance and, through his resurrection, ushering the human species into the culminating stage of its evolutionary development, in which it is called to live more fully in the eternal happiness of God in association with the risen Christ. Conversely, I argue that accepting evolution leads to dispensing with the need for traditional Christian beliefs in original sin and the "fall" of the human race from divine favor, as well as the belief that humans continue to experience the lifelong sinful concupiscence of fallen nature, beloved of many preachers. These doctrines, I argue, were accepted by Christians as originating within a Jewish culture that was deeply preoccupied with sin (and with sacrificial atonement for sin) and that understood the puzzling phenomenon of death as a divinely imposed punishment for a sin of disobedience against the Creator. As Genesis 2:17 sums it up, "In the day that you eat of it you shall die." However, this explanation, and its implications, is no longer required now that death has come to be accepted not as a mystery that requires a religious explanation but as a fact of evolutionary life that affects all living things.

In chapter 4 I recall the alternative theological tradition that the incarnation would have taken place even if original sin and the Fall had not occurred, as in Scotus, Hopkins, Teilhard de Chardin, and others, and I propose that a fresh, modern relevance is given to this possibility by the elimination of our first parents' fall from grace so that what was previously a speculation can now in an evolutionary context serve as the preferred line of theological reflection on the incarnation. At the same time, this provides an opportunity to offer a critique of the various theories of soteriology, or salvation theology, which have been elaborated in the Christian community from its earliest time as an attempt to account for the death of Jesus as somehow making up for the original sin by appeasing an injured God and providing a remedy for the initial human disobedience to God. A further consequence of dispensing with the traditional beliefs in original sin and the Fall is that there is no longer a need for the doctrine of atonement, because this interprets the death of Jesus as a way of making up for original sin, that is, as a sacrifice that makes reparation to an injured god and thus remedies the sinful state of humanity.

Not only the scientific discovery of the evolutionary significance of death but also the persistent dissatisfaction with the way in which the doctrines of original sin and concupiscence have found expression in Christian thinking provide good reasons for seeking, as I do in chapter 5, a new theological paradigm to account for God's share in human ills and tragedies, culminating in death, which may do more justice to evolution. In preference to modern approaches by way of process and kenotic theology, whose god, I observe, knows neither the Trinity nor the incarnation, I argue that once God has decided to create nondivine beings, notably including human freedom, he cannot but respect the intrinsic characteristics and activities of such beings.

The community of men and women who share the evolutionary progress brought about by the risen Christ to survive death forms the subject of chapter 6, the church in evolution, which has similarities with Schleier-macher's ecclesiology in drawing on human religious experience. Those who are saved have, either knowingly or unknowingly, accepted Christ's message of universal altruism in imitation of God and are thus accepted into Christ's evolutionary fellowship, either in anticipation of his life or as a later reflection of it. Because it is central to Christian belief to consider the church and its Eucharistic celebration as intimately and essentially linked, this chapter also considers the subject of the Eucharist in an evolutionary context, which involves an analysis of the nature of the Last Supper and of how the remembrance of this has been understood and celebrated in the church's succeeding worship. Given the earlier conclusion to which I argue—that as a result of accepting evolution the theme of sacrifice, and especially the idea of Christ's offering his death in propitiatory sacrifice to his offended father for the original sin and fall of humanity, is no longer a requirement of Christian belief—I submit that acceptance of evolution also renders the sacrificial dimension of the Eucharist no longer appropriate, but that its sacramental dimension, which consists of the continuing presence of the risen Christ who gave his body and blood to his disciples to effect the promised new covenant, provides a continuing and indispensible source of inspiration, life, and power to the eschatological community.

In the final chapter I sum up what might be viewed as the main characteristics of a theology of evolution as it pertains to other traditional Christian beliefs and ethical thought. I further argue that trying to preserve the traditional beliefs in original sin, the fall of humanity, and the death of Jesus as an expiatory sacrifice to appease an offended God, whether these beliefs are maintained in their traditional form or are subjected to various modernizing attempts to make them more acceptable, serves only to strain the belief of believers and the credulity of nonbelievers. Clinging to outmoded beliefs in any form also neglects the opportunity called for by Pope John Paul II to provide a much-needed ministry to people "struggling to integrate the worlds of science and religion in their own intellectual and spiritual lives."

The exploration that I undertake here to locate Christian belief in an evolutionary setting may appear to some unduly negative, but it would be highly regrettable if it were concluded that evolution, or this study, were judged to have simply destructive or reductionist consequences for Christian beliefs, such as doing away with original sin and questioning the sacrifice of the redemption. On the contrary, I wish to argue that there is very good reason for biological evolution to be welcomed by Christians for the positive and enhanced alternative appreciation it can offer to Christian reflection. This is particularly the case in the new, central understanding that I propose of the evolutionary twin purpose of the incarnation. This is partly to lead the human species to a higher form of ethical activity based on imaging the altruism of the triune God as exemplified in the teaching and life and death of Jesus. It is also to usher humanity through evolutionary death into a closer and richer sharing in the divine life by being associated with the victory that Jesus achieved in combating human death through his resurrection. Christ's death on the cross and his resurrection thus constitute a significant cosmic event that profoundly affects the evolutionary progress of the human species.

It would be unlikely that what is essentially a pioneering, personal exploration of the implications for Christian beliefs with the acceptance of biological evolution should be devoid of error, misunderstanding, and simple mistake. Nevertheless, it appears to me to be a worthwhile endeavor to undertake, not only in response to the challenge of Pope John Paul II with which I began, but also in light of the definition that I offer in my final chapter of what is involved in the reflection that we describe as theology. More than Anselm's definition of "faith seeking understanding," which runs the risk of being an abstract exercise divorced from any cultural contexts, I prefer to understand theology as a continuing dialectic between belief and experience, which involves what I have in earlier writings described as the continuing attempt "to make experience-sense of faith and faith-sense of experience." Because our common human experience is being faced with a major advance in our scientific understanding of human origins, intellectual integrity invites us to place that experience alongside our past and present religious beliefs, and in the process to hope to cast light on both. As I remarked earlier and repeat below, "the dialectical activity of submitting experience to the bar of belief and of submitting belief to the bar of experience is today a requirement of every believer, on pain of leaving their experience unanchored and their belief unsubstantiated."

The composition of this work has necessitated a considerable amount of discussion over the years between me and various colleagues and friends, with the risk of my becoming something of a bore on the subject of evolutionary theology. As a completed personal exploration of how Christian beliefs can be reassessed positively and instructively in an evolutionary context, I offer it now partly as an apology and partly in the hope that it will make some contribution in providing an answer to the urgent questions raised by Pope John Paul II, while in the process providing some help to those who are, as he expressed it, "struggling to integrate the worlds of science and religion in their own intellectual and spiritual lives."

The two texts that I have placed at the beginning of this study are intended to sum up the central theological message that I draw from evolution. The opening phrase from the prayer of Saint Ignatius Loyola, "Lord, teach me to be generous," can be read now as a reference to the divine altruism of the Trinity humanly expressed by Christ to be imaged in the life of the ordinary Christian. And the verse from Saint John's Gospel (10:10), "I have come that they may have life," may now be seen as embracing the entire divine evolutionary purpose of the incarnation as it unfolds in human history.

NOTE

1. Letter of His Holiness John Paul II to Reverend George V. Coyne, SJ, Director of the Vatican Observatory, June 1, 1988, www.vatican.va/holy_father/john_paul_ii/letters/1988/ (accessed September 22, 2010).

CHAPTER ONE

Accepting Evolution

HE RELATIONSHIP BETWEEN science and religion has long been a topic of debate and dispute, and nowhere more markedly in modern times than as it concerns the scientific account of evolution. Considerable attention is regularly given to the question of whether Darwinism and religion are in principle compatible, and in recent times distinguished contributions have been made by Peacocke, Ward, Polkinghorne, McGrath, Pope, Haught, and others that defend religion against polemical attacks in the claimed name of modern evolutionary theory.[1] In a comprehensive article on evolution in the encyclopedic *Christianity: The Complete Guide*, Gerd Theissen explains and comments on the threats that evolution is considered to pose to theology with the opening remark that "for many people the notion of evolution is an argument against Christian faith, but for others it is a challenge to formulate that faith more credibly."[2] By contrast, James Patrick Mackey is of the view that the popular animosity between evolution and religion is overrated and exaggerated, constituting nothing more than a false myth of a war to the death between science and religion. The disputes, he roundly declares in words that have a ring of truth, go back as far as Leucippus and Democritus and more recently surround Galileo and Darwin and "were not in fact disputes between religion and science at all. Rather were they disputes between, on the one hand, current establishment views representing that inextricable mixture of science and theology which has . . . been shown to be the norm in Western philosophy as a whole and, on the other hand, emerging views that, as part and parcel of the normal advance of knowledge, challenged some important part of the establishment view in each case."[3]

So far as concerns the predominance of evolution in this tension between science and religion, however this is conceived, Antje Ackelén notes that "the evolutionary perspective is today taken for granted in many respects and applied in many different areas, including epistemology, psychology and religion."[4] It should be noted, however, that her inclusion here of religion does not refer to the introduction of an evolutionary perspective into the study of religion, but rather to examining in evolutionary terms the causes for the development, survival, or decline of religion in different cultures or, put more simply in the words of John Durant, examining the idea "that religious beliefs may have biologically useful consequences."[5] There appears, indeed, an apparent unwillingness to consider the theological consequences that result from accepting the idea of evolution, apart from the issues identified by Celia Deane-Drummond in observing that "Darwin's theory seemed to remove all need for a Creator God, diminish any sense of divine providence in the wake of evolutionary ills and suffering, and qualify the importance of humans by situating human life as a brief episode in a long and complex evolutionary history," an agenda that helps to explain why "most of the debates [about religion and evolution] have focused on how far evolutionary theory is compatible with theological concepts of God as Creator, divine providence over creation, and theological anthropology, whereby humanity is perceived as being in a special sense the image of the Creator."[6] John Polkinghorne identifies several further reasons why, as he expresses it, "too many theologians fail to treat what science has to offer with the appropriate degree of seriousness," including the reluctance to become involved in an area of detailed technical knowledge and expertise with which theology is not intrinsically connected, and in some cases, influenced by Barth, "an ideological disinclination" to find truth, or general revelation, outside the pages of divine revelation.[7]

CATHOLIC RESPONSES TO EVOLUTION

As Durant noted, religious discussions and controversies raised by the new doctrine of biological evolution focused on three issues: the interpretation of scripture, the relationship between God and nature in terms of creation and providence, and the status of human beings.[8] Karl Rahner comments on early Catholic views of the new hypothesis of biological evolution: "From the middle of the [nineteenth] century until the first decades of the twentieth, the theory of evolution was almost unanimously rejected by theologians and by some it was explicitly declared to be heretical."[9] Zoltan Alszeghi chronicled the stages in the official Catholic response to the new science, beginning in 1860 with the condemnation by a local church synod in Cologne of evolution in any form as "completely contrary to Scripture and the faith."[10] That same year the First Vatican Council planned to condemn any theory involving polygenism, or the descent of the human race from more than one original pair, but the hasty conclusion of the council due to the Franco-Prussian War prevented any formal consideration being given to the subject. In 1909 the Pontifical Biblical Commission issued a detailed statement (DS 3512-19) that stressed the literal historical and factual truth of the first three chapters of the book of Genesis. In 1941, Pope Pius XII addressed the Pontifical Academy of Sciences on the subject of creation and observed that the many riches of paleontology, biology, and morphology had not to date contributed anything clear and certain on the problems concerning the origins of humanity. "Therefore," he concluded, "all we can do is leave to the future the reply to the question whether one day science, enlightened and guided by revelation, will be able to provide safe and definitive results on such an important subject."[11]

Returning in 1948 to the historical status of the early chapters of Genesis, the Biblical Commission observed more guardedly that their literary genre was quite unusual and problematic and judged that "to state a priori that their narratives do not contain history in the modern meaning of the word would easily lead to thinking they were not at all historical, whereas they relate basic truths presupposed in the economy of salvation in a simple and figurative language adapted to the understanding of a less developed people, at the same time as the popular description of the origins of the human race and of the chosen people" (DS 3864).

The first major Catholic statement on biological evolution was issued two years later in 1950 in the encyclical letter *Humani generis* of Pope Pius XII. This included a wide-ranging criticism of modern theological tendencies in which the pope approved of numerous requests for religion to respect the sciences, provided that this applied to demonstrable scientific facts. Caution, however, he observed, was required regarding "hypotheses" or "conjectural opinions" even if they relied on science in some measure, which affected doctrine contained in the Bible, or "tradition." Hence, the pope continued, "the Church's teaching authority does not forbid that the doctrine of 'evolution,' so far as it enquires into the origin of the human body from already existing and living matter—for the catholic faith bids us hold that souls are immediately created by God—be treated in investigations and discussions of experts in each field in accordance with the modern state of human sciences and sacred theology" (DS 3895-96).

The pope, however, went on to consider and to reject another conjectural opinion, that of polygenism. For the faithful, he warned, cannot accept the view that states that after Adam true human beings existed on earth who were not descended from him by natural generation as the universal protoparent, or that Adam refers to a number of protoparents, since it does not in the least appear how this view can be reconciled with what the sources of revealed truth and the actions of the church's teaching authority state on original sin, which proceeds from a sin truly committed by a single Adam and which has been transmitted to everyone by generation and exists personally within everyone (DS 3897).

In an allocution in 1966, Pope Paul VI referred to evolution no longer as a hypothesis but as a "theory," but he repeated the teaching of *Humani generis* that concerned what was termed by Karl Rahner a "moderate theory of evolution."[12] The most recent authoritative church statement on the subject was the observation of Pope John Paul II, in a message to the Pontifical Academy of Sciences on October 22, 1996, that, although Pope Pius XII had in his 1950 encyclical *Humani generis* referred to evolution only as "a serious hypothesis," it was now the case that "some new findings lead us towards the recognition of evolution as more than a hypothesis."[13]

It is remarkable that in its twentieth-century treatment of creation and human origins the 1994 *Catechism of the Catholic Church* makes no reference whatever to evolution, an omission that led Gabriel Daly to accuse it of "a near total disregard for the difficulties and doubts which beset the average modern believer of good will and critical intelligence."[14] In dealing with the creation of humans and their fall from divine grace, as derived from the narrative of the book of Genesis, the *Catechism* moves confusedly, he charges, between describing the language as often symbolic and accepting it as literal historical fact, to such a degree that he does not shrink from describing such a procedure as a way to "fudge the biblical issues."[15] Sharper than Daly's criticism is that of Joan Acker, who explains why she considers the *Catechism's* approach as an embarrassment in presenting its contents in "a Tridentine fundamentalist light."[16] In addition, Daryl P. Domning describes the *Catechism's* treatment of Adam and Eve as "a theological scandal to one and all."[17]

The absence of any reference to evolution in the *Catechism* was explained, however, by Bishop (now Cardinal) Christoph Schönborn, who had served as secretary to the *Catechism's* editorial committee and who subsequently coauthored with the chair of the commission preparing the *Catechism*, then Cardinal Ratzinger, a shared *Introduction to the Catechism of the Catholic Church*. Commenting on the presentation of creation in the *Catechism*, Schönborn described it as a theme that "has often been passed over for fear of entering into conflict with scientific opinions and theories regarding the origins of the universe." He added that "a particularly delicate subject is original sin," which had occupied the attention of a special commission for some time. On their deliberations and conclusions he reports only that "it cannot be the task of the Catechism to represent novel theological theses which do not belong to the assured patrimony of the church's faith. Consequently, the Catechism limits itself to setting forth the sure doctrine of faith."[18]

By referring to "novel *theological* theses," Schönborn seemed to have in mind various modern attempts made by Catholic theologians to reinterpret the traditional doctrine of original sin, partly as a consequence of the advances in evolutionary science.[19] Neither in the *Catechism* nor in Schönborn's explanatory chapter as secretary to its editorial committee, however, is there any reference to the scientific theory of evolution as having any contribution to make to the church's account of humanity's origins. This turned out to be not entirely surprising in view of the fact that in 2005 Cardinal Schönborn made an astonishing intervention in the American educational controversy on the relative merits of evolution and "intelligent design," an intervention that can only be interpreted as an outright attack on evolution. On the op-ed page of the *New York Times* (July 7, 2005), Schönborn airily dismissed as a "rather vague and unimportant letter" the late pope's formal message to the scholars of the Pontifical Academy of Sciences (a description he would hardly have used during the pontiff's lifetime), in which John Paul II had described evolution as more than a hypothesis, and then the Austrian cleric proceeded to reject the whole neo-Darwinian position as being not at all compatible with Christian faith. In an interesting refutation of Schönborn's position, the director of the Vatican Observatory later more accurately described John Paul II's declaration on evolution as "epoch-making."[20] Further serious criticism of Schönborn was expressed by Pawel Kapusta, and his views were debated in the conservatively minded American publication *First Things* (October 2005–January 2006).[21]

Not long before the *Catechism* was published, Schönborn's editorial colleague, Cardinal Ratzinger, delivered a set of Lenten homilies in Munich on the subject of the story of the Creation and the Fall that he described as "a creation catechism for adults," which contained some reference to evolution.[22] He included in his third homily on the subject of creation and evolution a section in which he considered the scientific possibilities of physical evolution, but he responded without further comment with a strong counterstatement of the need for faith in a positive creation of humanity by God and in its salvation by Christ.[23] In dealing with sin the cardinal contented himself with deploring the way in which today "sin has become everywhere a suppressed subject, but everywhere we can see that, although it is suppressed, it has nevertheless remained real."[24] Nothing is said to explain, far less to comment on, modern attempts, both scientific and theological, to provide an alternative explanation of the original literal account of the sin described in Genesis 3. For any thinking Catholic who wishes to come to terms with modern evolutionary science, the homilies and their subsequent publication must have constituted a disappointment at a lost opportunity.

By contrast to the Catholic *Catechism*'s and its authors' approach, Pope John Paul II expressed a positive attitude to evolution in his comments on the occasion of a 1988 Vatican conference to celebrate Isaac Newton's scientific work.[25] The pope noted the serious need to help people "struggling to integrate the worlds of science and religion in their . . . intellectual and spiritual lives," and with reference specifically to biological evolution he asked the very searching question, "Does an evolutionary perspective bring any light to bear upon theological anthropology, the meaning of the human person as the *imago Dei*, the problem of Christology—and even upon the development of doctrine itself?" In this area he saw how important the need was for an "intense dialogue with contemporary science," but he also noted disappointedly that this "has, on the whole, been lacking among those engaged in theological research and teaching."[26]

EVOLUTION AND CHRISTIAN ETHICS

One field of Christian theology that has recently seen some systematic examination in light of evolution is that of Christian ethics. In his study *Human Evolution and Christian Ethics*, Stephen J. Pope states that "the field of Christian ethics does not pay much attention to scientific treatments of human evolution," and he sets about defending Christian ethics against the reductionizing criticisms of some sociobiologists, while recognizing that "knowledge of evolution makes a modest but real contribution to our understanding of Christian love."[27] A topic that plays a central role in Pope's study is the doctrine of humanity as created in the image of God, a belief that has traditionally ascribed to human beings a unique significance and dignity surpassing that of other animals.[28] As such, Pope comments, it "provides the basis of a strong ethic of human dignity, from which flow a set of human rights, both positive entitlements and negative immunities, that protect and promote human well-being."[29] Nor does this Christian doctrine need to depend solely on revelation or on the immediate creation of every individual soul by God, as tradition has explained it. As Pope argues, in a more modern scientific approach we can accept that "the evolutionary process generated the development of important and distinctive human capacities, notably to understand and to love, that constitute the natural basis for the affirmation that we are made in God's image."[30]

Pope is clear that the human capacities to know and to love are as much a part of the original evolved human constitution as are the predispositions to seek one's own interests at the cost of others and to compete for resources. As he observes, "Evolutionists overstate their case when they see nature as nothing but the scene of conflict and therefore dismiss cooperation as derivative and altruism as illusory. . . . Nature itself is pervaded by symbiosis, interdependence, and cooperation."[31] To such an extent he maintains that, "if human beings are naturally moved by social emotions, then perhaps pity, empathy, and other pro-social feelings are not simply laid on top of a substrate that is essentially antisocial. If this is the case for human beings, then our first-person experience of caring for others is neither illusory nor derivative from self-concern."[32] And, as chapter 2 shows, Pope's examination of the sociobiological attempts to explain, or explain away, human altruism as it is commonly understood uncovers an understanding of this human characteristic that is not as skeptical or as cynical as many evolutionists today maintain.[33]

In his final chapter Pope explores what evolution might imply for the ethical dimensions of the central aspects of life found in sex, marriage, and the family. This involves asking "whether there is an evolutionary basis for the moral norms advanced by the natural-law tradition of Christian ethics, and whether there might be evolutionary support for modifying these norms in some ways." He proposes that "contemporary natural-law ethics ought to attempt a critical and selective appropriation of evolutionary views of sex, marriage, and the family in the light of its inclusive vision of the human good."[34] After surveying a variety of views, he argues that "we are naturally primed to receive and give love," but its expression requires training and education that will take us beyond loving only our kin and friends to be concerned also for the needy.[35] "Claims of kinship can be overridden by more urgent needs from other quarters."[36] By contrast with the traditional Catholic position on the God-given procreative finality built into human sexuality from the start, and the absolute moral conclusions to which this has inevitably led, Pope maintains that knowledge of evolution supports a greater sensitivity to concrete particularities in sexual ethics "because it does not draw such an intimate connection between the Creator's will and the natural reproductive end of sex."[37]

Another major Roman Catholic theological study in the field of evolution is that of John F. Haught, titled *God after Darwin: A Theology of Evolution*.[38] Haught judges that "contemporary religious thought has yet to make a complete transition into a post-Darwinian world," and he develops what he terms a theology of evolution as a way of "how to think about God in a neo-Darwinian context."[39] This leads him to concentrate largely on the nature and creative activity of God rather than on other Christian doctrines.[40] He notes that evolution has disclosed the continuity and interconnection of all cosmic reality, contrary to a previous conviction of sharp distinctions between different levels of being, and he also highlights the random character of natural selection as challenging traditional ideas of divine providence.[41] His main concern, however, influenced by process theology, is to show how "God's power and action in relation to the world take the form of persuasive love rather than coercive force."[42] This, he considers, allows scope for spontaneity and randomness in nature and its mutations, and, as maintained by Teilhard de Chardin, looks not so much "up" to the God of the past and present as "forward" into the future to which God is drawing the world, a perspective that Haught develops systematically in terms of a theological metaphysics of the future.[43]

OTHER THEOLOGICAL RESPONSES TO EVOLUTION

Other Christian bodies do not have an authoritative teaching organ comparable to that claimed by the Roman Catholic Church, so assessing other Christian reactions to Darwinism is more a matter of considering the views of individual theologians or groups of theologians. Hans Küng contributes some useful remarks on the reactions of different Christian denominations to evolution.[44] A valuable survey is provided in Peacocke's study "Biological Evolution and Christian Theology—Yesterday and Today," in which he considers various conciliatory and reconciling approaches to evolution undertaken by Christian theologians.[45]

In England and within the Anglican Church, as Nick Spencer observed, when Charles Darwin's first major work arguing for evolution appeared, it "produced a range of strong reactions. These were by no means easily divisible into religious hostility and scientific acceptance. Some leading churchmen, such as Samuel Wilberforce, the Bishop of Oxford, were hostile; others, like Frederick Temple, future Archbishop of Canterbury, wholly encouraging."[46] Many religious-minded people were deeply shocked to hear that their privileged and unique status among animals was being questioned despite the biblical account of their special creation. At the public debate held in the Oxford Natural History Museum on June 30, 1860, the year after *On the Origin of Species* was published, Bishop Wilberforce, a forceful and fluent speaker who had been dubbed "Soapy Sam" by Disraeli, asked Thomas Huxley, in the absence of Darwin due to his poor health, "whether he was descended from an ape on his grandfather's or his grandmother's side," a debating gibe that cost him a measure of serious support.[47]

The leader of the Catholic Church in England, Henry Edward Cardinal Manning, gave a lead to his community on the subject of Darwinian evolution in a sermon he delivered in London in 1867 in which he attacked what he termed the "religion of science." In this he seemed to allude to the proposed but demeaning affinity between humans and their monkey forebears that was objected to by so many, including Bishop Wilberforce, and that, Manning alleged, traced mankind "to a progenitor among the least graceful and most grotesque of creatures."[48] By contrast, John Henry Newman, a recent convert to Catholicism, claimed to see "nothing in the theory of evolution inconsistent with an Almighty God and Protector." Indeed, it is commonplace to point to Newman's 1845 publication of *An Essay on the Development of Christian Doctrine* as a closely argued application in the history of ideas of the principle of evolution. As he explained to a correspondent, "I do not see that 'the accidental evolution of organic beings' is inconsistent with divine design. It is accidental to *us*, not to *God*." As a consequence he did not "have personally any great dislike or dread of this theory."[49]

In 1869 the respected Jesuit periodical the *Month* published no fewer than three detailed articles on "Difficulties of the Theory of Natural Selection," offering a critical review of the scientific arguments of Darwin's work in which the author, the distinguished Catholic biologist St. George Jackson Mivart, concluded that Darwin had not proved his case.[50] Somewhat less irenic was the review printed two years later by the *Month* of Darwin's final masterpiece, *The Descent of Man and Selection in Relation to Sex*, written by the Jesuit Father Alfred Weld, who duly continued the popular monkey gibe by titling his review "The Philosopher among the Apes" and described Darwin's theory as monstrous and his book as pernicious.[51]

In 1882, as a consequence of public petitions, Darwin was given national recognition in a public burial in Westminster Abbey "in a ceremony attended by the elders of science, state and church," a ceremony at which "whatever doubts they may have harboured, leading figures of the church declared their satisfaction that 'properly understood,' the evolutionary ideas that had seemed so inflammatory in the 1860s, were perfectly compatible with Christian doctrine."[52]

As Desmond, Moore, and Browne observe, "In general, Darwin's support within Anglicanism came from advanced liberals."[53] These included two influential Anglican theologians who clearly saw and positively accepted the Christian implications of evolution, F. R. Tennant and J. R. Illingworth. Tennant expressed his views in detail in the set of Hulsean lectures that he significantly titled *The Origin and Propagation of Sin*, in which, in the words of Peacocke, he "rejected the traditional pessimism about man, as it had been developed from the Bible by the combination of Genesis with the Pauline epistles."[54] As Tennant explained, evidently choosing his language with delicacy, the explanation of the origin, propagation, and universality of sin in the human world offered by ecclesiastical doctrine "presupposes certain assumptions which it is becoming increasingly difficult to defend."[55] Not, Tennant was at pains to make clear, that he wished to deny the reality of sin in the lives of human individuals: That was one thing, but "the original sin with which it is confounded or which is alleged to be its source, is quite another thing."[56] What evolution opened to our consideration, he explained, was

> an alternative view of man's original condition. What if he were flesh
> before spirit; lawless, impulse-governed organism, fulfilling as such the
> nature necessarily his and therefore the life God willed for him in his
> earliest age, until his moral consciousness was awakened to start him,
> heavily weighted with the inherited load, not, indeed, of abnormal and
> corrupted nature, but of non-moral and necessary animal instinct and
> self-assertive tendency, on that race-long struggle of flesh with spirit. . . .
> On such a view, man's moral evil would be the consequence of no defec-
> tion from his endowment, natural or miraculous, at the start; it would
> bespeak rather the present non-attainment of his final goal."[57]

Given such a positive attitude to the idea of evolutionary human development, it is not surprising to find that Tennant had considerable fault to find with four factors comprising the traditional doctrine of the Fall: "the conceptions, namely, of an original state of goodness, of the transition from it to the act of evil, of the derangement of the whole nature by an act, or even a course of sin, and of the hereditary transmission of a disturbance so acquired."[58] He concluded his dismissal of the doctrine of original sin and the Fall with the claim that "the worthiest view of the meaning of the Incarnation—that which finds in it an absolute and eternal purpose of God—utterly transcends all questions of a Fall, and even the relation of Christ to human sin."[59]

In so writing, the Cambridge theologian demonstrates his descent from the broad evolutionary sympathy of the collection of Anglican divines who together comprised what became known as the *Lux Mundi* group led by Charles Gore that produced the series of studies in the religion of the incarnation of the same name.[60] Drawing on the Anglican Tractarian current of thought that stressed the incarnation, these authors found the new doctrine of evolution congenial to their theological temper, and this was particularly the case in the reflections of J. R. Illingworth.[61] The latter, in his chapter of *Lux Mundi* titled "The Incarnation and Development," looked to evolution to cast light on the Christian doctrine of the incarnation in its full breadth, including the divine immanence of the Logos in creation as contrasted with what he judged as various partial presentations of Christianity encountered through previous history. Such partial presentations included for Illingworth, in a remarkable indictment of Protestantism, "the general tendency of thought since the Reformation."[62] As he continued,

> the Reformers, from various causes, were so occupied with what is now called Soteriology, or the scheme of salvation, that they paid but scant attention to the other aspects of the Gospel. And the consequence was that a whole side of the great Christian tradition, and one on which many of its greatest thinkers had lavished the labours of a lifetime, were allowed almost unconsciously to lapse into comparative oblivion; and the religion of the Incarnation was narrowed into the religion of the Atonement. Men's views of the faith dwindled and became subjective and self-regarding, while the gulf was daily widened between things sacred and things secular; among which latter, art and science, and the whole political and social order, gradually came to be classed.[63]

By contrast, Illingworth recalled the rich traditional development of Christology, including the atonement as only one aspect of it, and felt able to pronounce in an evolutionary context that "in scientific language, the Incarnation may be said to have introduced a new species into the world— a Divine man transcending past humanity, as humanity transcended the rest of the animal creation, and communicating His vital energy by a spiritual process to subsequent generations of men." Perhaps daringly, he explained what he considered to be the reason "why the Atonement has often assumed such exclusive prominence in the minds of Christian men" by pointing to the profound personal experiences of human sinfulness and divine forgiveness that appear to be unique to Christianity: the "sense of forgiveness" and "the consequent rebound of the enfranchised soul" of many Protestant believers that evidences "the entrance of an essentially new life into the world, quickening its palsied energies, as with an electric touch." Such people, Illingworth proposed, have felt that the atonement "was the secret of their own regenerate life, their best intellectual apology, their most attractive missionary appeal; and so have come to think that the other aspects of the Incarnation might be banished from the pulpit and the market-place, to the seclusion of the schools."[64]

But this, he went on, has proved to be a fatal mistake. Truth cannot be mutilated with impunity. And this gradual substitution of a detached doctrine for a catholic creed, has led directly to the charge which is now so common, that Christianity is inadequate to life; with no message to ordinary men, in their ordinary moments, no bearing upon the aims, occupations, interests, enthusiasms, amusements, which are human nature's daily food.[65] Indeed, Illingworth appeals to evolution as a further instance of how "secular thought has so often corrected and counteracted the evil of a Christianity grown professional, and false, and foul."[66]

In the later collection of essays published to mark the centenary of *Lux Mundi*, Alasdair Heron charged that one of the real concerns of the original collection of essays was not so much to provide a symposium on Christology as it was an attack on Protestantism. Illingworth's essay, which Heron considered perhaps the finest chapter in the entire volume, was, Heron judged, "far from just to the Reformers," although Heron did admit "there is certainly some truth in it, though still onesided, as a characteristic of certain tendencies in Post-Reformation Protestantism."[67]

THEOLOGICAL IMPLICATIONS OF EVOLUTION

It is a fact worth noting that, apart from some of them devoting considerable attention to a new form of what could be termed postevolution apologetics, as we addressed in the introduction, Christian theologians in general today, in contrast to Tennant and Illingworth, do not appear to be much concerned about the wider implications for Christian beliefs in actually accepting Darwinism. Thus, notwithstanding their spirited defense of religion as the occasion required, McGrath, Macquarrie, Küng, and others do not in their systematic theological writings give much space to evolution, particularly as may concern its doctrinal implications. Even, according to Stephen Pope, in spite of his drawing attention to the subject, the writings of John Paul II himself "are wanting in evolutionary terms," based on the fact that he appears to hold "that any adequate account of human dignity has to rely on belief in the separate, intentional, and direct creation of each human soul by God."[68] Such a view, the American philosopher

Pope argues, that "God infuses a soul created from nothing into prepared human matter, thus creating a person," amounts to an unacceptable form of dualism.[69] In fact, according to Pope, although John Paul II "acknowledged that evolution is 'more than a hypothesis,' his philosophical phenomenology and biblical interpretation showed no influence of evolutionary thinking of any kind."[70]

It is true, of course, that the evolutionary theology of Pierre Teilhard de Chardin focused on Christ and had much to say about his role in evolution, as well as notoriously appearing to cast doubt on the traditional doctrine of original sin, as will be discussed later. In his final writings Teilhard de Chardin provided his definitive description of how the world is converging, moving toward "an evolutive summit" that he called omega point, which coincides with the universal, cosmic Christ, the incarnate God at the head of creation.[71] In other words, "the differentiation of beings (which is the immediate term of their individual perfection) is no more than the preliminary to an ever closer and more spiritual union of the elements of the Universe. The *unique attraction* of Christ animates this great effort towards self-concentration made by created Spirit."[72] However, Teilhard de Chardin's Christological interest is more on the impact of Christ as omega point of the evolving universe than on the constitution and activity of Christ himself.

Likewise, the study of Ilia Delio titled *Christ in Evolution* stresses Christology in showing how our present time is characterized by a new awareness and encouragement of global consciousness, and how this is stimulating a recovery and a fuller appreciation of an expanding cosmic Christology, which she explores through the mystical insights of a number of past and present theologians.[73] As she concludes, "We must discover Christ as new life within us; we must allow ourselves to be changed to a new level of consciousness, a new level of transcendent love, and a new vision of the world. . . . The risen Christ is the inner power of this evolutionary universe that impels us to go forward into a greater unity in love despite the forces of separation."[74] Powerful as Delio's Christological vision is, it contains little about the work of Christ and his personal evolutionary achievement in his life, death, and resurrection as we will explore.

The views of Tennant and Illingworth described earlier, then, may be considered exceptional in positively embracing evolution into their doctrinal syntheses. Yet even these theologians restricted themselves to criticizing the doctrines of the Fall and of the atonement without necessarily or explicitly noticing an intrinsic connection between these two traditional beliefs, such that if there were no fall, there was then no need for atonement or any further consequences for other beliefs. It appears to be the case, however, as I explore here, that evolution uncovers the traditional doctrine of original sin as almost a loose theological thread, so that when one pulls on it other doctrines connected with it also begin to unravel. Haught, then, seemed to be correct when he observed that "it is not yet evident that theology has thought about God in a manner consistent with the data of evolution. Powerful voices in the religious world continue to hold the idea of an absolute reality as far away from evolution as possible. And even theologians who have assented notionally to the compatibility of Darwin and theology have often failed to address the difficulties involved in such a novel union of ideas."[75]

The purpose of this book, then, is to begin to undertake this challenging task of considering what consequences for Christian theology might result from accepting the truth of human biological evolution. This will involve exploring the evolutionary significance of creation and of the incarnation, as well as of the emergence and role of ethics and of religion in the development of the human species. It will also entail assessing aspects of some traditional Christian beliefs and, where necessary, putting them aside in order to make room for a more contemporary evolutionary theology. Thus, as this book discusses, there has long been widespread dissatisfaction over the doctrine of original sin and the Fall as traditionally interpreted and understood. With the acceptance of evolution, I will argue, it follows that there is now no need for this traditional doctrine. Moreover, if such is the case, then there is no tragic human condition of sinfulness, far less "concupiscence," which needs to be remedied or repaired in order to restore a relationship of harmony between humanity and God. This in turn implies that there was no necessity for God to become human for the purpose of redeeming humanity from its dismal state or for a God-man to offer himself in atoning sacrifice to make up for sin. And the impact of this on Catholic belief in the Eucharistic and other doctrines needs corresponding assessment.

More positively and fundamentally, an alternative reason for the incarnation is then required, and this is provided by an evolutionary theology that proposes that the motive for the Word becoming flesh was not to save humanity from any inherited congenital sinfulness; it was for Christ to lead and conduct the human species through the common evolutionary fate of individual extinction to a new level of living with God. Nor was this done by the offering of Christ as an expiatory sacrifice to placate an injured God; it was achieved by Christ's freely confronting death and winning through to a new phase of existence to be imparted to his fellow humans in their evolutionary destiny to share fully in the life of God.

It should not come as a surprise that Christianity and Christian theology may need to acknowledge their need to evolve in order to survive alongside our growing scientific appreciation of the world in which we live and to fit themselves so as to continue to express in new scientific circumstances and in however faltering a way the complexity and richness of God's ongoing creative design. One of the fundamental questions—indeed, a foundational question—that Pope John Paul II asked of an evolutionary perspective is whether it brings any light to bear "even upon the development of doctrine itself." With this perspective in mind, we begin our exploration of Christianity in evolution by addressing the first of the questions that John Paul II addressed to evolutionary science: what light it might have to throw on the Christian doctrine of humanity as created in the image of God.

NOTES

1. Peacocke, *Theology for a Scientific Age*; Ward, *God, Chance and Necessity*; J. Polkinghorne, *Exploring Reality*; McGrath, *Dawkins' God*; Pope, *Human Evolution and Christian Ethics*; Haught, *God after Darwin*; Haught, *Making Sense of Evolution*.
2. Theissen, "Evolution," 448.
3. Mackey, *Scientist and the Theologian*, 26–27.
4. Ackelén, "Science and Theology," 1098.
5. Durant, "Darwinism and Divinity: A Century of Debate," in Durant, *Darwinism and Divinity*, 6.
6. Deane-Drummond, *Christ and Evolution*, 24.
7. Polkinghorne, *Theology in the Context of Science*, 5; and ibid., 7.
8. Durant, "Darwinism and Divinity," 19.
9. Rahner, *Hominization*, 29, also see 26.
10. Alszeghi, "Development in the Doctrinal Formulations of the Church," 14.
11. *AAS* 33 (1941): 506–7.
12. Rahner, *Hominization*, 62; Alszeghi, "Development in the Doctrinal Formulations of the Church," 16.
13. *AAS* 89 (1997): 188.
14. Daly, "Creation and Original Sin," 82.
15. Ibid., 94–96, and 104.
16. Acker, "Creationism and the *Catechism*," 6.
17. Domning, "Evolution, Evil and Original Sin," 15.
18. Schönborn, "Short Introduction to the Four Parts of the *Catechism*," 70–71.
19. See, e.g., Vandervelde, *Original Sin*; and below, chapter 7.

20. Coyne, "God's Chance Creation," 6.
21. Kapusta, "Darwinism from *Humani generis* to the Present," 27–42 at 36 and nn. 75–76.
22. Ratzinger, *"In the Beginning . . . ,"* ix (the German original published in 1986 was based on a series of 1981 Lenten homilies).
23. Ibid., 54–58.
24. Ibid., 63.
25. Letter of His Holiness John Paul II to Reverend George V. Coyne, SJ, Director of the Vatican Observatory, June 1, 1988, www.vatican.va/holy_father/john_paul_ii/letters/1988/ (accessed October 30, 2009).
26. Ibid., accessed September 22, 2010.
27. Pope, *Human Evolution and Christian Ethics*, 36, and 249.
28. Ibid., 195.
29. Ibid., 197. See also 197–200.
30. Ibid., 208. On evolution and the *imago Dei*, see chapter 2.
31. Pope, *Human Evolution and Christian Ethics*, 150.
32. Ibid., 14.
33. Ibid., 215. See chapter 2.
34. Pope, *Human Evolution and Christian Ethics*, 297.
35. Ibid., 308, and 309–10.
36. Ibid., 311.
37. Ibid., 313.
38. Haught, *God after Darwin*.
39. Ibid., 2, and 146.
40. But see later, in chapter 3, on his comments on original sin.
41. Haught, *God after Darwin*, 26.
42. Ibid., 44.
43. Ibid., 87, and 90–96.
44. Küng, *Beginning of All Things*, 90–95.
45. Peacocke, "Biological Evolution and Christian Theology."
46. Spencer, *Darwin and God*, 76.
47. Ibid., 104.
48. Manning, *Sermons on Ecclesiastical Subjects*, vol. 3, 46–47.
49. Quoted in Cornwell, *Newman's Unquiet Grave*, 236. See also 11.
50. Mivart, "Difficulties of the Theory of Natural Selection," (July 1869): 35–53; (August 1869): 134–53; (September 1869): 274–89.
51. Weld, "Philosopher among the Apes," 77, 100.
52. Desmond, Moore, and Browne, *Charles Darwin*, 103; Kitcher, *Living with Darwin*, 1.
53. Desmond, Moore, and Browne, *Charles Darwin*, 70.
54. Peacocke, "Biological Evolution and Christian Theology," 112; Tennant, *Origin and Propagation of Sin*.
55. Tennant, *Origin and Propagation of Sin*, 3.

56. Ibid., 9.
57. Ibid., 11.
58. Ibid., 24.
59. Ibid., 50.
60. Gore, *Lux Mundi*.
61. Peacocke, "Biological Evolution and Christian Theology," 110–11; Illingworth, "Incarnation in Relation to Development," 181–214.
62. Illingworth, "Incarnation in Relation to Development," 182.
63. Ibid., 183.
64. Ibid., 210–11.
65. Ibid., 211.
66. Ibid., 212.
67. Heron, "Person of Christ," 99–100.
68. Pope, *Human Evolution and Christian Ethics*, 170; cf. 206.
69. Ibid., 171, 173.
70. Ibid., 199.
71. Teilhard de Chardin, "The Christic," in *Heart of the Matter*, 92. See 90–94.
72. Teilhard de Chardin, "My Universe," in *Heart of the Matter*, 205.
73. Delio, *Christ in Evolution*, 27–31.
74. Ibid., 136–37.
75. Haught, *God after Darwin*, 87.

CHAPTER TWO

Evolution, Altruism, and the Image of God

S DISCUSSED IN the last chapter, Pope John Paul II once asked a series of challenging theological questions regarding evolution: "Does an evolutionary perspective bring any light to bear upon theological anthropology, the meaning of the human person as the *imago Dei*, the problem of Christology—and even upon the development of doctrine itself?"[1] This chapter aims to answer the question whether an evolutionary perspective can throw any new light on the meaning of the Christian doctrine of the *imago Dei*, or of the human person as created in the image of God. A major puzzle for many sociobiologists in understanding the process of natural selection among humans is how to find an evolutionary place and role for altruism, or for generous other-centeredness, as distinct from self- or group interest. This chapter proposes that from an evolutionary perspective the idea of altruism can provide a fruitful, fresh approach to the doctrine of the image of God by exploring the idea of humanity's being created in the image of God's own altruism and by suggesting that this also correspondingly throws light on the nature of human altruism.

UNDERSTANDING THE IMAGE OF GOD

The verses in Genesis (1, 26–27) that describe God's creating humankind in the divine image and likeness are among the most quoted and reflected upon passages of the Bible, and over the centuries they have been understood and explained in a variety of ways.[2] As we seek first to understand the verses in their original context in the book of Genesis, it is clear that this passage forms the climax of the narrative that begins with the creation of light and culminates in the creation of the human race. After crafting the physical universe and the plant and animal kingdoms, "God said, 'Let us make humankind in our image, according to our likeness; and let them have dominion over the fish of the sea, and over the birds of the air, and over the cattle, and over all the wild animals of the earth, and over every creeping thing that creeps upon the earth.' So God created humankind in his image, in the image of God he created them; male and female he created them."[3]

The clear role of man and woman here, as von Rad expresses it, is to be God's representative in the world, maintaining and enforcing God's dominion over the earth and animals.[4] Such a role for men and women implies a unique relationship and partnership between humans and God as they fulfill their God-given mission in creation.[5] As the Hebrew Bible became adopted by the Christian community as part of the revealed word of God, however, the Genesis verses referring to humans being created in the image and likeness of God were seized upon by early theologians who had been influenced by Greek philosophy and metaphysics, and the passage was given a special anthropological interpretation based on what was considered the unique characteristic of humanity being placed above all other creatures, its possession of the power of reasoning. Thus, in his commentary on the book of Genesis, Augustine pointed out the significance of humanity's being made in God's image so as to have dominion over the fish and birds "and other animals lacking reason." Because of this we should understand that humanity was made in God's image in possessing something that made it superior to irrational animals, namely, "reason, or mind, or understanding, or any more suitable term" (cf. Eph 4:23–24; Col 3:10).[6]

The Bible had revealed, however, that God decided to create humankind in his image and also in his likeness, and some theologians followed the Christian thinker Irenaeus in seeing a distinction rather than an accumulation in these two terms. In this way they applied the divine image to humanity's natural endowment of reason, which was retained even after original sin and the Fall, and the divine likeness to a further divine gift of the Spirit in creation, which humanity lost as a consequence of the Fall but subsequently regained in Christ.[7] In the course of theological history, however, the Irenaean distinction between image and likeness lost favor, but the central idea remained that the divine image that was created in humanity related to the power of rationality, and this was given further powerful support through the influence of Aquinas. In true Aristotelian fashion he explained that "some things have a likeness to God, firstly and most generally insofar as they exist, secondly insofar as they are alive, and thirdly insofar as they are thinking or intelligent. . . . So, obviously only intellectual creatures are according to the image of God properly speaking."[8]

Mirroring God

A major departure from the traditional understanding of the image of God in humanity as being a constituent of the human makeup occurred when Luther emphasized that being made in God's image was not a human possession or a human component. It constituted more of a relationship between the human creatures and their divine creator, whereby they could "image" or mirror the divine being. The implication was that being made in God's likeness was a precarious possession: If humans were to turn away from God, as they did when they were sinning, then they would cease to reflect God, and God's image would cease to exist in them—as had happened with Adam, according to Luther—until it might be restored in Christ.

In the wake of Luther's *Ninety-Five Theses*, Calvin appeared to follow the main current of theological tradition when he explained that "the image of God extends to everything in which the nature of man surpasses that of all other species of animals." However, it is not just in the possession of certain unique attributes that humanity images God, according to Calvin, but in the way in which humans are free to exercise those attributes in a manner reflecting God's own activity, should they so choose. Thus, he continues, "Accordingly, by this term is denoted the *integrity* with which Adam was endued when his intellect was clear, his affections subordinated to reason, all his senses duly regulated, and when he truly ascribed all his excellence to the admirable gifts of his Maker."[9] This new Protestant emphasis on the human activity of imaging God enables Grenz to explain, "For Calvin the *imago dei* does not lie primarily [n.b.] in the possession of the powers of reason and will but in their proper ordering and right functioning so that the human person mirrors God."[10]

From being an anthropological statement about the creation of humanity, the topic of *imago Dei* was later taken up from the Hebrew Bible into the center of Christian theology with Saint Paul's identification of Christ as "*the* image of the invisible God, the firstborn of all creation" (Col 1:15; cf. 2 Cor 4:4; Heb 1:3), and with Paul's further statement that God predestined those whom he foreknew "to be conformed to the image of his Son," so that he might be the firstborn within a large family (Rom 8:29). Through his human existence and actions, Jesus has presented us with a unique *eikon*, or created representation, of his heavenly Father, and we in turn are called to be associated with Christ as his brothers and sisters.

A Social Image of God

Traditionally the attempt to interpret how humanity can be understood as created in the image of God has concentrated on the divine nature, for example, on humanity as imaging the divine lordship of creation or as imaging the divine reason or, in the Protestant understanding, on how humans relate to the divine nature. A further approach developed, however, based on the understanding that it was the Trinity, and not just the single divine nature, that lay at the heart of God's creating humankind, an approach that has become known as the "social conception of the image of God."[11] Christians contemplating the Genesis account of the creation of humanity in the image of God had always been to some extent conscious of their belief in this creator God as being a trinity of persons and even perhaps as operating as such. For instance, Augustine commented on the wording of Genesis: "In making other creatures God said 'let there be . . .,' whereas in creating humanity God said 'Let us make . . . ,' in order to hint, so to speak, at a plurality of persons on account of Father, Son and Holy Spirit. But he immediately indicates that the unity of the godhead is to be understood when he says 'And God made. . . .'"[12] Viewing God according to this social model of the Trinity as comprising three interrelated divine persons leads one to appreciate the meaning and significance of personhood, both divine and human, as concurrently individual and communitarian, and to accept with Grenz that "'personality' has more to do with relationality than with substantiality and . . . the term stands closer to the idea of communion or community than to the conception of the individual in isolation from or abstracted from communal embeddedness."[13]

The fullest expression of this social understanding of God is found in the theology of the Greek term *perichoresis*, or in Latin *circumincessio*, which refer to the mysterious inner life of the Blessed Trinity, in which the Father, the Son, and the Spirit lovingly interact as equal and equally divine, yet constitute a single divine essence and sharing the one godhead.[14] Christian theology arrived at this complex concept, largely developed by John of Damascus in the seventh century, through attempting to understand how the Father, the Son, and the Holy Spirit, which are all attested to in the New Testament as divine, are interrelated in such a way that the unity or uniqueness of God is not compromised. God is understood to be at heart relational, or in essence a trinity, a community of divine persons sharing their life and their love fully and eternally with one another. It is this triune God of whom humanity was created to be the image; men and women were called, in other words, to reflect God by becoming in their own way a loving community of mutually related, caring persons. As Grenz commented, "The ultimate foundation for human relationships resides in the eternal dynamic of the triune God. Thus, humans fulfil their purpose as destined to be the *imago dei* by loving after the manner of the triune God."[15]

The International Theological Commission

This survey of the history of the Christian doctrine of humanity being created in the image of God can usefully close with an examination of the recent treatment of the subject by the Catholic International Theological Commission (ITC), published in 2004, titled *Communion and Stewardship: Human Persons Created in the Image of God*.[16] According to the ITC, prior to Vatican II the theme of *imago Dei* had become neglected in Catholic thought, but on the eve of the council it was being reconsidered, and now the ITC wished "to reaffirm the truth that human persons are created in the image of God in order to enjoy personal communion with the Father, Son and Holy Spirit and with one another in them, and in order to exercise, in God's name, responsible stewardship of the created world" (no. 4). Put more briefly, "communion and stewardship are the two great strands out of which the fabric of the doctrine of the *imago Dei* is woven" (no. 25).

These two aspects of the doctrine—human beings sharing communion with the divine Trinity and with each other, and the human sharing of God's governance of physical creation as God's steward—form the substance of the ITC theological reflection, expressed in regrettably sexist language, whose aim as a whole is, through focusing on humanity as made in God's image, "to reaffirm the divine truth about the universe and about the meaning of human life" (no. 5). Beginning by surveying the contributions of Genesis to the theme of human beings' creation in the image of God and their creation as man and woman, the ITC comments that the human is essentially a relational being who "exists in relation with other persons, with God, with the world and with himself" (no. 10). It goes on to add the New Testament enrichment that "since it is Christ himself who is the perfect image of God, man must be conformed to him in order to become the son of the Father through the power of the Holy Spirit" (no. 12). This process of individuals being conformed into the likeness of Christ occurs through their own personal history and their sacramental life. "Created in the image of God and perfected in the image of Christ by the power of the Holy Spirit in the sacraments, we are embraced in love by the Father" (no. 13).

The ITC document traces the history of interpreting the doctrine of humanity created in the image of God much along the lines that have been previously discussed. It was with the Second Vatican Council that the doctrine was given a central place in Catholic theological anthropology, in the proposition that "the *imago Dei* consists in man's fundamental orientation to God, which is the basis of human dignity and of the inalienable rights of the human person" (no. 22).[17] Moreover, "on the basis of the doctrine of the image of God, the Council teaches that human activity reflects the divine creativity which is its model (GS 34) and must be directed to justice and human fellowship in order to foster the establishment of one family in which all are brothers and sisters (GS 24)" (no. 23). Since the Second Vatican Council, the doctrine has developed, according to the ITC, in a number of ways, including the ideas that the *imago Dei* is not completed in creation but is in a continual process of development in Christ, as intimated in Romans 8:29, that it is linked to the idea of the natural moral law insofar as through imaging God—"in his very being man possesses a participation in the divine law"—and that it is orientated toward the future fulfillment of God's design for the universe and humanity (no. 24).

One of the two major developments in the ITC document is its exploration of the social nature of God and how through humanity's radical likeness to God the divine Trinity plans to share its own inner communion of life with and among its human creatures. "Human beings are created in the *imago Dei* precisely as persons capable of a knowledge and love that are personal and interpersonal. It is of the essence of the *imago Dei* in them that these personal beings are relational and social beings, embraced in a human family whose unity is at once realized and prefigured in the church" (no. 40). The communitarian point is worth stressing. "Christian revelation led to the articulation of the concept of person, and gave it a divine, christological and Trinitarian meaning. In effect, no person is as such alone in the universe, but is always constituted with others and is summoned to form a community with them" (no. 41). It follows, then, that humanity's being made according to the image of God, as described in the Genesis account of creation, applies not just to each individual human being but to the human race as a whole. "In this sense, human beings share the solidarity of a unity that both already exists and is still to be attained" (no. 43). The ITC acknowledges the earliest Christian interpretation of the verses of Genesis as indicating that humans are "distinguished by their intellect, love and freedom" from the other bodily beings with which they share the world, but it goes on to add that it is through this distinctiveness that "they are ordered by their very nature to interpersonal communion" (no. 56).

The other major theme that is developed in the ITC treatment of the image of God refers to humans occupying "a unique place in the universe according to the divine plan . . . the privilege of sharing in the divine governance of visible creation" (no. 57). The biblical imagery of stewardship shown in Christ's parables (cf. Mt 25:14; Lk 19:12) is used to develop this role of humans in relation to physical creation in terms of service rather than of mastery (no. 60). This enables the ITC to undertake two tasks: to remedy past attitudes of exploitative domination and abuse of creation that have been ascribed, it is now claimed, to misunderstanding Genesis, and to counter modern scientific designs on the human genetic makeup and human reproduction by claiming, "Human beings exercise this stewardship by gaining scientific understanding of the universe [cf. 62–70], by caring responsibly for the natural world (including animals and the environment) [cf. 71–80], and by guarding their own biological integrity [cf. 81–94]" (no. 61).

This provides the Catholic Church with its first detailed statement regarding evolution, in which the ITC recalls how in 1996 Pope John Paul II recognized evolution as "more than a hypothesis," while it cautioned that "this cannot be read as a blanket approbation of all theories of evolution," particularly when they touch on the doctrines of the creation ex nihilo and the creation of man in the image of God (no. 64). In addition, the ITC statement includes a welcome observation on the nature of "divine providential causality," which radically differs from created causality in kind, and not only in degree (no. 69), and which it claims can provide an "account of the special creation of the human soul within the overarching plan of the triune God to share the communion of Trinitarian life with human persons" (no. 70).

THE EVOLUTIONARY CHALLENGE OF ALTRUISM

This review of how the doctrine of human creation in the image of God has developed and come to be understood in Catholic Christian theology enables us to begin to consider an answer to Pope John Paul II's question of what light evolutionary reflection can throw on the idea of humanity as made in the image of God: We now turn to one of the major ethical discussion points raised by evolutionary science itself, namely the role and origin of human altruism. It is instructive to begin with the wider context of modern evolutionary thought regarding ethical behavior as this is considered to have developed in the evolving human species.

The Dawn of Ethics

In *The Descent of Man*, Charles Darwin (1809–82) ascribed the evolution of the human species to his wider principle of natural selection, which A. G. N. Flew summarized as "a massive case for saying that species have evolved, and that natural selection has been—and is—the main instrument of this evolution."[18] In the course of applying this to the human species, Darwin referred to a "moral sense or conscience" that he conjectured had evolved in early humanity and that he envisaged as originating in the common social instincts or feelings that "lead an animal to take pleasure in the society of its fellows, to feel a certain amount of sympathy with them, and to perform various services for them."[19] Central to this, Darwin felt, would be the growing awareness of being a member of a community and of being influenced in one's actions by the community's wishes and its approval or disapproval of one's personal behavior.[20] In this way, he argued, the sense of morality would emerge as a human characteristic acquired by the progenitors of humankind favoring the survival of the community and encouraging "through natural selection, aided by inherited habit," the acquiring of such social qualities as "sympathy, fidelity, and courage."[21] As he concluded, with copious practical illustrations, "As man is a social animal, it is almost certain that he would inherit a tendency to be faithful to his comrades, and obedient to the leader of his tribe; for these qualities are common to most social animals. He would consequently possess some capacity for self-command. He would from an inherited tendency be willing to defend, in concert with others, his fellow-men; and would be ready to aid them in any way, which did not too greatly interfere with his own welfare or his own strong desires."[22]

Not that Darwin considered that such human moral development progressed unimpeded or that human moral behavior was universally positive: He noted that the human individual's actions would be determined "unfortunately very often by his own strong selfish desires." However, he seemed to remain on the whole a moral optimist, observing that "as love, sympathy and self-command become strengthened by habit, and as the power of reasoning becomes clearer, so that man can [n.b.] value justly the judgments of his fellows, he will feel himself impelled, apart from any transitory pleasure or pain, to certain lines of conduct."[23] As H. J. Gensler observed, in this way "our primitive morality becomes more rational and less instinctive."[24] Dixon in his turn observed that "Darwin sought to overturn the utilitarian assumption that humans were naturally motivated by self-interest rather than by instincts of love and sympathy."[25] So much so, Darwin himself concluded rather grandly, that "he might then declare . . . I am the supreme judge of my own conduct, and in the words of Kant, I will not in my own person violate the dignity of humanity."[26]

Darwin considered the evolving moral sense of human individuals a distinct asset to any community, which would tend to result in that community's surviving and flourishing. "A tribe including many members who, from possessing in a high degree the spirit of patriotism, fidelity, obedience, courage and sympathy, were always ready to aid one another, and to sacrifice themselves for the common good, would be victorious over most other tribes; and this would be natural selection."[27] However, it need not necessarily follow that for Darwin tribal success was the point of ethics, that is, as some of his supporters and followers argued, that those actions are to be morally commended which promote group survival, and those actions which detract from such survival are for that reason to be morally condemned. The law of natural selection may be universally applicable in its descriptive sense, but it does not follow that it also applies in a prescriptive sense.[28] It has become commonplace to note that, with the arrival of humanity on the evolutionary stage, the entire future and shape of the world and its evolution, including the future, shape, and evolution of the human species, are subject now to human decision; yet it does not necessarily follow that such decisions must be ethically dictated by such cosmic future or, indeed, by the idea of cosmic survival. There could be other moral considerations to be taken into account. As Flew observed, "All those who in martyrdom witness to their conviction that survival can sometimes be too dearly bought do not thereby rebel against Nature's law of self-preservation. Rather they demonstrate that no such law obtains; or, at any rate, that if it does, the human animal does not fall within its scope."[29]

Darwin himself, in fact, argued that it was humanity in its specifically primeval state that saw actions as good or bad "solely as they obviously affect the welfare of the tribe," which was why he commented that "this conclusion agrees well with the belief that the so-called moral sense is aboriginally derived from the social instincts, for both relate at first exclusively to the community."[30] But it should be noted that he is referring here to the human moral sense in a primitive phase of its development, in its aboriginal stage. In fact, for Darwin the human moral sense has evolved into becoming "a highly complex sentiment." It originated in the social instincts shared by most animals and was in its early stages largely guided by social approval and disapproval, as discussed earlier, but over and above all that it came to be also "ruled by reason, self-interest, and in later times by deep religious feelings, and confirmed by instruction and habit" to become what we experience today as our moral conscience.[31] Hence Darwin was prepared to envisage individuals at a later stage of evolution reaching moral conclusions that are not necessarily determined by, or to be identified with, group interests. As he observed,

> The social instincts, which no doubt were acquired by man as by the lower animals for the good of the community, will from the first have given to him some wish to aid his fellows, some feeling of sympathy, and have compelled him to regard their approbation and disapprobation. Such impulses will have served him at a very early period as a rude rule of right and wrong. But as man gradually advanced in intellectual power, and was enabled to trace the more remote consequences of his actions; as he acquired sufficient knowledge to reject baneful customs and superstitions; as he regarded more and more, not only the welfare, but the happiness of his fellow-men; as from habit, following on beneficial experience, instruction and example, his sympathies became more tender and widely diffused, extending to men of all races, to the imbecile, maimed, and other useless members of society, and finally to the lower animals— so would the standard of his morality rise higher and higher.[32]

Küng usefully draws attention to the emergence of human empathy in this development when he explains that "with the evolution of strategic thought there also developed a capacity for empathy, a feeling for the fears, expectations, and hopes of others, a fellow feeling that became basic to human social behavior."[33]

It is impossible to reconcile the moral sympathy that Darwin expresses in the previous passage for various "useless members of society" with the selective program of later social Darwinism, which claimed to have his support for morally preferring both individual choices and social policies that favored only the socially useful and which countenanced eliminating those who were not so favored. "Survival of the fittest," which Darwin had originally used as a purely explanatory equivalent of the phrase "natural selection" to refer to situations of development viewed retrospectively, became in the systematic thought of his contemporary, Herbert Spencer, tantamount to a moral program for society, at its worst accepting remorselessly and morally approving those actions that would favor its best members and would send the weakest to the wall. In such situations *best*, of course, is a thoroughly ambiguous word, partly presuming a dynamic of progress that one is morally obligated to support, and partly offering a naturalistic mental glissade from a factually desirable state of affairs to a morally obligatory situation.[34] As Ruse comments succinctly, "Natural selection cares only about winners, not about the best."[35] Pope judges this "infamous ideological use of evolution . . . [as] the antithesis of Christian ethics."[36] And as L. Dupré explained, "The so-called 'survival of the fittest' does not mean the *best* survive in this game of chance. But the *toughest*."[37]

In his famous introduction of the naturalistic fallacy that argues from actual states of affairs to infer their moral desirability, G. E. Moore explicitly instanced Spencer's evolutionary ethics.[38] And Copleston wrote of Spencer that he seemed "never to have understood clearly that the process of evolution, considered as an historical fact, could not by itself establish the value-judgments which he brought to bear upon its interpretation. For example, even if we grant that evolution is moving towards the emergence of a certain type of human life in society and that this type is therefore shown to be the most fitted for survival, it does not necessarily follow that it is morally the most admirable type."[39] Flew pointed out the simple fallacy: "To say within the terms of Darwinian theory that in natural selection the fittest must survive is to utter only a tautology. But this can be mistaken to be an urgent practical imperative, categorically demanding that we make every sacrifice to ensure that they in fact do."[40]

Darwin's defender and champion, and a distinguished and respected intellectual in his own right, Thomas Huxley (1825–95) brought welcome clarity to the ethical implications of evolution in his 1893 Romanes lecture, "Evolution and Ethics." For one thing, he summarily rejected any tendency to social Darwinism in observing "the unfortunate ambiguity of the phrase 'survival of the fittest.' 'Fitness' has a connotation of 'best'; and about 'best' there hangs a moral flavor."[41] This being so, he argued in an important passage,

> the practice of that which is ethically best—what we call goodness or virtue—involves a course of conduct which, in all respects, is opposed to that which leads to success in the cosmic struggle for existence. In place of ruthless self-assertion it demands self-restraint; in place of thrusting aside, or treading down, all competitors, it requires that the individual shall not merely respect, but shall help his fellows; its influence is directed, not so much to the survival of the fittest, as to the fitting of

as many as possible to survive. It repudiates the gladiatorial theory of existence.[42]

For Huxley, in other words, "the ethical process is in opposition to the principle of the cosmic process, and tends to the suppression of the qualities best fitted for success in that struggle."[43] In principle ethics and evolution are eventually in competition, according to Huxley, and the individual's innate drive in self-assertion, which is essential for survival, appears intrinsically hostile to that genuine concern for other individuals that is considered central to the whole idea of ethics. This contrast, and conflict, between evolution and ethics leads Huxley to acknowledge "the pressing interest of the question, to what extent modern progress in natural knowledge, and, more especially, the general outcome of that progress in the doctrine of evolution, is competent to help us in the great work of helping one another?"[44] No great Christian apologist—he is recognized as having coined the term *agnosticism*—he was emphatic about the need for an ethical approach to evolution, on which his last words may be considered: "Let us understand, once for all, that the ethical progress of society depends, not on imitating the cosmic process, still less on running away from it, but in combating it."[45]

Genetic Dominance

The new science of sociobiology has transformed our understanding and grasp of Darwinian evolution largely through the discovery of the gene and the identification of its primary role in natural selection. As McGrath explained the change, "The neo-Darwinian synthesis is grounded in the assumption that small random genetic changes (mutations) over long periods of time occasionally have positive survival value. Organisms possessing these favorable mutations should have relative advantage in survival and reproduction, and they will tend to pass their characteristics on to their descendants."[46]

The influential E. O. Wilson, described by Ruse as "the doyen of today's American evolutionists," roundly claimed that the time has come for ethics to be "biologicized," and in this he was certainly correct in maintaining that ethical reflection as well as moral behavior must be continually "earthed" in our human biological history and constitution.[47] Whether, however, ethics can be reduced simply to biology, as Wilson seems at least inclined to contend, is much more arguable, and this involves considering his positions on the role of the gene as central to natural selection and on his view of altruistic human behavior as being intrinsically unfavorable to natural selection, the two aspects of sociobiology that are most pertinent to this study.

In the opening chapter of his major work, *Sociobiology: The New Synthesis*, significantly titled "The Morality of the Gene," Wilson identifies natural selection as "the process whereby certain genes gain representation in the following generations superior to that of other genes located at the same chromosome positions."[48] Because of this, evolutionary priority is now accorded to genes rather than to the Darwinian organism, whose function is now recognized as not being to reproduce itself in some enhanced mode. Rather, Wilson argued, "it reproduces genes, and it serves as their temporary carrier."[49] According to this version of evolutionary theory, various activities of the human organism may involve different human feelings, attitudes, and motivations, but these are simply orchestrated behavioral responses that have been "designed not to promote the happiness and survival of the individual, but to favor the maximum transmission of the controlling genes."[50]

In her study of the roots of human behavior, Mary Midgley shows approval of some of Wilson's sociobiological positions, coupled with scant respect for others.[51] So far as concerns his claim for the dominant role of the gene, Midgley charges that from regarding the genes as engineers of human behavior he moves to identifying the genes as "containing the point of the whole operation."[52] For all the human "awe and wonder" that Wilson rightly shows that the existence of deoxyribonucleic acid (DNA) must elicit from us, Midgley maintains that this should not lead us to depreciate the individual humans who will spring from it as if these were in some sense less worthy of respect.[53] On the contrary, one might contend in agreement with Midgley, if the stuff of which we are made is so awesome, how much more so are we who are astonishingly intricate unique permutations of it. "What a piece of work is a *man*," Shakespeare pointed out, not a gene! Moreover, she observes, genes and DNA are names given by scientists to "specific little bits of complex goo." However, "little bits of goo, however complex, cannot design or engineer anything." In other words, she takes philosophical exception to language that ascribes purpose to what is, after all, not a totality, but just a working part within a whole.[54]

It was to emphasize the primacy accorded by Wilson and other evolutionists to genetic activity that Richard Dawkins introduced the popular, not to say notorious, modern myth of "the selfish gene" that systematically reduces everything and every activity to its own agenda of self-replication.[55]

Midgley found the idea of a selfish gene a bizarre one.[56] Similar misgivings, to say the least, are to be found in the writings of Keith Ward, who observed that the selfish gene theory "has great difficulty in accounting for the genesis of culture, of scientific understanding and [especially] the powerful sense of moral obligation."[57] Ward observes that "it seems a rather drastic procedure to pretend that all distinctive human characteristics (especially the development of consciousness, morality, rationality, science and art) can be adequately explained by showing that they were conducive to more efficient domination or reproduction." There is "a certain simplistic appeal," he observes dismissively, in attempting to explain all human culture in terms of one all-encompassing theory.[58]

Alister McGrath, the scientist-theologian, also references Dawkins's selfish gene theory in his forthright book *Dawkins' God*, in which he offers a sustained refutation, not prescinding from the personal, of the "famously aggressive atheism" that Dawkins claimed to derive from his central scientific principles.[59] Interestingly, McGrath appears less critical of the idea of the selfish gene than Ward is, and he even offers some defense on behalf of Dawkins against the strictures of Midgley, which was that describing a gene as selfish is anthropomorphic thinking, definitionally vague, and philosophically lazy. Although McGrath judged that Midgley was making "a reasonable point concerning the validity of metaphorical or analogical language," nevertheless he noted that Dawkins's own point was that "genes behave *as if* they are selfish. . . . [T]heir dynamics resemble those of consciously selfish agents."[60] On this it is difficult to avoid the final comment that the metaphor and its designedly sensational popular attractiveness are now greatly weakened, and the plot thins considerably with the acknowledgment that one didn't really *mean* that genes have designs or selfish schemes to ensure their survival at all costs.[61] Moreover, what could be readily inferred from the selfish gene theory—that all human behavior is determined by the gene's single-minded resolve to perpetuate itself—is invalidated when one reads that Dawkins maintained stoutly, as McGrath acknowledged of him, that human beings are *not* the prisoner of their genes but are capable of rebelling against such a genetic tyranny.[62]

Even when one can discount for purposes of serious reflection the imagery of the gene being remorselessly single-minded in all its activities and influences, there can still remain in some sociobiological writing a more pervasively vague notion of purpose, a purpose that is ascribed uncritically, or at least unconsciously, to nature itself in the whole process of natural selection with its apparent implication of choice. Of course, we can reflect, with McGrath, that the use of purposive language in the whole enterprise of describing and reflecting on evolution, from Darwin onward, is only a fruitful metaphor, which expresses in an imaginative parallel with intelligent purpose and persistence a dynamic process of so-called selection that happens to occur blindly in nature. Yet the very term *natural selection* is to some extent an unfortunate one. In spite of its original usefulness to Darwin in offering a contrast with the term *artificial selection* that is deliberately engineered by horticulturalists and stockbreeders, natural selection can easily be misunderstood as ascribing to nature some capacity for choosing among available lines of reproduction. Yet, as Flew pointed out, "the whole point of natural selection is, one is tempted to say, that it is not selection at all"; one could even urge, he adds, that as an expression it is self-contradictory. Indeed, he would contend, in reality there is no design, only its empty appearance.[63] It is therefore disconcerting to read Wilson describing human feelings of love, hate, aggression, and so on as operating in blends "*designed* . . . to favor the maximum transmission of the controlling genes."[64]

Egoism and Altruism

The need for particular care in scrutinizing any temptation to ascribe purpose to genes or to nature, even metaphorically, becomes more important as one considers the other main plank of Wilson's sociobiological program identified earlier, that of "biologizing" ethics.[65] What Wilson judged to be "the central theoretical problem of socio-biology" is "how can altruism, which by definition reduces personal fitness, possibly evolve by natural selection," or, as he expanded it, how can one explain in evolutionary terms "the surrender of personal genetic fitness for the enhancement of personal genetic fitness in others."[66] The term *altruism* was introduced by August Comte to contrast with the idea of egoism.[67] Literally meaning "for the other," altruism is commonly applied to human behavior that is directed at voluntarily helping others with no purpose or prospect of recompense or reward for oneself. Occasionally it is taken to include the idea that what one does altruistically entails a cost to oneself, but apart from the acceptance of the obvious opportunity costs, such self-sacrifice is not essential to the original idea of altruism, which is more one of contrasting action performed for others with action undertaken for one's own sake. Dixon noted that "Comte trumpeted it as one of his great scientific discoveries that humans were innately altruistic. He contrasted this with the traditional theological teaching that humans were innately selfish and sinful."[68]

Pope observes, however, that "Christian ethicists do not often use the word 'altruism,' because the term is not morally helpful" since it is capable of expressing extremism and fanaticism as well as helpful behavior.[69] In addition, when the term was first introduced by Comte, Christian theologians objected to it as an antireligious and positivist move, although later it gradually became identified by religious writers "as a synonym for Christian love."[70] Edwards acknowledges the theological work that has focused on the central role of altruism, but he also judges that altruism can be abused, since "indiscriminate calls to altruism and self-sacrifice can function to maintain oppression," and more importantly, he claims, altruism as located in God does not do justice to love as viewed from the perspective of Trinitarian life, which, Edwards maintains, has more to do with "mutual and equal relationships."[71] However, not only altruism but even calls to love can be abused in some situations, so rather than avoid the term, what is called for is a continual critical awareness of the demands of particular human situations where it is involved or invoked. In addition, as I shall argue, the richness of divine personal interaction is perfectly capable of being described in terms of *mutual* altruism among the persons, which stresses the element of complete self-giving that is the essence of God. Moreover, the central significance of altruism in contemporary sociobiological reflection and discussion on human evolution renders it perfectly appropriate and topical theologically, such that, considered in the context of contemporary reflection on human evolution, the term takes on a particular ethical significance, indeed, a central significance, in becoming capable of describing the mission of Christ in the incarnation and, indeed, in identifying the divine purpose of creation and its intended destiny.

Ruse makes the valuable point, for clarity's sake, that altruism has been given a special sense by sociobiologists, who distinguish between, on the one hand, what is commonly considered altruism in the sense of doing good with no strings attached, or what Ruse calls "literal altruism," and on the other hand, the idea of mutual cooperation and working together, where the idea of doing good is accompanied by some recompense. "In this sense," Ruse explains, "evolutionary altruism is a metaphorical sense of the term" that points to the biological strategy of cooperation between individuals within the same group to the long-term advantage of the group in terms of survival.[72] Human beings had to get good at cooperating and working together in order to survive; in other words, they had to get good at "biological altruism." As Ruse concludes, "By working together humans succeeded, and those that worked together more successfully tended to have more offspring than those who did not. Hence, down through the ages we evolved as highly successful 'altruists.'"[73]

Among various attempts at explaining such altruism, one approach invokes the ideas of kinship and group selection. Wilson explains that above the level of the individual various lineage groupings are to be found—siblings, family, extended family, tribe—and that "if selection operates on any of the groups as a unit, or operates on an individual in any way that affects the frequency of genes shared by common descent in relatives, the process is referred to as kin selection."[74] It seems to make evolutionary sense, then, for an individual to act altruistically toward others if they all belong to a recognizable group sharing the same genes, because the genetic opportunity costs for the individual, or what is given up by the individual personally, will be compensated for in other members of the group, or in the group as a whole, either then or later. "Blood relatives cooperate or bestow altruistic favors on one another in a way that increases the average genetic fitness of the members of the network as a whole, even when this behavior reduces the individual fitnesses of certain members of the group."[75] This is Darwinian natural selection operating at the level of the group rather than of the individual organism.

In addition, however, to explaining how altruistic behavior aimed at helping others can be genetically significant in benefiting one's kin or blood relatives, sociobiologists also entertain the possibility that altruistic kindness can redound on oneself or that, even without individual hope of reward or return, multiplication of altruistic activities can shape a group over time for its evolutionary betterment. Interestingly, Darwin recognized that humanity's moral sense evidently operates on a variety of reasons and motives, including what he assessed as the "low motive" for the early human being of learning that "if he aided his fellow-men, he would commonly receive aid in return."[76] It is this low motive of which Darwin appeared to be less critical morally when he wrote that "we are led by the hope of receiving good in return to perform acts of sympathetic kindness to others," and then added that this feeling of sympathy "will have been increased through natural selection; for those communities, which included the greatest number of the most sympathetic members, would flourish best, and rear the greatest number of offspring."[77]

It may appear difficult to avoid the conclusion from these arguments which aim to explain—or explain away—what is ordinarily viewed as altruism, that human beings are being conned by their genes into being altruistic, or having a moral sense. This could appear to underlie the exploration of Ridley into *The Origins of Virtue* and the evolution of cooperation, in which he was impressed by "the surprisingly social nature of the human animal" and set out to explain how this could have come about in evolutionary terms.[78] Contrary to the common perception of life as one of continuous competition, he concluded that "life has become a team game, not a contest of loners."[79] Yet it turns out to be a team game played and conducted by all its members with only one dominant purpose, that of genetic interest. In other words, "selfish genes sometimes use selfless individuals to achieve their ends."[80] Indeed, individual humans may at times consider that they are being altruistic to a fellow human, acting generously without an ulterior motive or the prospect of return in mind. If so, however, it appears, according to Ridley, that they are being deluded by their genes to act in this way.

In so interpreting all human behavior as gene-centered and gene-determined, however differently the individual agent might perceive such personal conduct, Ridley's approach is similar to that of Wilson in discounting the significance of individual motives. Indeed, Wilson observed that the "theory of group selection has taken most of the good will out of altruism," particularly when one considers what he calls mutually advantageous "tradeoffs of reciprocal altruism."[81] It has even been suggested that a Good Samaritan situation can be advantageous for the Samaritan as well as for the victim for whom he cares, should their situations come to be reversed sometime in the future. Indeed, it is even possible that altruistic genes will develop in the course of time, which may result in varying degrees of unselfish, altruistic behavior on the part of individuals, resulting in overall survival and enhancement of the group.[82]

Central to these considerations must be the idea of human motivation, but in her criticism of Wilson, Midgley claimed to search in vain for his views on humanity's internal experiences of purpose, intention, motivation, and the like, and she charged that he "scrupulously avoids any discussion" of them.[83] Yet his reference to altruistic individuals trading with each other must, she considered, involve motivation and a calculation of comparative profit.[84] Indeed, agreeing with Midgley, one may conclude that it is difficult to see how Wilson can accord any genuine reality to such human phenomena as motivation and choice, given his earlier claims for the centrality of the gene's selective power and his overarching criterion of potential genetic fitness. In fact, Wilson appears to dismiss freedom to act or to abstain from acting as illusionary in ways similar to Freudian, Marxist, and other forms of determinism. This appears to be implied by his explanation that "the hypothalamic-limbic complex of a highly social species, such as man, 'knows,' or more precisely it has been programmed to perform as if it knows, that its underlying genes will be proliferated maximally only if it orchestrates behavioral responses that bring into play an efficient mixture of personal survival, reproduction, and altruism."[85]

Ridley is another popular writer on sociobiology whose approach to human motivation leaves a considerable amount to be desired. As he observes reductively, "what matters to society is whether people are likely to be nice to each other, not their motives."[86] He entertains a somewhat scrupulous choice of possibilities in observing that "a true altruist would not give a gift, because he would realize that he was either motivated by vainglory of doing good or expecting reciprocation." Nor, in spite of his protestation to the contrary, is Ridley to be absolved of cynicism in proposing this as a total account of what might be involved in what appears to be unguarded generosity.[87] He oversimplifies moral situations by making a common error in identifying the idea of self-interest with that of greed, and he appears determined to explain simple generosity in terms of some calculated or hoped for return, if only on the feeble ground of an enhanced reputation.[88]

Concerning the relationship between egoism and altruism, or the tension that can arise between self-interest and the common good, Ridley finds much of relevance in the modern development of game theory, and particularly in the prisoner's dilemma, which, he claims, provides "nothing less than an understanding of why people are nice to each other."[89] Game theory, Ridley explains, "is concerned with that province of the world where the right thing to do depends on what other people do."[90] In the case of the prisoner's dilemma, the scenario is that each of two prisoners charged with a crime is promised leniency if he betrays his accomplice's guilt, and each tries to work out the options available to his accomplice, in order to conclude what he himself should then do. The facts are that, if one betrays the other, one's own sentence will be reduced, but the other's sentence will be increased, whereas if neither betrays the other they will both receive an equal smaller sentence. The problem of the prisoner's dilemma, Ridley comments, is how "to get two egoists to cooperate for the greater good, and to eschew the temptation to profit at the other's expense."[91] He observes that "both would be better off if they stayed silent, but each is individually better off if he defects." Hence, he concludes "it is rational to be selfish" and "cooperation is illogical."[92]

Yet, Ridley acknowledges, in spite of this unavoidable conclusion, people do cooperate frequently, and often apparently against their own interests. The way to understanding this logical contradiction, he observes, lies in the discovery that much depends on whether the prisoner's dilemma game was played on only one occasion or whether it was played frequently. In the latter case, a new dimension apparently opens to influence the decisions made, namely, the desire to cooperate. "Played repeatedly and discriminatingly, the game always favors the good citizen."[93] What this appears to indicate is the survival significance of human beings evolving the ability to cooperate and to work in mutual trust in such a way that, despite frequent lapses owing to shortsighted egoism, Ridley concludes, "instinctive cooperativeness is the very hallmark of humanity and what sets us apart from other animals."[94] Ultimately, however, for Ridley this all appears to be the work of calculation for survival, if not the self-centered calculation of individuals and groups, then the latent metaphorical calculation of the ever-manipulative gene at work in what Schloss critically describes as being "sincerely though erroneously convinced of one's good intentions."[95] What appears to be centrally involved is creating a reputation for trustworthiness and a sense of fairness, and at least giving the impression of acting altruistically in this way toward others, always in the ultimate egoistic purpose of long-term survival of oneself and one's genes. The moral ambivalence, to put it mildly, is clear in Ridley's conclusion that "the human mind contains numerous instincts for building social cooperation *and* seeking a reputation for niceness."[96]

Room for Real Altruism

Not all sociobiologists, however, are so skeptical, or indeed so cynical, about genuine altruism. Rolnick does conclude that "rather commonly, biologists have recently defined altruism solely in terms of sociobiological assumptions regarding reproductive value." However, he also notes important work by Batson and Shaw that challenges "the fairly common assumption among psychologists (and sociobiologists) that the motivation for all intentional action, including the intention to help others, is egoistic."[97] Midgley writes approvingly that as sociobiology has developed, "the crude rhetoric of selfishness has been toned down."[98] Frans de Waal argues with many illustrations for the existence of an evolved altruistic trait in all animals, including humans.[99] And Andrew Brown reflects interestingly on how sociobiologists were shocked to discover from their research "how altruism can prosper in a world where it seems that only selfishness is rewarded."[100] If this is so, and a place can be found for genuine altruism as a feature of ordinary human behavior, with no strings attached as it were, then it would be a mistake to maintain that human evolution is just one more instance of "nature red in tooth and claw." There is room for human evolution in terms of genuine moral experiences, insights, and actions that make room for generosity and empathy in living.

Moreover, welcome clarification on human motivation in an evolutionary context is provided by Pope's useful identification of four areas in which he considers that much modern sociobiological writing is significantly defective. These areas are *reductionism*, which explains higher human capacities in terms of biological or genetic principles, ultimately genetic fitness and the selfish gene;[101] *determinism*, which considers the human mind "no more than a biological means by which irresistible genetic forces determine external acts," thus concentrating on one causal factor of action and neglecting all others;[102] third, a disregard for the contribution of *culture* to human consciousness and choice, such that "the amazing plasticity and variety of the human emotional constitution . . . needs culture of some kind or another to be actualized," and "even fundamental genetically based inclinations can be overridden by other factors"[103]; and finally a preference for invariably explaining human actions in terms of self-concern and *egoism*.[104]

This last in particular, which highlights the whole issue of human motivation and intention, is something that many, if not most, sociobiologists appear almost to take for granted. As Pope remarks, "The predominant assumption in sociobiology is egoistic, maintaining that human behavior is always or almost always motivated ultimately (often unconsciously) by self-concern and that apparent altruism is illusory."[105] Ruse warns us, it is true, in contrast to Ridley, that "the claim is not that humans are hypocritically consciously scheming to get as much out of each other as they possibly can whilst perhaps pretending to be nice. But rather that humans do have a genuinely moral sense and awareness of right and wrong . . . which motivates them."[106] Even if this is the case, there is a need to emphasize it by recognizing and maintaining the clear distinction offered by Pope between, on the one hand, conscious intentions, desires, and motives, which are not illusory and which can include altruism in the ordinary meaning of that term, and, on the other hand, "biologically based instinctual proclivities, inclinations and drives," the stuff of sociobiology, which can evidently influence, but not determine, the activities of conscious reflection, motivation, and decision.[107] In other words, as he concludes importantly, "a great deal of human experience seems to make sense only if human nature has evolved in such a way as to include not only egoistic inclinations but also capacities for genuine altruism and related affective capacities like empathy, sympathy, and compassion."[108] In developing this line of reflection, Pope would certainly merit the approval of Midgley by confirming her comment on altruistic behavior that "it is important that we understand such actions for what they are, as done with the motives that they actually are done with, rather than distorting them to fit a tidy theory."[109]

The observation of Dixon is relevant here that some scientists still today, such as Wilson and Dawkins, mistakenly believe "that Darwinian evolution has always been thought of as a process favoring ruthless selfishness. In fact . . . it was recognized by Darwin himself, and by virtually all other scientific writers throughout the Victorian period too, that instincts of sympathy, cooperation, and love were just as much a product of nature, and in certain circumstances, just as necessary for survival, as were instincts of aggression, competition, and self-preservation."[110]

Colin Grant reaches similar conclusions after a thorough, detailed examination of the altruism literature. He describes and evaluates the experiments of Batson and his colleagues, based on the hypothesis "that altruism is a reflection of empathy," and concludes with them that "in spite of the predominant assumption that human beings are characterized fundamentally by self-interest, regnant in academia and trumpeted in popular culture, the evidence shows that people do act with concern for others. That such behaviour persists against such massive insistence that it is folly indicates that something like what we call altruism is present in human life at a profound level."[111] Grant's study, however, of what he claims to be the link between altruism and Christian ethics is theologically thin in a Trinitarian as well as a Christological dimension. A recognition of this richer concept of God would not only help to protect the exercise of altruism, in God as in humans, from allegations of more or less inevitable latent egoism, on which Grant appears preoccupied, but it could also help to defend the traditional Christian theology of divine impassibility against being dissolved into process theology, as he considers and I discuss in a later chapter.[112]

It may be possible to sum up this contrast between egoism and altruism by noting that, to account in evolutionary survival terms for human moral behavior, Darwin found the origin and basis of morality in the social instincts of early humans, whereas many modern sociobiologists have concentrated on what they term reciprocal altruism, or what is more accurately termed farsighted, or gene-dominated, mutual egoism. Recent work argues from game theory, and specifically the intricacies of the prisoner's dilemma, that the human race has evolved a sentiment of social trust that, when it is practiced, is a much more effective device for racial survival than is overt selfishness.[113] Ultimately, however, it appears that science has not, or not yet, accounted for the development of the quite unique human moral sense, perhaps mainly because it just cannot handle human motives. Boehm commented that in sociobiology genuine altruistic behavior "has remained an ultimate mystery," partly, it appears, because human altruism in all its fullness and potentiality is beyond the competence of sociobiology.[114] Pope, for instance, advises us that as a matter of fact "the particular norms of altruism promoted by various cultures may or may not contribute to the inclusive reproductive success of those individuals who are its members."[115]

Commenting on the sociobiological displacement from human purpose to genetic purpose and agency, Schloss remarks that "the loss of agency, at organismal not to mention mental levels, has profound implications for understanding morality."[116] It is one thing to experience and develop a primitive sense of loyalty to the groups to which one may belong, motivated at least partly by concern for self- or group survival; it is something further to come to recognize and to respect the competing interests of individuals with whom one may share membership of a group but who may also be individuals who belong to other groups, or perhaps to no groups at all. The single motive that does appear to dominate much of modern sociobiological thought is the conviction of Hobbes, rejected by many of his contemporaries, that everything humans do is dominated by sheer self-interest, an idea that Midgley characterized as "crude psychological egoism."[117] Darwin may have expressed the matter rather idealistically, but at least he had a view of human morality that went far beyond evolutionary survival through egoism when he wrote,

> As man advances in civilization, and small tribes are united into larger communities, the simplest reason would tell each individual that he ought to extend his social instincts and sympathies to all the members of the same nation, though personally unknown to him. This point being once reached, there is only an artificial barrier to prevent his sympathies extending to the men of all nations and races. If indeed, such men are separated from him by great differences in appearance or habits, experience unfortunately shews us how long it is, before we look at them as our fellow-creatures.[118]

The enormous leaps in logic contained in this disarming conjectural narrative serve only to confirm the conclusion of Poulshock that "as the Darwinian paradigm continues to find more and more universal application, it still faces serious challenges with regard to explaining altruism, ethics and morality."[119] Polkinghorne sums up the situation well when he comments,

I believe that all human beings have a degree of moral knowledge that exceeds what science may be able to explain in terms of evolutionary strategies for survival and gene propagation. Notions of kin altruism (protecting and propagating the family gene pool) and reciprocal altruism (helping an associate in the expectation of an eventual return) are enlightening and no doubt express part of the truth. The same could be said of game-theoretical maximal strategies, such as tit-for-tat (respond to others as they do to you). However, these insights do nothing to explain the kind of radical altruism that impels someone to risk their own life in the attempt to rescue an unknown and unrelated person from drowning. Anthropological accounts of diverse societies help us to see how cultural effects can mould the shape of public morality, but I am unable to believe that my ethical convictions, for example that torturing children is wrong and that there is a duty of care to the weak, are just conventions of my society. They are facts about the ethical reality within which we function as morally responsible persons.[120]

IMAGING THE DIVINE ALTRUISM

Given this understanding of the origin and potential of altruism in the process of human evolution, it is attractive within a theological context, I now suggest, to recognize that the source and primary analogue of all altruism must be God's and to develop from that realization a theology of altruism. It is not uncommon for short versions of the Christian catechism to begin by asking "Why did God make you?" and to answer the question in terms of how God expects us to behave, such as our being created to know, love, and serve God in the present life and, as a result, to be happy with God forever in the life to come. Such replies, however, in expressing what is expected of us in creation can have the undesirable effect of obscuring the really fundamental answer to the question of why God made us: It was simply to share his life with us.

A THEOLOGY OF ALTRUISM

We are entirely the product of divine altruism, the effect of the sheer creative generosity of the Supreme Being. The fifth-century theologian whom we know only as Pseudo-Dionysius the Areopagite made much of the Neoplatonic idea that it is of the nature of goodness to communicate itself, a theme taken up by Aquinas and other theologians in the Latin maxim *bonum est diffusivum sui*, that is, "the good spreads itself."[121] When this insight is applied to the divine work of creation, it is captured clearly by Keith Ward in his explanation that "God creates the world out of overflowing goodness," which enables us to appreciate the simple unconditional reply to the catechism question of why God made us: namely, to share his life generously with humanity.[122] Moreover, as we have become more aware that God is essentially social as Father, Son, and Spirit, as discussed in the first part of this chapter, we are correspondingly in a position to appreciate more how, in bringing us into existence, God plans to share with us, and among us, his own eternal life, that dynamic love that is, as it were, continuously circulating in the life of the Trinity, which earlier generations identified as the divine *perichoresis* into which we are to be caught up.

Originating in God, altruism also epitomized the moral teaching of Jesus, God become man, who continually proclaimed his father's unconditional love for his human creatures, exemplified this throughout his own life, and is forever inviting his fellows to show that they take after their father (Mt 5:45) by exercising on their own part complete selfless altruism toward God and each of their neighbors (Mt 22:3–40). As Meier summarized the teaching of Jesus, "If one joins together all the authentic sayings that deal with mercy, compassion, forgiveness, and similar obligations towards others, the results portray a Jesus who stressed the need to show mercy without measure, love without limits."[123] It follows that a major purpose of God's decision to become a member of the human species was precisely to reveal the human face of divine altruism and to teach humankind what selfless altruism means and entails. Daryl P. Domning expresses this well when he observes that God "knew that we would eventually need an incarnate example of perfect, divine altruism to show us how to transcend our original selfishness."[124]

Jesus's moral teaching on what altruism involves, and his appeal to his fellow humans to imitate his own archetypal human altruism, can thus be seen as a major evolutionary step in the moral advancement of the human species. Unhappily, however, it ran up against the buffers of human sin in Jesus's own contemporaries, meeting with endemic self- and tribe-centeredness and the collective refusal to look beyond one's selfish interests to a wider horizon of generosity and solidarity, which we saw earlier in this chapter that Darwin recognized would be so difficult.[125] Huxley also alerted us to this when he observed,

> The practice of that which is ethically best—what we call goodness or
> virtue—involves a course of conduct which, in all respects, is opposed to

that which leads to success in the cosmic struggle for existence. In place of ruthless self-assertion it demands self-restraint; in place of thrusting aside, or treading down, all competitors, it requires that the individual shall not merely respect, but shall help his fellows; its influence is directed, not so much to the survival of the fittest, as to the fitting of as many as possible to survive. It repudiates the gladiatorial theory of existence.[126]

In accepting the violent death thrust upon him, Jesus held out to his fellow humans an abiding example of supreme altruism in living out his unselfish loyalty to his understanding of his father and to his father's will.

As discussed earlier in this chapter, the individual's innate drive for self-assertion, which seems essential for survival, appears intrinsically hostile to that genuine concern for other individuals that is considered central to the whole idea of ethics and is at the heart of altruism. Sin emerges as humanity's yielding to evolutionary selfishness and declining to accept the invitation to self-transcendence; it is a refusal to transcend oneself in the interests of others. As Daly expressed it succinctly, "Refusal to love constitutes the essence of sin."[127] It can be argued, then, that part of the role of ethics, and of the example and appeal of altruism, is to train the human evolutionary urge by focusing it on others and on their interests rather than exclusively on one's own.

It is significant, however, to note that work is being done in sociobiology to show that a place can be found for genuine human altruism as a feature of ordinary behavior and that it would be a mistake to maintain simply that human evolution is just one more instance of "nature red in tooth and claw." As I expressed it earlier, there is room for human evolution in terms of genuine moral experiences, insights, and actions that make room for generosity and empathy in living. If humanity has at its heart some rudimentary sense, or inkling, of regard for others, as Darwin observed, then a case can be made for arguing from such a natural disposition to be concerned for one's fellows to a recognition that inserted in human beings is an image of the primordial altruism that is central to the life of God, as I have developed this. Indeed, it becomes possible, and attractive, to propose that humanity is created to image God as supremely and essentially altruistic. As dynamic, circulating, interpersonal love is central to the nature of God conceived as a community of persons, likewise an innate concern among humans for their mutual welfare can be identified as a distinctive feature in which they are created to image God, not only as individuals, but also as a species.

In such a case, we cannot just regard Jesus as simply saving us from the evolutionary drive to be solely egoistical. It would be appropriate in evolutionary terms to view Jesus more positively as inserted into the human species for the purpose of building upon the human image of God's altruism that has been created in all men and women. He is thus conceived by Paul as *the* image of God (Col 1:15), providing a "prime example" and reminding us of the importance of complying with what is deeply human and divine within us as the moral driving force of our creaturehood. As in many other ethical instances, the purpose of divine revelation then becomes that of, on the one hand, confirming and reinforcing a moral insight that is already accessible to human reason and, on the other hand, enriching that insight by locating it in the context of an all-pervading design of divine life and love. Here the theological awareness of divine altruism giving rise to human altruism serves to confirm and strengthen the awareness of human genuine altruism that is evident to some of those involved in sociobiological exploration, as discussed earlier, while at the same time providing an enveloping and transforming religious context to enrich that ethical awareness.

The upshot of these reflections, then, is to suggest that as our understanding of God and of the divine triune nature has expanded or deepened, and with it our understanding of what constitutes human personality and human community, so our grasp of how humankind can be understood to image God can reach new dimensions and depths in imitating the divine altruism. In other words, God created humankind in the image of his own altruism. In this theological development we can, in response to the question of Pope John Paul II with which I began this chapter, witness to a fresh nuance of the traditional doctrine that humans are all created in the image of God. We are invited to imitate in all our actions within the human species the altruistic solidarity and community of the divine Trinity, and in the process, as Romans 8:29 tells us, we are called to be daily conformed to Christ, who is the prime image of God's own altruism.

As so conceived, altruism is not just one expression of trying to lead a good life, but as other-centeredness, or neighbor love, it is the common element of what actually constitutes a good life, to be found also in God's creative enterprise and in the self-giving achievement of Jesus. As such, wherever and whenever it is to be found, human altruism or generosity, the breakout from evolutionary self-obsession, can be seen as a reflection of, and participation in, the creative altruism and agape of God himself and as either an anticipation or a replica of the generous human love by which Christ won our way through death, as a step in the evolutionary development of the human species. Altruism can, in fact, be identified as the divinely inspired moral evolutionary goal of the human species, a goal that conjecturally countless human individuals have in fact achieved in the course of their lives, even if only partially or occasionally, and whether or not they were aware of Jesus and his teaching and example. Certainly in the teachings, life, and death of Jesus, we may consider, is to be found the definitive and all-exhaustive act of human altruism as imaging God's. As totally non-self-centered and other-serving, human altruism ushers the evolving human species to a new level of existence and moral activity whose purpose is to increase the solidarity of the human race as collectively and individually created in the image of an altruistic God and, as such, destined to share fully in the inner richness of the divine life.

NOTES

1. Letter of His Holiness John Paul II to Reverend George V. Coyne, June 1, 1988. An earlier version of this chapter was printed in *Theological Studies* 71 (2010): 677–701.
2. See the informative and stimulating study of Grenz, *Social God and the Relational Self.*
3. Gn 1:26–27. All biblical quotations are from NRSV.
4. Von Rad, *Genesis*, 55–58.
5. Scullion, "Creation-Incarnation," 7–28, at 9.
6. Augustine, *De Genesi ad litteram*, 20, 30 (Migne, *PL* 34:292). Unless otherwise indicated, translations are mine.
7. Irenaeus, *Adversus haereses*, 5, 6, 1 (Migne, *PG* 7:1137–38); 5, 16, 22 (Migne, *PG* 7:1167–68); Kelly, *Early Christian Doctrines*, 171.
8. Aquinas, *Summa Theologiae* I, q. 93, a. 2.
9. Calvin, *Institutes*, I, xv, 3. Emphasis added.
10. Grenz, *Social God and the Relational Self*, 169.
11. Ibid., 304.
12. Augustine, *De Genesi ad litteram*, 3, 19 (Migne, *PL* 34:291).
13. Grenz, *Social God and the Relational Self*, 4. See Mahoney, *Challenge of Human Rights*, 99–111.
14. Grenz, *Social God and the Relational Self*, 316–17. On the relevance of *perichoresis*, see also Edwards, *God of Evolution*, 21–28.
15. Grenz, *Social God and the Relational Self*, 320.
16. ITC, *Communion and Stewardship.*
17. Vatican Council II, *Gaudium et spes*, paras. 24, 34.
18. Flew, *Evolutionary Ethics*, 12.
19. Darwin, *Descent of Man and Selection in Relation to Sex*, 18.

20. Ibid., 151.
21. Ibid., 199.
22. Ibid., 167.
23. Ibid., 167–68.
24. Gensler, "Darwin, Ethics and Evolution," 121–33, at 122.
25. Dixon, *Invention of Altruism*, 137.
26. Darwin, *Descent of Man and Selection in Relation to Sex*, 168.
27. Ibid., 203.
28. Flew, *Evolutionary Ethics*, 18; see 33–34.
29. Ibid., 33.
30. Darwin, *Descent of Man and Selection in Relation to Sex*, 182.
31. Ibid., 203.
32. Ibid., 190–91.
33. Küng, *Beginning of All Things*, 192.
34. See Sewell, *Political Gene*.
35. Ruse, "Significance of Evolution," 500–510, at 501.
36. Pope, *Human Evolution and Christian Ethics*, 82.
37. Dupré, "Intelligent Design," 169–80, at 170.
38. Cited in Dixon, *Invention of Altruism*, 369.
39. Copleston, *History of Philosophy*, 140.
40. Flew, *Evolutionary Ethics*, 36.
41. Huxley, *Collected Essays*, vol. 9, *Evolution and Ethics and Other Essays*, 1–116, at 80.
42. Huxley, *Evolution and Ethics and Other Essays*, 81–82.
43. Ibid., 31.
44. Ibid., 79.
45. Ibid., 83.
46. McGrath, *Dawkins' God*, 34.
47. Ruse, "Evolutionary Ethics Past and Present," 27–49, at 36; Wilson, *Sociobiology*, 562.
48. Wilson, *Sociobiology*, 3.
49. Ibid.
50. Ibid., 4.
51. Midgley, *Beast and Man*, xvii–xviii. On Midgley's controversy with Dawkins, see the lively chapter 5 of Brown, *Darwin Wars*.
52. Midgley, *Beast and Man*, 90.
53. Ibid., 100–101.
54. Ibid., 90–91. See 99.
55. Dawkins, *Selfish Gene*.
56. Midgley, *Beast and Man*, 102. See Midgley, *Evolution as a Religion*, 143–50.
57. Ward, *God, Chance and Necessity*, 90.
58. Ibid., 71.
59. McGrath, *Dawkins' God*, 12.

60. Ibid., 41–42.

61. Grant explores the whole idea and language of metaphor as the background invoked by Dawkins in referring to the gene as "selfish." See *Altruism and Christian Ethics*, 57–70.

62. McGrath, *Dawkins' God*, 46. See Dawkins, *Selfish Gene*, 1989 ed., 200–201.

63. Flew, *Evolutionary Ethics*, 15.

64. Wilson, *Sociobiology*, 4.

65. Ibid., 562.

66. Ibid., 3, and 106.

67. Pope, *Evolution of Altruism and the Ordering of Love*, 5.

68. Dixon, *Invention of Altruism*, 5.

69. Pope, *Evolution of Altruism and the Ordering of Love*, 227–28.

70. Dixon, *Invention of Altruism*, 371.

71. Edwards, *God of Evolution*, 16.

72. Ruse, "Evolutionary Ethics Past and Present," 502.

73. Ibid., 503.

74. Wilson, *Sociobiology*, 106.

75. Ibid., 117.

76. Darwin, *Descent of Man and Selection in Relation to Sex*, 201.

77. Ibid., 163.

78. Ridley, *Origins of Virtue*, 5.

79. Ibid., 14.

80. Ibid., 20.

81. Wilson, *Sociobiology*, 120, and 114.

82. Ibid., 120.

83. Midgley, *Beast and Man*, 113.

84. Ibid., 127.

85. Wilson, *Sociobiology*, 4.

86. Ridley, *Origins of Virtue*, 21.

87. Ibid., 120.

88. Ibid., 260–61, and 137–38.

89. Ibid., 53. See Ruse, "Evolutionary Ethics Past and Present," 43.

90. Ridley, *Origins of Virtue*, 57.

91. Ibid., 224.

92. Ibid., 54, 57.

93. Ibid., 225. See Binmore, *Natural Justice*.

94. Ridley, *Origins of Virtue*, 249.

95. Schloss, "Evolutionary Ethics and Christian Morality: Surveying the Issues," 1–24 at 12.

96. Ridley, *Origins of Virtue*, 262.

97. Batson and Shaw, "Evidence for Altruism," 107–22; Rolnick, "Darwin's Problems," 307.

98. Midgley, *Evolution as a Religion*, x.

99. De Waal, *Age of Empathy.*

100. Brown, *Darwin Wars,* 1–21.

101. Pope, *Evolution of Altruism and the Ordering of Love,* 94.

102. Ibid., 95.

103. Ibid., 106, 107.

104. Ibid., 109–14.

105. Ibid., 110.

106. Ruse, "Evolutionary Ethics Past and Present," 502.

107. Pope, *Evolution of Altruism and the Ordering of Love,* 111.

108. Ibid., 114.

109. Midgley, *Beast and Man,* 129; cf. Midgley, *Evolution as a Religion,* 146–50.

110. Dixon, *Invention of Altruism,* 3.

111. Grant, *Altruism and Christian Ethics,* 45, and see 44–50; and ibid., 225–26.

112. Ibid., 191–217; see chapter 5, this volume.

113. Ridley, *Origins of Virtue,* 54–57, 224–45; Binmore, *Natural Justice.*

114. Boehm, "Explaining the Prosocial Side of Moral Communities," 78–100, at 80.

115. Pope, *Evolution of Altruism and the Ordering of Love,* 10.

116. Schloss, "Evolutionary Ethics and Christian Morality," 5.

117. Mahoney, *Challenge of Human Rights,* 11–14; Midgley, *Ethical Primate,* 5.

118. Darwin, *Descent of Man and Selection in Relation to Sex,* 187–88.

119. Poulshock, "Leverage of Language on Altruism and Morality," 114–31, at 129.

120. Polkinghorne, *Theology in the Context of Science,* 64.

121. Pseudo-Dionysius, *De divinis nominibus,* 4.20 (Migne, *PG* 3:720); Aquinas, *Summa Theologiae,* I, q. 5, a. 4 ad 2.

122. Ward, "Christian Ethics," 224–49, at 225.

123. Meier, "Jesus," 78:23.

124. Domning, "Evolution, Evil and Original Sin."

125. Darwin, *Descent of Man and Selection in Relation to Sex,* 190–91.

126. Huxley, *Evolution and Ethics and Other Essays,* 81–82.

127. Daly, *Creation and Redemption,* 1.

CHAPTER THREE

The Evolutionary Achievement of Jesus

N THE PREVIOUS chapter I offered a response to a question that Pope John Paul II once addressed to evolutionary science, whether an evolutionary perspective would throw any light on Christian beliefs, specifically on the significance of the human person as created in the image of God. In answer, I proposed that human altruism, which puzzles many evolutionary scientists, can provide a theological link between God and his human creature in that altruism originates in the life of the divine Trinity of persons as they interact in self-donation to each other and are operative in the work of creation, and that this divine altruism is expressed in the act of creation and finds an image in the human creature to provide a basis and a potential for transforming members of the human species into a mutually caring community imaging God's own community of love. All this is operative through the supremely altruistic teaching and death of Jesus Christ, who is, according to Paul, "*the* image of God" (Col 1: 15). In this way the Word became a member of the human species for the purpose of teaching his fellows how to live a truly ethical life against the inherent evolutionary tendency to competitiveness and self-centeredness by instructing us, and also inspiring us by his own example, to live a life of complete altruism. This, I suggest, is the common link between the inherent and creative generosity of God, the devoted life of his son, and the life in Christ concentrated on the service of God and neighbor that is the evolutionary calling for God's human creatures who are created bearing the image of an altruistic God.

In this chapter I turn to another, related, theological question put to evolution by Pope John Paul II on the same occasion: Does an evolutionary perspective bring any light to bear upon what he described as "the problem of Christology"?[1] The pope is not clear what precisely the nature of the problem is. In her study *Christ and Evolution*, Celia Deane-Drummond explores the implications of Darwinism for Christology, and does so largely in a way that is influenced by the works of von Balthazar and his attraction to theodrama and by the works of Bulgakov with his emphasis on wisdom.[2] Her introductory chapter, "The Challenge of Darwinian Evolution," provides a very readable summary account of the modern scene of evolutionary science.[3] She tends to understand any modern challenge posed by the incarnation as stemming from the fact that we now appreciate that God united himself with a human nature that had evolved and is still in evolution. She asks, "How might Christ's human nature and divine nature be related, given current understanding of humanity in evolutionary terms?" and "Is there a way of expressing belief in the divinity of Christ that also allows for an understanding of human nature as radically embedded in evolutionary history?"[4] However, she does not make clear just why human evolution as such should be considered as creating a new challenge to Christology, traditionally understood as the assumption of human nature (in whatever state it may be) by the Word of God.

Part of a reply to the pope's question presumably will lie in any contribution that evolution can offer, not just to the constitution of Christ as God-man, viewed in traditional terms as a hypostatic union, but more specifically to the role of Christ within God's purpose in creation. Accordingly, I aim in this chapter to examine what I call the evolutionary achievement of Jesus: That is, in his accepting death as a human being and in his rising from the dead, he achieved a new phase of evolutionary existence for the human species, into which he could then usher his fellow humans. In this way he would save them from individual death and extinction, which appeared to be the evolutionary fate of all living things, and would impart to humans through their association with him that richer share and eternal communion in the divine Trinitarian life that is God's evolutionary design for them.

SAVING HUMANITY FROM DEATH

Such a major step forward for our species indicates from the start that the evolutionary role of Jesus was incomparably more than as an ethical exemplar and leader, valuable as that is, and as Enlightenment thinkers envisaged him, if they considered him at all positively. In an informative passage, McGrath draws attention to the strong preference on the part of some modern theologians, including Rashdall, Lampe, and Hick, partly influenced by the study of religions, for the exemplarist approach to the life and death of Jesus rather than for what had become the traditional atonement approach. At the same time he points out what he considers to be the significant weakness of mere exemplarism.[5] In accepting the violent death thrust upon him, Jesus held out to his fellow humans an abiding example of supreme altruism: living out his unselfish loyalty to his understanding of his father and to his father's will. What needs highlighting in an evolutionary theology, however, is that the life and death of Jesus enable one not merely to recognize his ethical message and acknowledge the Enlightenment appreciation of his moral leadership but to grasp the additional, indeed central, point that Jesus actually achieved something in his dying. Wright explained this by observing that "he would defeat evil by letting it do its worst to him."[6] Jesus triumphed over death, and his death was more than a striking moral example of the extent to which altruism could draw one; it was also in evolutionary terms a cosmic achievement for humanity, taking our species through the evolutionary cul-de-sac of individual extinction to enter into a newer form of human living. He not only liberated humanity from self-centeredness, instilling in us the moral values of peace, justice, freedom, and truth, but also rescued us from the evolutionary destiny of individual death.

The sequence of the Easter Mass portrays his achievement as a victorious cosmic combat: *Mors et vita duello Conflixere mirando; Dux vitae mortuus Regnat vivus* (Death and life met in a wondrous duel; the leader of life died and lives victorious). In his dying Jesus was impelled by his divine and human altruism to break through death to a renewed life and to open this evolutionary advance for the rest of humanity.

DISPENSING WITH ORIGINAL SIN

Stressing as I have done that the death and resurrection of Jesus have had the evolutionary cosmic effect of providing a remedy for human death, the universal fate for individuals that is apparently essential to the advance of evolution through natural selection, appears to be at variance with the traditional biblical and Christian doctrine that what Jesus brought about through his death was the saving of the human race from original sin and the Fall. Stressing that Jesus in his death and resurrection saved humanity from death rather than from sin, it follows that fundamental questions are thereby raised about the traditional Christian beliefs positing an original sin and Fall and interpreting the death of Jesus as a remedy for that moral Fall on the part of early humanity. As Haught commented, original sin "for many Christians is the most difficult religious teaching to square with

Darwinian evolution."[7] This does not mean that in evolutionary theology there is no place for human sin and weakness, no room for divine grace and forgiveness, or no room for the incarnation, death, and resurrection of Christ. On the contrary, as this chapter examines. But it does mean that in an evolutionary theology there is no need for the idea of an early collective lapse of the whole of humanity from divine grace through an original sin of its protoparents, nor for the idea that God became man in order to restore through his death this fallen humanity to its original state of divine friendship. Such a development raises questions about the origin and purpose of those traditional doctrines of the Fall and redemption, quite apart from the inherent difficulties that have been often felt in trying to understand and accept them.

The Origin of the Fall

In her study of modern sociobiology, Patricia A. Williams identifies three strata in the formulation of the Christian belief in the Fall: the original text in Genesis 2:4 to 3:24, the theological reflections produced on this by Paul in chapter 5 of his epistle to the Romans, and the further theological interpretation of Paul that was elaborated by Augustine of Hippo.[8] To this last stratum the Catholic tradition would add the subsequent official formulation of the doctrine of original sin as drawn up by the Council of Trent (DS 1510–16), which has been summarized most recently in the *Catechism of the Catholic Church* (nos. 379–421).

Starting from the present situation, we find the *Catechism* explaining that "the account of the fall in Genesis 3 uses figurative language, but affirms a primeval event, a deed that took place at the beginning of the history of man" (no. 390). According to this, in figurative terms God had created humanity in a relationship of divine friendship, requiring only that the first human couple in the garden of Eden abstain from eating of the tree of the knowledge of good and evil, on pain, as God is depicted as threatening, that "in the day that you eat of it, you shall die" (no. 396; Gn 2:17). Genesis goes on to inform us that our protoparents disobeyed God, thus committing the first human sin, a sin that had the effect of destroying their harmonious relationship with God, and also as a result destroying the original harmony that had existed within the human beings themselves as well as the harmony between man and woman and between humanity and creation (no. 400).

The *Catechism* continues (no. 402) that "all men are implicated in Adam's sin, as St Paul affirms" (Rom 5:12), and it appeals to the Council of Trent to explain "the fact that [Adam] has transmitted to us a sin with which we are all born afflicted" (no. 403). It notes that "the transmission of original sin is a mystery that we cannot fully understand." The *Catechism* adds a new explanatory term, *human nature*, which is not to be found in the council text, when it explains that Adam and Eve's sin "affected the human nature that they would then transmit in a fallen state. It is a sin which will be transmitted by propagation to all mankind, that is, by the transmission of a human nature deprived of original holiness and justice" (no. 404). This human nature would be "fallen," the *Catechism* explains, not just because it is deprived of "the original holiness and justice" in which Adam and Eve were initially created, but now it is also "wounded" in its natural powers, and it is "inclined to sin—an inclination to evil that is called 'concupiscence'" (no. 405), as had been taught and explained by the Council of Trent. A moralizing conclusion of this Catholic doctrine of "concupiscence" is then drawn by the *Catechism* in observing that "ignorance of the fact that man has a wounded nature inclined to evil gives rise to serious errors in the areas of education, politics, social action and morals" (no. 407).

The Tridentine Teaching

As we saw in the first chapter of this book, the *Catechism* completely ignores the development of evolutionary science and its explanations of human origins, being content to repeat and expand slightly the teaching of the sixteenth-century Council of Trent. If we go behind the teaching of the *Catechism* to the council's 1546 "Decree on Original Sin" on which the *Catechism* draws, we are informed that Adam had disobeyed God's command in paradise and as a result had "incurred God's anger and indignation and therefore death with which God had earlier threatened him" (DS 1511). The council went on to explain that Adam's sin harmed all his descendants, as Paul had stated in Romans 5:12, a passage that followed Saint Augustine and the Latin Vulgate Bible in understanding that death spread to all men in Adam "in whom [*in quo*] all sinned." The implication of this inclusion of all men in Adam was that all future humans, who were descended in solidarity from the first human being, were therefore somehow implicated in Adam's sinful deed. As a result, the council had to find a way of explaining how Adam's sin could have automatically spread to all of his descendants, and this it did by defining that "Adam's original sin was spread to everyone and is in everyone not just by imitation but by propagation" or "by generation" (DS 1513–14).

Having thus accounted for the origin, nature, and transmission of the original sin, the Council of Trent went on to deal with its effect in every subsequent human being, explaining that, although the guilt of that inherited original sin is totally removed from individuals by baptism, nevertheless something of that sin remains in them, the celebrated innate sinful desire, or concupiscence. As it stated, "this Synod affirms and experiences the fact that concupiscence or 'tinder' (*concupiscentia vel fomes*), remains in the baptized." In this reference to concupiscence, the council was picking up the Pauline exhortation to the baptized in Romans 6:12 that even after they have been saved from sin they should "not let sin exercise dominion in your mortal bodies, to make you obey your passions," literally "the concupiscences (Greek *epithumiais*) of your body." Elsewhere Paul refers to such concupiscence, or "sinful desire," as something that was in general forbidden by the Mosaic commandment "thou shalt not covet" (Rom 7:7; Ex 20:17), a prohibition that was extended from the original commandment against coveting one's neighbor's wife and possessions to the forbidding of all expressions of covetousness or sinful desiring, or all concupiscence. Further, in the subsequent passage, Paul, the convert of Christ, appeared still to experience personally "sin that dwells within me" (Rom 7:17, 20). Thus the Council of Trent viewed Paul as teaching that even all baptized human beings still remain throughout their lives vulnerable to the stirrings of sin within them.

Fuel for Sin

This Pauline concupiscence, which in his opinion continued to exist and to be experienced even after justification, was developed in subsequent theology in terms of concupiscence as the *fomes* of sin, that is, "tinder" for sin, the two terms being regarded by the council as synonymous (DS 1515). The word *fomes* is a classical Latin term for "kindling wood," perhaps best conveyed today by the idea of "fuel," which is connected with the Latin term meaning "to favor" and is at the root of the English term *to foment*, or "to stir up." It was this traditional view of concupiscence as fomenting sin, or as the *fomes peccati* believed to exist in everyone resulting from original sin, of which Martin Luther made so much in his early attack on the selling of indulgences. Those pursuing this trade of releasing souls from purgatory and from the penalties of sin in exchange for a set price, he charged, "speak as if the only sins were actual sins, and as if the remaining *fomes* was not an uncleanness, not an impediment, not a reason for delaying entry into the Kingdom (*Haec omnia ita loquuntur, quasi non sint peccata nisi actualia, ac si fomes relictus nulla sit immundicia, nullum impedimentum, nullum medium quod moretur ingressum regni*)."[9]

As a consequence the ensuing papal bull of Pope Leo X, the famous *Exsurge Domine* of 1520, which listed and condemned statements from Luther's writings, picked up his reference to the now traditional *fomes peccati* and condemned him for stating erroneously that "the tinder wood of sin (*fomes peccati*), even if no actual sin is present, delays the soul leaving the body from entering heaven" (DS 1453). It was with this current dispute with Luther in mind that the bishops at Trent in their "Decree on Original Sin" dealt with postbaptismal concupiscence, or the traditional "*fomes peccati*" (fomenter of sin), by conceding that inherited concupiscence does remain after baptism, but denying that it is sin in the real sense of the term and that as such it can keep one out of heaven, as Luther was accused of maintaining (DS 1515).

The Origin of Original Sin

The formal teaching of the Council of Trent, then, is that Adam's original sin is inherited by everyone through procreation and that its guilt is forgiven by the conferring of baptism, yet something of its results remains even in the baptized, experienced as concupiscence or sinful desires, fomenting or fueling sin in each of us. On this several comments can be offered, the first crucially relating to where it all starts, namely, to what Paul meant in Romans 5:12 when he used the Greek phrase *eph' hō* relating to Adam's action. Augustine and others, including the council fathers at Trent, relying on the Old Latin translation, took this to mean in Latin *in quo*, or "in whom," with the clear implication that everyone had sinned in Adam. Most exegetes today understand this phrase as using the common Greek preposition *epi* to imply succession rather than inclusion, thus giving the meaning "since when" all have sinned rather than "in whom" all have sinned.[10] We must conclude that if this is the original Pauline meaning, it removes from divine revelation any reference to Adam's descendants being incorporated in solidarity "in him" (*in quo*), and as a result it dispenses with the conclusion that the whole of succeeding humanity has been condemned en masse as a sort of "condemned mass in Adam," as Augustine and others explained.[11] J. N. D. Kelly delivers his considered verdict in explaining how the Old Latin version of the New Testament (which had influence only in the West) gave "an exegesis of Rom 5, 12 which, though mistaken and based on a false reading, was to become the pivot of the doctrine of original sin."[12]

As a consequence of this reflection, it follows that there is now no need for theology to find a method by which to explain how all Adam's offspring inherit his original sin. Trent's insistence that Adam's original sin was transmitted among all subsequent human beings by propagation, or by generation, rather than simply by imitation (which Pelagius was considered to have maintained) was clearly due more to the theological polemic of Saint Augustine against Pelagius and his supporters than to Paul's writing centuries earlier. The Council of Trent's teaching on original sin (DS 1512) appealed to the sixth-century Second Council of Orange, which itself drew explicitly on Augustine's views on original sin, including his quotation and his understanding of what he considered Paul's *in quo* and what he considered its implications (DS 371–72; *Catechism* no. 406). Augustine himself, under severe pressure from Pelagian sympathizers, found himself denying vehemently that he had "invented original sin."[13]

Perhaps he was protesting too much. As Edward Yarnold observes of Augustine in his book *The Theology of Original Sin*, the "traditional Catholic expression . . . [of original sin] is to a large extent that saint's thought."[14] John Muddiman puts the point more sharply: "It is well known that the New Testament basis for the Augustinian doctrine is meagre, namely Romans 5:12 in the Vulgate translation, and a great deal even then has to be assumed."[15] Here, as elsewhere, then, we would do well continually to bear in mind the remark of Heikki Räisänen that "theology would gain from a distinction between historical exegesis and contemporizing theological interpretation; otherwise it runs the risk of only getting back from exegesis what it has first put into it."[16] He also adds a remark that may be particularly applicable these days to the subjects being considered here: "It is seldom realized how vast a difference it would make if critical points made by common sense and careful exegesis were really taken seriously." Augustine's insistence on original sin was, in fact, influenced by his implacable opposition to Pelagian claims for moral self-sufficiency, as well as by Augustine's own humiliating struggle for chastity and his pessimistic theology of human sexuality. As I have commented elsewhere, it is not surprising that the troubled Augustine saw in human disruptive sexual experience "not only the terrible effects of original sin, but also the very channel through which that sin was transmitted from generation to generation."[17] Behind the explanation added to the Council of Trent's teaching by the modern *Catechism* that original sin is part of human nature, as discussed earlier, we can discern the continual stress laid by Augustine on the ruinous effect on human nature of Adam's sin, which brought about what he describes in one passage as "human nature's total collapse" (*ut ruina eius natura humana esset totaliter collapsa*).[18]

The question, then, is to what extent Augustine misunderstood or embellished Paul's views and added his own contribution in terms of original sin to shape what later became the formal Catholic teaching on the Fall and its consequences. Williams inclines to the view that for Augustine "the disobedience of Adam and Eve leads to a much greater disaster than Genesis 2 and 3 actually describe." Indeed, in addition to mistakenly reading Paul as judging that all humanity have sinned "in" Adam—with all the consequent elaborate need to explain how this can happen—Augustine "inflates the original nature of the first couple, exaggerates the character of their sin, and amplifies their punishment."[19] Moreover, Fitzmeyer observes that in fact Paul's teaching does not use the term *original sin*, which is a creation of Augustinian times, and "it does not say all that the Tridentine decree says," the Tridentine additions being obviously due to the mind and authority of Augustine.[20] Because of its central theological significance, the point is worth stressing. As Fitzmeyer continues, providing textual references to Augustine as well as other authorities,

> "Original sin" is a Christian idea, which builds on what Paul teaches in this paragraph, as he exploits the implications of the causal connection between Adam's sin and the sinfulness of human beings in the etiological story of Genesis 3. Paul never explains how that causality works or how Adam's sin is transmitted. When Augustine opposed Pelagius, who had been teaching that Adam influenced humanity by giving it a bad example, he introduced the idea of transmission by propagation or heredity. He also introduced the idea of *gratia sanans*, "healing grace," and *gratia elevans*, "elevating grace." With the introduction of those ideas into the debate, the story in Genesis 3 about Adam's sin was then recast in terms of "the Fall": Adam fell from grace, from a supernatural status.[21]

In other words, Fitzmeyer points out, the most that Romans can actually say is that "through his sin Adam began the common sinning of humanity; he was the author of that malevolent force. . . . [B]ecause of the very essence of Sin, derived from Adam, the power of Death has entered the world of humanity."[22]

Coping with Concupiscence

A second comment that can be offered on the doctrine of original sin and the Fall as developed from chapter 5 of Romans through Augustine and the Council of Trent to the modern *Catechism* relates to the whole idea of concupiscence, or Paul's forbidden desire, of which even so complex and encyclopedic a theologian as Karl Rahner commented that "the concept of concupiscentia . . . is undoubtedly one of the most difficult in dogmatic theology."[23] Kelly distinguishes two aspects of Augustine's account of original sin that the latter claimed to base on Paul. One aspect, which as previously noted was discredited, is humanity's sharing collectively in Adam's sin (*in quo*), allegedly on Pauline authority. The second aspect of Augustine's theology to which Kelly then draws attention is that as a consequence of our sharing in Adam's rebellion against God, "human nature has been terribly scarred and vitiated," and of this "the most obvious symptom . . . , apart from the general misery of man's existence, is his enslavement to ignorance, concupiscence and death."[24]

Regular reference to humanity's sinful failings as a melancholy consequence of our fallen nature is a prevalent element of Christian teaching, and especially of Christian preaching. Brian Hebblethwaite's description is typical of many when he writes of the doctrine of the Fall, "We affirm, with the tradition, that man, through the pressures both of heredity and environment *and through the corruption of his will*, falls very far short of the divine intention, and stands in need of redemption."[25] It is not an emphasis that is exclusive to the Protestant (and Augustinian) tradition, though it may be found more congenial there, and it may have been his Protestant background, as well as a touch of depressiveness, that led John Henry Newman to ascribe so much importance to what he identified as the "anarchical condition of things"; he considered that "the doctrine of what is theologically called original sin becomes to me almost as certain as that the world exists, and as the existence of God."[26] Reflecting on this regular sin-laden refrain of Christian reflection, as expressed also by the *Catechism*'s emphasis on the presence of inflammatory concupiscence throughout the modern world, Daly was not beyond suggesting that "the section of the Catechism dealing with original sin seems to have been designed specifically to support the revanchist program which is being imposed on the Church of today."[27]

Indeed, such stress on human sinfulness could not have been more emphasized than it was by Pope John Paul II, speaking in Italian in a general audience on October 8, 1986, on "The State of Man in Fallen Nature."[28] The pope expounded on the teaching of the Council of Trent and its vocabulary of *fomes* and concupiscence, and he explained,

> In the condition in which nature finds itself after sin, and especially because man is more inclined to evil than to good, one speaks of a "spark

of sin" (*fomes peccati*), from which human nature was free in the state of original perfection (*integritas*). This "spark of sin" is also called "concupiscence" (*concupiscentia*) by the Council of Trent, which adds that it also continues in man justified by Christ, therefore even after holy Baptism. . . . As a consequence of original sin, concupiscence is the source of the inclination to various personal sins committed by people through the evil use of their faculties (these sins are called actual, to distinguish them from original sin). This inclination remains in man even after holy Baptism. In this sense everyone bears in himself the "spark" of sin.

The pope did go on to add, in welcome terms as not every gloomy preacher harping on our fallen sinfulness appears aware, that "human nature is not only 'fallen' but also 'redeemed' in Jesus Christ, so that 'where sin increased, grace abounded all the more' (Rom 5:20)." Although regrettably the pope did not expand on this strong and badly needed corrective to the predilection among preachers for dwelling on our fallen human nature, he did end on an encouraging note by observing that it is our redeemed state that "is the real context in which original sin and its consequences must be considered." In other words, one might say, Saint Paul warned his readers that, even for the baptized, life is a tough moral struggle against our unruly feelings, which can stir up sin in us if we allow them to, yet we do have the continual help of the generous grace of Christ to encourage us and to enable us to resist and overcome those feelings. We are, after all, as the popular hymn expresses it, not fallen: We are "ransomed, healed, restored, forgiven."

In fact, if the concept of biblical and Pauline concupiscence, which later became identified as the *fomes peccati*, or the fomenter of sin, was understood as a permanent remnant in all individuals of their collective and successive sharing in Adam's original guilty act, even after baptism, then, once that solidarity of all human beings with Adam in his original act of sin is no longer considered as part of divine revelation, the theological basis for the idea of concupiscence as the resulting relic and regular fomenter of sin within us all simply no longer exists. It does not follow from this, of course, that after baptism humans do not experience the stirrings of sin in their lives. Paul does not in fact make an organic connection between our unruly desires and the sin of Adam as if the desires were an inevitably inherited consequence of that sin, but he does warn Christians against the continuing force of those desires. Moreover, when the bishops of Trent directed their attention to what they considered the concupiscence inherited by Adam's offspring, they candidly stated that they both "acknowledged and felt" it (*fatetur ac sentit*), accepting the internal stirrings of sin not only as a fact of revelation but also as a sad experience of even episcopal life. An echo of this Tridentine theme is found in the writings of the bishops of the Second Vatican Council regarding their understanding of concupiscence (a term they did not use) when they observed, "What is known to us through God's revelation is consonant with our experience. Looking into our hearts, we also find ourselves with a leaning towards evil."[29] Consequently, although it now appears that we cannot claim as part of divine revelation that concupiscence, or Vatican II's "leaning towards evil," is a relic of a state of sin inherited from Adam that is operative in everyone to foment sin or that is active as what Pope John Paul II described as the spark that can ignite to produce sin, nevertheless the reality of rebellious feelings regularly stirring us toward sinning in our daily lives remains an undeniable fact of Christian experience. But our human moral frailty and unruly desires require a different explanation from that offered by the Council of Trent when it viewed them as the result of an original sin and collective fall of early humanity that has reverberations continuing in individual lives.

The Old Testament Story

Considering the source of Paul's theological elaborations in the simple narrative of chapter 3 of Genesis provides us with a much sparer picture of what is depicted as happening in Eden. Williams observes, "As ... almost all scholars of the Hebrew Scriptures agree, there is no fall in the narrative."[30] In more detail, Fitzmeyer views the same chapter in Genesis, which became traditionally viewed as the story of the Fall, as teaching only "the loss of God's trust and friendship by Adam and Eve because of their transgression and disobedience. ... [I]n that etiological story there is not a hint of a 'fall' from grace or original justice, as patristic and later scholastics eventually formulated it."[31] It is not too much to conclude from this that the "fall" is a later fantasy, and "fallen nature" a theological fiction. The question then arises, why should this have happened?

FINDING A NEW EXPLANATION

Fitzmeyer refers to Genesis 3 several times as an "etiological story" that, he explains, "sought to explain how this sinful condition of humanity first emerged. It tells how Adam and Eve brought sin into the world; yet the etiology of that account teaches that sin has been around as long as humanity has: its genesis and origin are not in God, but from human beings."[32] Such etiological stories are a common feature of the Hebrew Bible that aim to provide apparently historical origins for various Israelite institutions and features, such as place names and popular traditions. Carmichael expresses well that the idea of etiological myth is "a sophisticated attempt to account for current reality by inventing a mythical past."[33]

Explaining Death

It was within this etiological context that von Rad in his classic commentary on the book of Genesis observed that the original purpose of the primeval history was to proclaim "first of all with impressive one-sidedness that all corruption, all confusion in the world, comes from sin."[34] Daly confirms this in explaining an etiological myth as "a myth which is constructed to account for present human experience," an explanation which is applied by Paul Ricoeur to the myth of the Fall insofar as "its function is to posit a 'beginning' of evil distinct from the 'beginning' of creation, to posit an event by which sin entered into the world and, by sin, death."[35]

Indeed, the explanatory role of the book of Genesis is explained by Westermann as the "book of beginnings" that provides a primal history of the beginning of the world, which is followed by a patriarchal history of the development of human community, the whole acting partly as "the prelude to the story of a people whose history begins in the Exodus."[36] In the words of Clifford, "Genesis is concerned with origins."[37] Within that perspective of explaining origins, Genesis chapters 2–3 have a particular role, Westermann observes, and he identifies the question that informs the narrative as, "Why are those created by God limited by death, pain, toil, and sin?"[38] In other words, the purpose of the early chapters of Genesis, from the seven days of creation through the disobedience of Adam and Eve to their sentencing and expulsion from paradise, was to give an acceptable account of the origin of the world as stemming from a loving creator, while providing an explanation of the undoubted experienced miseries of life that obviously could not be simply ascribed to such a God. Such an explanation is provided in summary form, for instance, by the observation in the Book of Wisdom (2:23–24): "For God created us for incorruption, and made us in the image of his own eternity, but through the devil's envy death entered the world, and those who belong to his company experience it." How was Hebrew culture to account for the existence of disasters, evils, and, above all, death and human extinction as facts of earthly life, if all is to be referred back to a good and loving God?

Explaining all this as the outcome of human wickedness was an approach that was evidently congenial to the Israelite temperament and mentality, while at the same time, it is worth noting, drawing on that mentality to explain all human ills as the consequence of sinful disobedience could only serve to confirm and reinforce such a pessimistic attitude about life. In his essay on the atonement in the collection *Lux Mundi*, Lyttelton observed about the idea of sin, "Of this conception the Bible, the most complete record of the religious history of man, is full from the first page to the last. Throughout the whole course of Jewish development, the idea that man has offended the justice of God was one of the abiding elements in the religious consciousness of the race."[39] Von Rad answered the question of how these ills could take place with the simple answer that "the Yahwist, from the most varied kinds of building material, formed in the primeval history (chs. 2 to 11) a story of mankind's increasing alienation from God."[40] John McKenzie takes a similar line in describing this early unit in Genesis 2–11 as providing a "panorama of wickedness."[41] Commenting on how strongly "the OT is aware of the universality of sin," he continues, "the consciousness of the universality of sin grows with Israel's historic experience; the shattering events of the fall of the Israelite monarchies and of the exile leave the survivors of early Jerusalem with *a sense of sinfulness that is almost excessive.* Where Yahweh punishes so severely, guilt must be great indeed." [42] It is not surprising, then, that, as McKenzie concludes, "the removal of sin and guilt is a matter of vital concern in the religion of the OT."[43] A similar line is taken by N. T. Wright in recognizing the near obsession with sin that is found in Israelite history. As he wrote, "If Israel's God was to deliver his people from exile, it could only be because he had somehow dealt with the problem which had caused her to go there in the first place, namely, her sin. The question of how this was to be done looms so large in various aspects of her life, culture and ritual that it is easy to think of the method of dealing with sin (centred, what is more, on the individual), as the major focus of Judaism."[44]

An Evolutionary Fact

With the modern development and acceptance of the science of evolution, however, an alternative explanation has become available to account for human sin and for what have been traditionally considered its consequences of disasters and death, an explanation that dispenses with the need to construct an etiology, or a myth and theological elaboration, that invokes an original sin and the collective fall of humanity to account for these phenomena. To take the centrally significant phenomenon of death, which the Genesis 2 narrative was largely constructed to explain, it is clear that everything centers on the threat uttered by God in Eden regarding the tree of the knowledge of good and evil that "in the day that you eat of it you shall die"(Gn 2:17). As we have seen Wisdom point out (2:23–24), God "made us in the image of his own eternity, but through the devil's envy death entered into the world." Death is thus viewed as the divinely imposed penalty for human disobedience. Paul summed it up by observing that "death is the wages of sin" (Rom 6:23). But whereas in traditional Christianity death has always been perceived as a penalty, in evolution through natural selection the death of individuals, not just of humans, is rather seen as a biological necessity and a requirement. Without individual deaths there would be no natural selection among the variety of random evolutionary developments that occur over time, no processes of variation and specializing, and no surviving in response to environments. As Arthur Peacocke observed in his study *Theology for a Scientific Age,* "Biological death of the individual is the prerequisite of the creativity of the biological order."[45] In fact, he concludes, "the statistical logic is inescapable: new forms of matter arise only through the dissolution of the old: new life only through the death of the old."[46]

An evolutionary account of God's work of creation, then, does not require a theology of sin and punishment to account for natural and human disasters in the way in which the Bible invariably explains these, whether as the curses on disobedient Adam and Eve, the deluge destroying the earth's sinful inhabitants, the plagues to punish recalcitrant Egypt, the punishments of the people of Israel in Sinai and in the age of the Judges, or the cataclysm of the Israelites in their enforced exile to Babylon for abandoning their god. Even in modern times there is no lack of theologians who continue to explain natural tragedies as divine retribution for human sin, as the founder of Methodism, John Wesley, viewed the Lisbon earthquake of 1755. How could a loving and all-powerful God condone such wanton suffering and loss of life? The inevitable Hebrew reflex was to say they could only be the visitations of divine wrath as the just punishment for human sins. If such events are now to be considered the unavoidable results of evolution, however, as a process of cosmic trial and error and survival, this can be considered as a more intellectually satisfying explanation.

It is obviously noncontroversial, as Denis Edwards acknowledges, that "the cosmology assumed by the biblical author does not have authority for a Christian today." However, it does not automatically follow that, as he continues, "what have authority for today's Christian theology are the theological insights contained in the biblical narratives."[47] The connection between the two—biblical narrative and emerging theological insight—is too close for the former to be capable of correction while the latter remains unaffected. Among the salvific truths about God the creator and the work of creation, which Edwards claims to find communicated in the creation narrative as we have it, is "the reality of human sinful rebellion against God, bringing alienation from God, from other human beings, and from creation itself."[48] In other words, he does not see a need to recognize that the biblical narratives that express a mistaken cosmology connected with the phenomenon of death have given rise to misleading or mistaken "theological insights" relating to the alleged original sin and fall of humanity.

The conclusion of this chapter is that original sin and the fall of humankind is not a truth in the descriptive sense. They started as an etiological myth in Israelite culture to explain the phenomenon of death, which depicted human mortality as the result of human disobedience to God, as related in Genesis: "In the day that you eat of it you shall die" (Gn 2:17). For all his tangential developments of the myth, Augustine was apparently clear on its central point, that "the condition of human beings was such that if they continued in perfect obedience they would be granted the immortality of the angels and an eternity of bliss, without the interposition of death, whereas if disobedient they would be justly condemned to the punishment of death."[49]

As established earlier, however, there is no biblical warrant for considering that a first sin had a cataclysmic effect on the whole of human nature, far less that such an effect was inherited by every subsequent human being by being transmitted from generation to generation through sexual intercourse. Nor is there any scriptural ground for maintaining that even when the collective guilt of such sin is dispelled by baptism there remains in all the baptized an inherent weakness, or concupiscence, that incites everyone to succumb to their unruly feelings. Moreover, with the development of modern evolutionary science, that particular myth, and all the accretions that it gathered in the course of theological history, are no longer necessary, death being recognized as an essential biological process that applied to all living entities well before the advent of humanity and that has naturally encompassed all human beings since their first arrival on the cosmic scene. It may well be true that at some stage in human evolution something went badly wrong, morally speaking. But there are no grounds for claiming that it was a single moral catastrophe that implicated all subsequent human beings and alienated the Creator and still reverberates through the whole of humanity. What went wrong was that men and women began to sin, and kept on sinning, making moral choices that were out of harmony with the cosmic design their creator had in mind.

Haught is outspoken in rejecting the biblical account of original sin: "Evolutionary science . . . has rendered the original cosmic perfection, one allegedly debauched by a temporally 'original' sin, obsolete and unbelievable."[50] As the previous discussion testifies, it has no revelationary, far less historical, warrant, and the obvious conclusion appears to be that it would be more theologically appropriate now to drop it as unnecessary and cumbersome religious baggage, as the final chapter in this volume proposes in more detail.

BAFFLING DEATH

It is clear that the pivotal event in the Christian Gospel and the center of its preaching must be the resurrection of Jesus from the dead. Peter preached the resurrection of Jesus to his fellow Jews in Jerusalem on the day of Pentecost (Acts 2:24), and so did Paul in the equivalent Gentile scenario on the Areopagus in Athens (Acts 17:18, 31). Jesus's return from the dead, however, was not simply a singular event that happened to him. It had cosmic repercussions betokening that the resurrection of Jesus was an evolutionary breakthrough for humanity. In other words, the profoundly good news is that through Jesus human beings are being saved from the evolutionary fate of individual mortality. As Roger Trigg has written, "Resurrection lies at the heart of the Christian Gospel, not just as something which once occurred for Christ, but as a hope held out to each and every individual."[51]

As we consider the New Testament, a major emphasis that we become aware of is that we are saved by Jesus from sin. However, this depends on a causal link in Israelite thinking and religion, inherited by Christianity, between sin and death such that death was envisaged as entering into human history as the penalty imposed by God for the sin of disobedience committed by our first parents. As I show, however, in light of our growing understanding of evolution, dying is a fact of evolutionary life and does not require any further explanation, as opposed to the Jewish/Christian explanatory account of the Fall. Consequently, if the death of Jesus is construed as in some way a saving death, this is not necessarily interpreting it as a move to save and redeem humanity from sin. Rather, the death of Jesus is a saving from death; it is a remedying for us humans of the evolutionary fact of death that requires the disintegration of some organisms in order to provide for the emergence of others. In other words, the evolutionary purpose of the death of Jesus, freely undertaken, was to conduct the human species beyond individual mortality and to introduce it to the final stage of everlasting fulfillment for which it is destined by a loving God.

It was not necessary that in such a project the death that Jesus experienced should be a violent one. However, the moral program to which he tried to introduce his fellows, as discussed in the last chapter—namely the imitation of God-originating altruism, or agape, as a prelude to a life of sharing the divine happiness—was one that met largely with resistance, and it aroused such antagonism among his contemporaries because of its personal, religious, and political implications that his fellow humans decided to destroy him. How Jesus might have passed through death peacefully had his earthly mission been successful we have no means of knowing, but his rejection and death by crucifixion not only enabled him to usher his fellow humans into sharing a richer life but also provided them with the example and inspiration of a death of suffering that provided for all time the supreme instance of human altruism and agape. Such a death confronting and overcoming human evolutionary dissolution gives to John Donne's lines an unexpected richness: "One short sleep past, we wake eternally, / And death shall be no more; death, thou shalt die."

Such a sharpening of the focus of the gospel to appreciate that it is more from death, from mortality, than from sin that Jesus is saving humanity might give a new relevance and vitality to preaching the gospel today. It is not uncommon to hear in several, especially Christian, quarters the plaint that these days people have lost a sense of sin. Part of my reaction to this as a historian of Catholic moral theology is to reply, "And not before time." In fact, one advantage that results from the postmodern general demise of deference to all sorts of authority in society is a certain maturing of many individuals in the face of moral chiding by church authorities so that what is happening for many grownups is not so much a loss of the sense of sin as the discovery of a sense of reality and of a sense of proportion in their lives and their religion.

Conversely, it does appear that what people in today's culture need most is not the recovery of a sense of sin but the acquiring of a sense of purpose in their lives, something to give a shape and objective to their personal existence. Among the attempts to provide an interpretation of the Fall and of original sin that might be more meaningful today, one view congenial to the evolutionary approach was provided by James Gaffney. In his *Sin Reconsidered*, Gaffney provides a reinterpretation of sin that views it not as a lapse from a primordial state of innocence and human perfection but as a striving of the individual to attain to a state where moral exertion is seen as "part of the normal and natural development of maturing human personalities, rather than as the legacy of a primordially wounded nature."[52] This view, that sin represents not paradise lost but paradise ungained, is one that becomes particularly agreeable in light of an article written by Roger Haight titled "Jesus and Salvation: An Essay in Interpretation." Haight provides a useful survey and classification of patristic contributions to an understanding of Jesus's saving work before offering an interpretation for today that includes providing an account for four phenomena: "for the foundational experiences of bewilderment at the ultimate meaning of existence, of the evil that characterizes human existence, of moral failure in one's own personal existence, and of finitude that is never secure, but only grows weaker with time and culminates in the apparent annihilation that is death."[53]

I suggest a simplification of Haight's requirement of any salvation theory so that it need account for only two of the four conditions that he lays down: namely, what he terms the experiences of "bewilderment at the ultimate meaning of existence" and of "finitude that . . . culminates in the apparent annihilation that is death." It does not seem necessary that a theory of salvation suitable for an evolutionary worldview account for what Haight identifies as bewilderment at the experience of evil and of personal moral failure, that is, of sin; for these appear more satisfyingly explained, as Gaffney argued, as moral immaturity on the part of the human species and of the individual members of the species, such as we saw Darwin and Huxley identify in chapter 2. In other words, what Haight helps to bring out is that God in Christ saves us from death as the ultimate apparent denial of meaning and striving in life and that what the saving God confers on humans through his risen Christ is a completion and fulfillment of their earthly existence. In fact, death is devastating enough for humans without any need to invoke sin. In a televised address on the evening of Princess Diana's tragic accidental death in 1997, Cardinal Hume observed as reported in the London *Tablet* (September 6, 1997) that "the human mind cannot understand death. We face it with fear and uncertainty, revulsion even; or we turn away from the thought for it is too hard to bear." It was to help us accept and overcome this that God became man. In the words of the beautiful preface 1 of the Mass for the Dead, "In Christ the hope of our resurrection has dawned, and though we are saddened by the certainty of dying, he consoles us with the promise of eternal life to come."

Approaching this evolutionary interpretation of the achievement of Jesus raises the theological question of inculturation, to which the church on occasion pays formal respect, but which it appears to find so difficult to acknowledge in practice. In noting the connection between the gospel and culture, the Second Vatican Council observed that in revealing himself to his people "God has spoken in terms of the culture peculiar to different ages."[54] The argument that I advance here implies that a concentration on sin is strongly characteristic of the historical Jewish culture that was inherited by Christianity, and that consequently when the Word became flesh, emerging Jewish Christianity adopted this theology of sin as the appropriate, almost self-evident, matrix in which to develop the articulation of the good news of the gospel. The idea of inculturation, however, alerts us to the possibility of distinguishing what may be the core elements of Christianity from what may be more contingently associated, depending on the culture involved. This does not necessarily imply that in any particular culture contingent factors are less significant than core factors. Nor does it suggest that there is some platonic or abstract form of Christianity that hovers in the air uninculturated and waits to be applied to particular cultures rather than being educed from them in some way, as Paul attempted to do with Greek culture. The work of the Greek Apologists resulted in a recognizably Greek form of Christianity that raised controversy surrounding charges of the hellenization of dogma, and it is also customary to speak of characteristically Western, or Latin, Christianity and Eastern Christianity, the former of which could be described as a blend of Jewish Christianity (as in the New Testament) and Augustinianism.

Cultures can be not only contemporaneous but also successive in history, and this implies that the gospel's internal dynamic drives it to find expressions appropriate to different centuries as well as to different regions. This consideration lies behind the theme of *aggiornamento*, literally "updating," which so motivated Pope John XXIII in convening the Second Vatican Council.[55] As we attempt, then, to inculturate the gospel in the third millennium we can best do so by identifying the human needs and the human resources of this new global culture and by presenting the truths of the gospel in the way most suited to responding to and meeting those needs and resources. I suggest that today the deepest human need is to find a meaningful explanation of life and to cope constructively with the prospect of death rather than to be convicted of sin, and that concentrating on the latter will not only alienate many of our contemporaries but also obscure the central fact of the good news of the gospel, which evolution now enables us better to appreciate: that Jesus voyaged through death and rose to a new life and that he offers all humans the prospect of living beyond their own death to a fuller, richer life. This fundamental point of the incarnation is brought to light in Hopkins's poem *On the Blessed Virgin Compared to the Air We Breathe*: "Men here may draw like breath / More Christ and baffle death."

NOTES

1. Letter of His Holiness John Paul II to Reverend George V. Coyne, June 1, 1988.
2. Deane-Drummond, *Christ and Evolution*.
3. Ibid., 1–32.
4. Ibid., 95.
5. McGrath, *Christian Theology*, 428–30. Deane-Drummond, *Christ and Evolution*, 34–36, adds the names of Peacocke and Barbour as additional liberal theologians dependent on Lampe for their exemplarism.
6. Wright, *Christian Origins and the Question of God*, vol. 2, *Jesus and the Victory of God*, 565.
7. Haught, *God after Darwin*, 145–46.
8. Williams, *Doing without Adam and Eve*, 77.
9. Luther, *Lutherswerke*, vol. 2, 572.
10. See Fitzmeyer, "Romans," 413–17.
11. Augustine, *Contra duas epistolas Pelagianorum*, 4, 4, 7 (Migne, *PL* 44:614).
12. Kelly, *Early Christian Doctrines*, 354.
13. Augustine, *De nupt et conc.* 2, 1, 25 (Migne, *PL* 44:245); Mahoney, *Making of Moral Theology*, 47.
14. Yarnold, *Theology of Original Sin*, 55.
15. Muddiman, "New Testament," 102–21, at 112.
16. Räisänen, "New Testament in Theology," 122–141, at 124.
17. Mahoney, *Making of Moral Theology*, 63; see 47.
18. Augustine, *Contra Iulianum opus imperfectum*, III.57 (Migne, *PL* 45:1275). Cf. "nature corrupted and condemned": *City of God*, XXII, 24, 1 (Migne, *PL* 41:788), 1071. The Catechism of the Council of Trent, aimed at helping parish priests communicate the teaching of the recent council, is probably influenced by Augustine in its comment in part 2, in which it defines baptism, that "by nature we are born from Adam children of wrath." Callan, *Catechism of the Council of Trent*, 163.
19. Williams, *Doing without Adam and Eve*, 42.
20. Fitzmeyer, "Romans," 408.
21. Ibid., 409.
22. Ibid., 411–12.
23. Rahner, "Theological Concept of Concupiscence," 347.
24. Kelly, *Early Christian Doctrines*, 363–64.
25. Hebblethwaite, *Incarnation*, 47 (emphasis added).
26. Newman, *Apologia*, 218.
27. Daly, "Creation and Original Sin," 110.
28. Found via internet search, using key term "John Paul II addresses, 8 October 1986," (accessed October 9, 2009).
29. Vatican Council II, *Gaudium et spes*, no. 13.
30. Williams, *Doing without Adam and Eve*, 44.

31. Fitzmeyer, "Romans," 409.

32. Ibid., 135; cf. 409.

33. Carmichael, *Origins of Biblical Law*, 40.

34. Von Rad, *Genesis*, 22.

35. Daly, "Creation and Original Sin," 102; Ricoeur, *Symbolism of Evil*, 243.

36. Westermann, *Genesis*, x–xi.

37. Clifford, "Genesis," sec. 2, para. 2.

38. Westermann, *Genesis*, 28.

39. Lyttelton, "Atonement," 276.

40. Von Rad, *Genesis*, 37.

41. McKenzie, "Aspects of Old Testament Thought," 77:1–178, at 126; cf. 28.

42. Ibid., 77:126 (emphasis added).

43. Ibid., 77:132.

44. Wright, *Christian Origins and the Question of God*, vol. 2, *Jesus and the Victory of God*, 272–73.

45. Peacocke, *Theology for a Scientific Age*, 62–63.

46. Ibid., 63.

47. Edwards, *God of Evolution*, 11.

48. Ibid., 12.

49. Augustine, *City of God*, 13, 1, 510.

50. Haught, *God after Darwin*, 149.

51. Trigg, "Theological Anthropology," 453–71, at 455.

52. Gaffney, *Sin Reconsidered*, 41.

53. Haight, "Jesus and Salvation," 235–43; and 244.

54. Vatican Council II, Pastoral Constitution on the Church in the World, 58.

55. O'Malley, *What Happened at Vatican II?*, 37–39.

CHAPTER FOUR

Incarnation without
the Fall

IN CHAPTER 3 I argue that with the acceptance of the evolutionary origin of humanity there is no longer a need or a place in Christian beliefs for the traditional doctrines of original sin, the Fall, and human concupiscence resulting from that sin and, further, that much more positively the evolutionary achievement of Jesus was to communicate the altruism of God to the evolving human species and to lead it through death and individual extinction to a richer experience of life by sharing in the altruistic love of the three-personed God. This approach argues against the mainline Christian tradition that the point of the incarnation, God becoming man, was to remedy the ruinous state of fallen humanity. The incarnation has been considered the central Christian doctrine traditionally viewed as God's merciful move to repair the fall of humanity and restore the original harmony between Adam's descendants and their creator. As the Easter liturgy exults, the fall was a *felix culpa*, a "fortunate offence," "a truly necessary sin of Adam, which has been undone by the death of Christ."

The offer of an evolutionary reinterpretation of the incarnation creates a new relevance for the surprisingly popular topic that was discussed as a matter of theological speculation during the Middle Ages: whether the incarnation would have taken place even if the fall of humanity had not occurred. Early in his treatment of Christology in the *Summa Theologiae*, for example, Thomas Aquinas chose to ask, "Whether, if mankind had not sinned, God would nevertheless have become incarnate." In response he noted that some theologians maintained that this was the case, but he himself considered preferable the view held by others that the work of the incarnation was ordained by God as a remedy for sin, this, he explained, being the only reason for it given in scripture.[1]

WHAT IF ADAM HAD NOT SINNED?

A modern writer on the incarnation has written succinctly, "Christ's coming to earth was not an afterthought, a plan B."[2] And a shrewd Jesuit friend of mine once closed a discussion with the comment that "the incarnation was too big to be a rescue job." Indeed, on reflection there may be something ridiculous, not to say mildly blasphemous, about the idea that Almighty God failed in his first attempt at creating human beings and had to try again by this time becoming human himself. As Karl Rahner once expressed it, the incarnation is "no fresh attempt on God's part in which he strives once more to achieve as redeemer in the world what he failed to achieve as creator of it."[3] However, medieval theologians found themselves faced with Augustine's confident assertion that God was working on a plan B when he asserted, "If man had not sinned, the son of man would not have come (*Si homo non peccasset, Filius hominis non venisset*)."[4] Augustine concluded this from Jesus's statement that "the Son of man came to seek out and to save the lost" (Lk 19:10), yet in a detailed study of patristic and scholastic sources on the subject, A. Michel uncovered an impressive number of Christian thinkers who took the opposite line and favored the idea that the divine plan for creation included God's becoming human quite apart from the sin of Adam.[5]

Among the fathers, Michel noted, none explicitly held that if Adam had not sinned the Word would nevertheless have become incarnate.[6] However, there may be indirect indications, he felt, that some fathers did entertain the idea as a possibility, and he based this among other considerations on their understanding of how according to Revelation Christ was "the firstborn of all creation" (Col 1:15) and the alpha and omega, "the beginning and the end" (Rv 22:13).[7] As if challenged by Augustine's bold claim, many scholastic theologians, including Albert the Great and Alexander of Hales before Aquinas, and Scotus and the Franciscan tradition after Aquinas, seriously considered the possibility that God would have taken on human nature even if humanity had not sinned and fallen from grace and required redemption. Many felt that the New Testament lists a number of reasons for the incarnation: to manifest God's glory, to reveal God's love, to teach human beings how to behave, to help human beings disengage from material concerns and concentrate on God, to provide them with a foretaste and anticipation of eternal life, and finally, to take away the sins of the world. However, the basic question considered was whether the last reason given, the redemption of the human race from sin, is the major reason for the incarnation, providing a basis for all the others, as Aquinas maintained.

The first writer identified by Michel as adopting the position that the incarnation would have taken place even if Adam had not sinned was the twelfth-century Benedictine abbot, Rupert of Deutz, who explained that all the difference that original sin made was that, rather than take on an impassible and immortal nature, the Word took on a possible and mortal one.[8] The influential Peter Lombard did not take the matter up, but Albert the Great, while acknowledging the lack of certainty, maintained that the Word would have become flesh even if mankind had not sinned. Alexander of Hales also thought it very likely, and Robert Grosseteste, bishop of Lincoln, agreed with Abbot Rupert.[9] It was against this background that Aquinas approached the question. Although, as previously mentioned, in his *Summa Theologiae* he concluded it more appropriate (*convenientius*) that the incarnation would not have taken place if Adam had not sinned, in his earlier commentary on the *Sentences* of Lombard he adopted a more tentative approach. There he considered it arguable (*probabiliter*) that the incarnation would not have occurred, but he also recognized as equally arguable (*etiam probabiliter*) the view that the incarnation would have taken place even without sin, because, as he pointed out, apart from liberating humans from sin it would have raised up human nature and brought about the consummation of the whole universe.[10]

It was with Duns Scotus in the fourteenth century that the idea of the incarnation taking place even without the Fall achieved a definitive form as a theological opinion. Michel comments that it became almost "a Franciscan doctrine"; in addition to Franciscans, distinguished non-Franciscan adherents included Gabriel Biel, Denis the Carthusian, Francis of Sales, and the Jesuits Salmeron and Suarez.[11] In his systematic survey of Scotus's theological teaching, Parthenius Minges extracts from Scotus's writings those passages that relate to his view that "even if humanity had not sinned the Son of God would have become incarnate."[12] Of these passages the most informative is Scotus's refinement of the traditional argument: "All the sources of Scripture and the Fathers can be expounded in the sense that Christ would not have come *as redeemer* if man had not fallen."[13] In other words, it was possible for Scotists to reconcile their view with that of those who understood the incarnation as occurring only as a consequence of sin by following the distinction introduced by Rupert of Deutz and understanding the incarnation following sin to envisage God's taking on a human nature that was possible and mortal as a result of sin, whereas if God had become human without Adam having fallen, the human nature taken on would have been like Adam's, impassible and immortal.[14]

Proof for such a theological position was considered to be found in scripture, especially the rich Christology of Colossians 1:15–21 that all things in heaven and on earth were created in him, through him, and for him. Similarly, the parallel between Christ as the firstborn of all creatures who holds all things together with the innocent Adam before the Fall could be read as indicating that the incarnation is connected with creation and as such is quite independent of the need for redemption.[15] In fact, Michel suggests, the Scotist position may also be supported by the phrase of the creed that describes Christ as coming "for us and for our salvation," which implies thereby a double motive, one for the incarnation and another for the redemption.[16] He then goes on to list the difficulties to which the more traditional view is subject, and after an exhaustive consideration of the evidence, including the later nuances of the Scotist and Thomist positions, he delivers his own final judgment that the view of Scotus is "acceptable" (*probable*) but that of Thomas is "more acceptable" (*plus probable*). In other words, he concludes, "from the viewpoint of reason, the Scotist opinion seems more satisfying; but from the viewpoint of faith based on revelation, the other opinion seems more imposing."[17]

CHRIST AS LORD OF CREATION

In modern times the most explicitly committed follower of Scotus's view on the incarnation was the Jesuit poet Gerard Manley Hopkins (1844–89), who in his studies and throughout his career was totally devoted to the thought of Scotus rather than to that of the more establishment-approved Jesuit theologian, Suarez, a commitment that earned Hopkins during his Jesuit studies the reprimand of manifesting "a somewhat obstinate love of Scotist doctrine."[18] The principal attraction that Scotus held for Hopkins lay in identifying and analyzing the unique "thisness" (*haecceitas*) of every individual thing, an approach that had strong affinity with Hopkins's own developing theme of "inscape" and that had helped to win for Scotus the accolade of "the subtle Doctor." For our purposes, however, it is sufficient to say that Hopkins identified with Scotus's view that the incarnation would have taken place even without the Fall. In his reflections on the Ignatian *Spiritual Exercises* and the divine work of creation, Hopkins observed that "the love of the Son for the Father leads him to take a created nature and in that to offer him sacrifice," and to note, "The sacrifice might have been unbloody; by the Fall it became a bloody one."[19] Likewise, Devlin draws attention to Hopkins's more detailed reflection on the work of creation in which the latter concluded that "the first intention then of

God outside himself or, as they say, *ad extra*, outwards, the first outstress of God's power, was Christ," a passage on which Cotter also expands in his study of Hopkins's Christology.[20] Such Scotist-inspired expressions were the outcome of Hopkins's ambition to present a totally Christocentric view of creation, and this was equally the dominant theme of another modern Jesuit thinker and writer whose influence and whose popularity have been more marked in recent times than those of Hopkins, the French evolutionary visionary Pierre Teilhard de Chardin (1881–1955).

It appears, in fact, that the cosmic Christology developed by Teilhard de Chardin has given fresh impetus to the Scotist and Franciscan idea that God would have become human even if original sin and the Fall had not occurred. As he wrote, "the most essential aim and criterion of Christian orthodoxy can be reduced to this one point: to maintain Christ *to the measure of and at the head of creation*."[21] On another occasion he described "the essence of Christianity [as] simply and solely belief in the unification of the world in God through the Incarnation."[22] Indeed, it is not infrequently felt that in his theology Teilhard de Chardin could be accused of "not fully including the mystery of sin and thereby failing to bring out the full import of the Redemption."[23] In fact, the thinking of Teilhard de Chardin is somewhat more complex. It is true that he almost despaired of the traditional account of original sin in the church's tradition. As he observed before 1922 in an unpublished article that was written at the request of a colleague, "It is apparent that today we are being irresistibly driven to find a new way of picturing to ourselves the events as a consequence of which evil invaded our world."[24] It was mainly on account of this article that was delated to the Holy Office and to his Jesuit superior in a still antimodernist Rome— an event that clouded his whole future reputation—that he was removed from teaching geology at Paris's Institut Catholique and was encouraged to take up geological work in China.[25]

It was not so much, however, that Teilhard de Chardin tried to do away with original sin as it was that he attempted to reinterpret it in a synthesis that combined the evil in the world with the threefold dimension of creation, fall, and redemption, which he envisaged were all operative in the evolution of the cosmos toward its Christological destiny. From his early studies in geology onward he developed a conviction that the whole cosmos and everything in it is in a continuous process of evolution, impelled internally from primeval matter and developing up to, and through, human consciousness to a point at which all created reality will culminate and achieve ultimate union and in the fullness of the divine presence become incarnate in Christ. As the divine creative initiative is lived out in such a progressive dynamic succession of stages of increasing complexity, each of them incomplete and striving, then the chance of evil, Teilhard de Chardin claims, is an inevitable accompaniment to the existence of all participated being. Evil is often the misfortune of something going wrong, which to the scientist considering evolution is seen as statistically inevitable.[26] Expressed much more technically,

> When cosmogenesis [the coming to birth of the world] is accepted, then . . . , for inexorable statistical reasons, it is physically impossible for some lack of arrangement, or some faulty arrangement, not to appear with a multitude which is still undergoing the process of arrangement—and that applies to every level of the universe, pre-living, living, and reflective. In such a system, which advances by tentative gropings, the laws of large numbers make it absolutely inevitable that every step toward order is paid for by failures, by disintegrations, by discordances: . . . Evil is thus a *secondary* effect, an inevitable *by*-product of the progress of a universe in evolution.[27]

It is this phenomenon that Teilhard de Chardin believed lay at the base of original sin. He wrote, "Original sin expresses, translates, personifies, in an instantaneous and localized act, the perennial and universal law of imperfection which operates in mankind *in virtue* of its being *'in fieri'* [in process of becoming]."[28]

In other words, original sin, for Teilhard de Chardin, is inseparable from creation; it is the unfulfilled aspect of all created reality. It is not, then, a matter of whether he could envisage the incarnation taking place without the Fall, as he understood the latter term—he could not envisage even creation (and therefore incarnation) without the Fall. In fact, creation, fall, and incarnation are for him three aspects of the single act of divine volition. "Creation, Incarnation and Redemption are seen to be no more than the three complementary aspects of one and the same process: Creation (*because* it is unifying) entailing a certain immersion of the Creator in his work, and at the same time (*because* it is necessarily productive of evil as a secondary statistical effect) entailing a certain redemptive compensation."[29] Hence for Teilhard de Chardin original sin is coextensive with creation. "If there is an original sin in the world, it can only be and have been everywhere in it and always, from the earliest of the nebulae to be formed as far as the most distant."[30]

In exploring such often tentative reflections, Teilhard de Chardin was always at pains—often literally—to be faithful to the church's teaching, even if at times he felt, or hoped, that he was in advance of its under-standing. He summed up his approach in a personal variant of the famous phrase of the Jesuits' founder, Ignatius of Loyola—which stressed the need for "thinking with the church" (*sentire cum Ecclesia*)—when he wrote "in what I am saying here, accordingly, my only wish and my only hope is to 'sentire'—or rather '*praesentire*'—*cum Ecclesia*,'" that is, to think ahead for the church.[31] In some respects at least this wish and hope were to be real-ized almost ten years after Teilhard de Chardin's death in the recognition of many that he was a hidden expert, or *peritus*, who influenced the think-ing of the Second Vatican Council.[32] In his lifetime he acknowledged that the way in which he interpreted the Fall and original sin could be viewed by some as "only a device for respecting an irksome dogma verbally, while emptying it of its traditional content," but he claimed that his interpreta-tion was entirely respectful of Christian thought and had more construc-tive possibilities.[33] There seems little doubt that he found the traditional depiction of the doctrine an embarrassment and its popularity a depress-ing element in Christianity. Writing in 1927 in *Le Milieu Divin*, which his biographer, Robert Speaight, described as "the essay which was to contain the essence of his spiritual doctrine" and which was officially disapproved of during Teilhard de Chardin's life, not being published until two years after his death, he observed that "our faith in the Kingdom of God has been disconcerted by the resistance of the world to good. A certain pessimism, perhaps encouraged by an exaggerated conception of the original fall, has led us to regard the world as decidedly and incorrigibly wicked. And so we have allowed the flame to die down in our sleeping hearts."[34]

His awareness that he was himself judged lacking in his appreciation of sin and evil, however, may have led to his adding in 1948 an appendix to what would become his masterpiece, *The Phenomenon of Man*, in which he assured the reader that he did not dismiss or diminish the problem of evil, nor did he deserve the charge of "naïve or exaggerated optimism." On the contrary, he responded, he was quite well aware of the "evil of disorder and failure," the "evil of decomposition," the "evil of solitude and anxiety," and the "evil of growth."[35] These Teilhardian forms of evil are explained and com-mented on by Mooney, who faults Teilhard de Chardin for insisting on tak-ing an exclusively positive approach to redemption, noting the similarity of Teilhard de Chardin's thought to that of Duns Scotus, "as well as its marked contrast."[36] The similarity lies in the fact that both theologians emphasize that "the primary motive of the Incarnation is not to counteract the effects of sin in the world, either original or personal, but to unite all reality, material and spiritual, natural and supernatural, divine and human, in the Person of the Incarnate Word, God's masterwork, the goal and crowning achievement of his goodness, power and love." Where they differ, Mooney notes, is in Teilhard de Chardin's explanation that this exaltation of Christ is also the primary motive of the redemption, apparently subsuming the suffering and death of Jesus into the whole creative process of evolution. "The whole question," Mooney rightly observes, "is whether salvation is to be conceived primarily as a reparation for sin or primarily as an elevating of created reality and a leading it to its fulfillment in union with God."[37]

Far from the incarnation, then, being at the service of the redemption, as Aquinas and the main current of Christian thinking tended to maintain, for Teilhard de Chardin the redemption was at the service of the incarnation, a stage in human evolution: "From the very origins of mankind as we know it, the Cross was placed on the crest of the road which leads to the highest peaks of creation."[38] In fact, the litany of evils noted earlier that Teilhard de Chardin produced to prove his recognition of evil itself are all manifestations of one sort or another either of the very process of evolution or of the statistical inevitability of "some unhappy chance" occurring in the course of evolution. This is the force of his conclusion that "indeed, if we regard the march of the world from this standpoint (i.e., not that of its progress but that of its risks and the efforts it requires) we soon see, under the veil of security and harmony which—viewed from on high—envelop the rise of man, a particular type of cosmos in which evil appears necessarily and as abundantly as you like in the course of evolution—not by accident (which would not much matter) but through the very structure of the system."[39]

When he then turned to consider the traditional Christian understanding of the origin of evil as expressed in the doctrine of original sin and the Fall, however, Teilhard de Chardin was much less confident. In his early work, *The Divine Milieu*, written in China in 1926–27, he noted the contribution of revelation insofar as "by revealing an original fall, Christianity provides our intelligence with a reason for the disconcerting excess of sin and suffering at certain points."[40] Later, near the end of his career in 1948, he asked whether to the eye of faith, not to science, the evil that we witness and are aware of "does not betray a certain excess, inexplicable to our reason, if *to the normal effect of evolution* is not added the *extraordinary effect* of some catastrophe or primordial deviation? On this question, in all loyalty," Teilhard de Chardin now confessed, "I do not feel I am in a position to take a stand."[41]

"FOR OUR SALVATION"

Daly observes that "there can be no understanding of what salvation might mean until we are clear about the condition from which we long to be saved."[42] The view that even if Adam had not sinned at the dawn of human history the incarnation would have taken place at some time and God would have taken on human nature and become one of us is a theological position that possesses some acceptability from tradition. As such, it is easy to conclude that, if in fact there was no original sin or fall from divine grace, as I have argued, then the incarnation without the fall becomes more than a would-have-been; it becomes what in fact happened. From theological speculation it becomes reality. A different line of approach to the same conclusion can be shown from examining the serious difficulties that arise from interpreting the incarnation as the way in which God chose to remedy original sin and to restore fallen humanity to divine friendship.

It may have been one of the disciples of Jesus who contemplated his dead master's body hanging on the cross on Calvary that Friday afternoon on whom it first dawned that this bloody corpse was a sacrifice to God. For the belief that the suffering and death of Jesus should be interpreted as positively sacrificial became a central theme in the early Christian community as it tried to come to terms with his mission brutally terminated by his execution. To all appearances, Jesus the Nazarene was got rid of by Jewish and Roman authorities as a convicted troublemaker. To the religious and secular authorities he was subverting the established religion and destabilizing the political situation; in his own mind and that of his followers he was a religious reformer who was being put to death because of his faithfulness to his teaching about the God of Israel and because of the quality of worship and behavior that he insisted God looked for from his people. As the fourth gospel reports Jesus saying at his Roman trial, "for this I came into the world, to testify to the truth" (Jn 18:37). In his tragic death, as in his life, Jesus bore faithful witness to the truth about God.

But was there more than that going on that day on Calvary? Could it be that in accepting his death Jesus was not just making a final statement of utter fidelity to his father, but that he was also asking something from God—even something in return for his death? In other words, was his death a sacrifice? The *Oxford Companion to the Bible* observes, "In the New Testament, particularly in Hebrews [5:1; 7:27; 9:12–14, 26], the death of Jesus is described as a sacrifice that definitively secures for the whole of humanity the effects (atonement, fellowship with God) that older sacrifices brought about only temporarily."[43] It was not only the letter to the

Hebrews, but more formatively for the future focus of Christian theology it was also Paul's letter to the Romans, that seemed to put at the center of the church's understanding of the death of Jesus the appreciation that as a result of that death all humanity is now restored to God's friendship; that is, all are justified, or made right with God, "through the redemption that is in Christ Jesus, whom God put forward as a sacrifice of atonement by his blood"(Rom 3:24–25; cf. 1 Cor 5:7). In his magisterial study of Christology, T. N. Wright observes that "very early within the Christian tradition a theological interpretation was given to Jesus' death." As he continues, "'Christ died *for our sins*' was already a traditional formula within a few years of the Crucifixion. Paul could write not long afterwards that 'the son of God loved me and gave himself for me' (1 Cor 15.3)."[44] As Wright summarizes it, such "atonement-theology . . . characterised the Church's understanding of Jesus' death from very early on."[45]

Israelite culture was steeped in the idea of sacrifice, its major religious activity, particularly the bloody slaughtering of animals, which were regularly offered to God to express a spectrum of human attitudes, whether as first fruit offerings of a herd or flock to symbolize the ownership of the whole by God; as peace offerings to establish, or reestablish, a favored relationship with God; or as sin offerings or guilt offerings to atone for a ritual impurity or a moral offence against God (Lv 1–7; Nm 15; Lk 2:22–24; Mt 5:23–24). The Israelite stress on sacrifice was culturally linked with the Jewish preoccupation with sin on which I commented in the previous chapter and provided a ritual mechanism for obtaining forgiveness for wrongdoing and absolution from guilt, about which the Jews were almost obsessively conscious. On occasion the Old Testament prophets condemned the people of Israel for being more concerned with their formalistic sacrifices to God than with behaving justly toward their fellows (Am 5:22–24; Is 1:11,16–17; Ps 51:17). As Hosea expressed it (6:6), "I desire steadfast love and not sacrifice, the knowledge of God rather than burnt-offerings," a sentiment echoed by Jesus in his own day: "Go and learn what this means, 'I desire mercy, not sacrifice'" (Mt 9:13). What the prophets and Jesus were emphasizing, however, was that religious sacrifices were no substitute for a morally good life; they were not thereby discouraging in principle the national practice of regularly offering sacrifice to God. For, as Wright concluded, in describing the range and types of sacrifices central to Jewish culture, "when questions of dealing with sin and enslavement were raised it was to the notion of sacrifice that Jews naturally turned."[46]

The Jewish culture and mentality that focused so much on sinful transgression and redeeming sacrifice was thus a ready source and encouragement of the interpretation of the Crucifixion of Jesus as a sacrifice, a redemptive act offered to God, a ransom, a sin offering, an expiation and atonement for sin, a reconciliation of estranged humanity. Not only Israel's ritual culture but also its literature was seen as pointing to sacrificially atoning interpretations of the violent death of Jesus, especially those passages in the book of Isaiah that were read as prophetic references to a future suffering "servant of the Lord" (Is 53): "Upon him was the punishment that made us whole. . . . The righteous one, my servant, shall make many righteous, and he shall bear their iniquities" (Is 53:5, 11). As C. H. Dodd observed, "When the early church came to grips with the problem presented by the extraordinary career and the tragic fate of its Founder, it turned for elucidation to these passages of Isaiah, which speak of a life of service and a martyr's death."[47] It was out of this prophetic vision and the widespread culture of sacrifice in the world of the Bible that soteriology developed as that branch of theology that studies Christ as savior (Greek *soter*) of humanity and took a variety of forms through the centuries, picking out ideas and allusions from the Bible and meditating on them in light of the culture of each age. It is instructive to examine how this broad current of Christian thought developed historically and can be evaluated today by contrast with the evolutionary context I proposed in chapter 3 that the voluntarily accepted death of Jesus on the cross can be interpreted as having another purpose, one that is richer and more positive than that of being a sacrificial sin offering aimed at restoring the fractured relationship between humanity and its creator.

An obvious objection to any attempt to relegate the atonement theology of the Crucifixion from the center of Christian beliefs is found in the fact that two of the gospels cite Jesus himself as offering this interpretation of his coming death. The gospel of Mark, followed by Matthew, envisioned a key significance to the statement ascribed to Jesus that the Son of Man came "to give his life as a ransom [*lutron*] for many" (Mk 10:45 = Mt 20:28), which has been described as "the theological climax" of the dramatic Markan journey of Jesus from Galilee to Jerusalem (Mk 8:22–10:52).[48] As Donahue and Harrington remark, "Rather than being a foreign body attached to the end of Mark 10:41–45, the 'ransom' saying provides the key to the whole passage and to Mark's Gospel as a whole. Moreover, the 'ransom' saying links Mark's Gospel to Paul's focus on the soteriological effects of Jesus' death and resurrection."[49]

It is clear also, as well as significant, that the Old Testament background to this statement of Jesus is the fourth servant song in Isaiah 52:13–53:12, which "contains the most extensive description of the Servant's sufferings and a theological interpretation of them as a sacrifice and an expiation for Israel's sins."[50] Wright is skeptical about the view that rejects the historicity of Jesus's "predictions of the passion," including the ransom atonement verse of Mark 10:45 = Matthew 20:28. He rejects its being regularly "dismissed . . . as reflecting early Christian apologetics and atonement-theology rather than anything characteristic of the mind of Jesus."[51] Yet Donahue and Harrington persuasively conclude that Mark 10:32–34 "is a very detailed Passion prediction, so detailed that it is hard to escape the impression that its wording reflects the episodes described later in the Markan Passion narrative."[52] In other words, the reference to ransom atonement ascribed to Jesus in Mark and repeated in Matthew should most likely be seen as a *vaticinium ex eventu*. It appears to be an alleged prophecy that has its origin in the early community's post-Easter attempt to understand the theological significance of why God permitted the Crucifixion, and to do so in the context of the deeply rooted Israelite traditions of death as the punishment for sin and of sacrificial atonement as the remedy for sins. There are good grounds for thinking, then, that the sacrificial reference to the death of Jesus found in Matthew and Mark originated from later reflection in the Christian community.

Varying Soteriology

It has been suggested by McBrien that the Isaian servant role "at first eagerly attributed to Jesus, was later abandoned as being too Jewish and, therefore, not readily understandable within the Gentile world." In its place other ideas from the Bible were developed instead, especially those of ransom and redemption, as warranted in the gospels' description of Jesus as being handed over to liberate humanity from the slavery of sin (Mk 10:45 = Mt 20:28; cf. Col 1:13–14; 1 Tm 2:6).[53] Put succinctly, McGrath observes that "Christ is seen as having achieved something which makes possible a new situation."[54] On this Macquarrie noted that "the Church has never formulated a doctrine of the atonement with the same precision with which it has tried to define the person of Christ. Instead, we find several explanatory models that have developed side by side. Even in the New Testament, a considerable variety of ways of understanding the atoning work of Christ is to be found."[55] Indeed, as Kelly commented, "modern students are sometimes surprised at the diversity of treatment accorded by even the late fathers to such a mystery as the Atonement."[56] In the early Apostolic fathers and Apologists, he notes, there is no shortage of references to

Christ as a revealer who saves humanity from ignorance and from error.[57] But Kelly concludes that apart from the late first-century Ignatius of Antioch we nowhere "meet with any real appreciation of the truth that through Christ's assumption of human nature the infusion of new life into fallen humanity has been made possible."[58] He emphasizes this by commenting that "Latin theology remained curiously backward and meagre in its treatment of the redemption."[59]

What might be considered to reflect more originality in expounding the specifically saving work of Christ was forthcoming in the work of Irenaeus (*fl.* 180), who viewed the work of Christ as "obtaining salvation for us, so that we might regain in Jesus Christ what we had lost in Adam, that is, being in the image and likeness of God."[60] Christ achieved this, according to Athanasius in the fourth century, by becoming "incarnate for our sakes, so that he might offer himself to the Father in our place, and redeem us through his offering and sacrifice."[61] In this sentiment Athanasius was creating a sacrificial soteriology that came to dominate subsequent Christian reflection, both Catholic, in the Council of Trent's decrees on original sin, justification, and the Mass, and Protestant, to the eloquent displeasure of Tennant as discussed in chapter 1.[62]

If there developed in time considerable agreement among theologians on what it was that Christ effected through his sacrificial death, there was a marked variety of ways to describe how he brought about this effect. A regular theme was that of hostility and conquest, with the identity of the defeated enemy varying.[63] The eleventh-century Easter liturgy sequence *Victimae paschali laudes* (Praise for the Easter Victim) celebrated how "death and life fought a wondrous duel; the leader of life died but is now alive and reigning." More commonly, the foe was Satan. Earlier, in a world that was considered to be peopled by warring spirits, including "the spiritual forces of evil in the heavenly places" (Eph 6:12), a popular view was that God in Christ waged and won a war against the devil to rescue from the latter's clutches the souls of fallen and condemned humanity, as strikingly illustrated in the medieval theme of "the harrowing of hell," which was based "rather tenuously," McGrath observed, on 1 Peter 3:18–22.[64] The unadorned story was that in their disobedience to God, Adam and Eve chose to make themselves and their descendants subject to the devil, but when the latter then claimed jurisdiction over the sinless Jesus, Satan was considered to be overstepping his authority; his power was broken and Jesus took over his jurisdiction.[65] Augustine explained the background more fully in observing that "by a kind of divine justice the human race was handed over to the power of the devil for the sin of the first man, which passes by origin to all who are born of the intercourse of the two sexes, and involves all the descendants of the first parents in its debt."[66]

A further ingenious development that no doubt appealed to some Christian minds was the theme of God outwitting the devil. By his successful temptation of Eve the latter had gained mastery over sinful humanity, but God then took human form and in turn deceived Satan into overreaching himself by claiming to have authority over Jesus as well as his fellow humans.[67] Setting a trap for Satan by concealing the divinity of Jesus under human appearance and luring the enemy into snatching at a baited fishhook or grasping at the bait in a mousetrap were diverting analogies that aimed to explain how in his incarnation and death Jesus had liberated humanity from the clutches of sin.[68] Astonishingly to modern believers, for instance, Augustine in a popular sermon recalled how Jesus likened himself in expelling demons to someone entering a strong man's house to tie him up and plunder his property (Mt 12:29). In pursuing the application of the verse to Jesus and Satan, Augustine asked, "So what did our Redeemer do to our captor? As our price he held out his cross as a mousetrap (*muscipula*); he placed his blood there as food. . . . By shedding the blood of someone who was not a debtor the Captor was commanded to give up those who were his debtors."[69]

Augustine's reference here to a "price" offered by Jesus to the devil illustrates an important development of the confrontation theory of salvation, one that took up and exploited the biblical idea of ransom, the term that Jesus himself is described as applying to his saving work (Mk 10:45 = Mt 20:28; cf. Col 1:13–14; 1 Tm 2:6). Basically the Greek words for "ransom" found in the New Testament, *lutron* and *apolutrosis*, derive from the simple verb *luein*, which means "to release," but they add the additional element of doing so at a cost. Daly observes that "the language of soteriology is replete with burnt-out metaphors."[70] Thus references today to the redemption achieved by Christ hopefully no longer retain any association with the term's original metaphorical force of ransom (Greek *lutron*) or of buying back (Latin *redemptio*). McBrien commented that in the development of soteriological thought "it has been an extraordinary misunderstanding to view this act of ransoming in more than *metaphorical* terms, as if it were some necessary payment demanded."[71] In New Testament times, Daly noted, writers "are content to employ the metaphor without driving it beyond its limitations." However, many of the fathers were unable to exercise this restraint and went on to ask the theologically fatal question,

"To whom was the ransom paid?" concluding that it must be the devil and thereby opening up a line of enquiry that produced an exotic and unbiblical mythology centered on "the Devil's rights."[72] Thus in a number of ways thinkers proceeded, as Dillistone expressed it, to "elaborate and embellish" the idea of a negotiated transaction undertaken to save humanity.[73] In fact, the effete metaphor ascribed to Jesus "to give his life a 'ransom' for many" (Mk 10:45) became an elaborate allegorical narrative, developing in real terms the idea that paying a ransom involves the releasing of captive prisoners back to their lord by payment of an agreed sum to their captor.

Thus Christ paid his blood and life to Satan as an agreed-upon exchange between God and the devil for the release of the captive human race to their original lord and master. Irenaeus writes how the Word "redeeming us by his blood gave himself for those who had been led into captivity."[74] More fully, Origen in the third century made much too of the metaphor, writing of Jesus delivering up his soul to the devil as ransom for the sinful humans over whom the latter claimed power, but who were released when Jesus in death overcame the devil.[75] In other respects Origen had more successful impact on subsequent soteriological reflection by introducing the theme of Christ's death as an act of vicarious substitution, or propitiatory sacrifice. "He is indeed," Kelly notes, "the first of the fathers to treat this aspect of the Lord's work in full detail, and he conceives of His death, not simply as an obedient surrender to God's will, but as an offering which has positive influence on the Father."[76]

Tertullian (c. 160–c. 225) had his own deeply influential contribution to add to the idea that, as prophesied in the suffering servant of Isaiah, Christ was punished for our sins. Applying his legal expertise in a number of areas he was able, Dillistone observes, "to clarify and confirm the doctrine and discipline of the Church."[77] This included transferring to theology the forensic idea of making reparation for offences in terms of giving satisfaction, although apparently Tertullian did not apply this to the work of Jesus as rendering satisfaction for our sins.[78] However, McBrien comments, "It was this legalistic approach that would influence much of Western theology for centuries thereafter."[79] For this would become the central point of the explanation of the redemption that came to be offered in the eleventh century by Anselm, the Italian abbot of Bec who became archbishop of Canterbury in the train of William the Conqueror after the Norman conquest of England. What has become the classic monograph *Cur Deus homo* (Why God Became Man) was Anselm's response to scholars among the secular clergy at the cathedral of Laon who considered that the whole idea of paying "ransom" raised serious questions about the power and the wisdom of God, not to mention the unpalatable idea of the devil having jurisdiction over fallen humanity above God.[80]

Honor Satisfied

Anselm's major move was to remove the devil from the soteriological scene and to concentrate on the need to make reparation for the offense committed against an infinite God, thus repairing the disruption of the order of creation that was brought about by the first humans in their sin. Obviously, Anselm proposed, compensation was required for the massive dishonor, insult, and injustice done by Adam to God, yet humankind in its sinful state could not even begin to offer anything like sufficient compensation or proportional recompense. Only God himself could bring this about by crossing the divide between God and man in the incarnation and then, as the sinless man/god, offering appropriate satisfaction to God in the form of accepting death—a death, of course, that Jesus himself did not merit as a sinful creature. By thus paying the debt humanity had incurred by sinning, and so giving satisfaction for sin, Christ canceled out the original dishonor, restored the divine order of creation, and redeemed humanity from its state of alienation from God. In other words, as Anselm himself summed it up, "man could not be reconciled except by a man-God who was capable of dying, through whose righteousness there might be restored what God lost through the sin of man."[81]

In later Protestant, or at least Calvinist, hands, Christ on Calvary became the substitute for humanity, punished by God the great lawgiver for our sins and in our place, as indeed Isaiah 53:5 seemed to have foretold, in a version of soteriology termed vicarious satisfaction. Wendel judged Calvin's description of the work of Jesus "a classic expression of the doctrine of satisfaction as it had been current ever since St Anselm. Everything in it is exactly in balance and harmony."[82] However, even in Calvin's text there appear at least hints of Jesus undergoing punishment as a substitute for sinful humans, which would come to be considered characteristic of later Calvinism. As he wrote, "Our Saviour Jesus appeared, having clothed himself in the person of Adam and taken his name and *put himself in his place*, in order to obey the Father and present his body before the righteous judgment of the latter; *to suffer the punishment that we had deserved*, in that flesh wherein the fault had been committed."[83] Such "substitutionary punishment," however, Macquarrie rejected as "sub-Christian," and Daly too had strong things to say about what he considered the "implicit blasphemy" of espousing "the notion of an offended God whose anger needs to be propitiated by human suffering."[84]

It is no great step to move from the basic position of Anselmian soteriology which requires the rendering of appropriate satisfaction to God, through Aquinas, to the sixth session of the Council of Trent in 1547, which decreed that among the several different causes of justification the meritorious cause is Jesus Christ, who "when we were enemies (cf. Rom 5:10) out of the great love with which he loved us (Eph 2:4) merited justification for us by his most holy passion on the wood of the cross and made satisfaction to God the Father on our behalf" (DS 1529).[85] Echoing this Anselmian and Tridentine doctrine, the 1994 Catholic *Catechism* has continued to teach (no. 615) that "Jesus atoned for our faults and made satisfaction for our sins to the father." Why Trent considered that satisfaction necessary is clear from the realization that through it "human beings from being unjust become just and from being enemies become friends" (DS 1528). In other words, not to belabor the point, Trent's teaching on justification depends basically on its teaching on original sin. In opening the decree on justification it noted that

> in order to understand the doctrine of justification truly and genuinely it is necessary that everyone acknowledges and confesses that when all humanity had lost their innocence in the sin of Adam, "became unclean" [Is 64:6] and (as the Apostle says) "by nature the children of anger" [Eph 2:3], as was expounded in the decree on original sin, they were to such a degree "slaves of sin" (Rom 6:20) and under the power of the devil and death, that not just the gentiles by the force of nature, but not even the Jews by the letter of the law of Moses could be freed or get up from that state . . . (DS 1521).

In concentrating on satisfaction for Adam's sin as the leitmotif of Christ's death, the Tridentine decree wisely avoided any reference to the theme of ransom or redemption (buying back), but there is a relic of the mythological interpretation in the allusion to sinful humans having been "under the power of the devil."

WHAT KIND OF GOD?

Taken together the Christian Church's doctrines of the Fall through Adam and the redemption through Christ constitute a great colossus of sin and salvation bestriding the Christian landscape for centuries, which constitutes a cosmic melodrama involving a cast of a rejected and injured, or unjustly treated, God, God's self-alienating human creatures, and God's only son, who became human and freely accepted a violent death at the hands of his fellow humans as a sacrifice offered to God for the purpose of making restitution for the outrage, achieving the reconciliation of sinful humanity to its creator, and restoring it to divine friendship. The story of how all this took place involved numerous twists and turns through the centuries and has finished by raising several difficult, if not disquieting, questions, some of which should now be considered. For one thing, McGrath notes that "justification was simply not a theological issue in the pre-Augustinian tradition," and it is quite evident how the intricate Reformation and Counter-Reformation marches and countermarches on the subject of justification depended on Luther's personal anxiety for his own salvation.[86] In fact, it is difficult to avoid the conclusion that McGrath has shown, perhaps inadvertently, that the whole tale of how to handle the justification of the ungodly has been very largely due to the personal preoccupations of Augustine and Luther in their day.[87] Yet we may well feel able to apply to more than Protestantism the strong strictures that we have seen Illingworth direct at the unbalanced and lopsided theology that resulted when "the religion of the Incarnation was narrowed into the religion of the Atonement," and as a consequence theologians "were so occupied with what is now called Soteriology, or the scheme of salvation, that they paid but scant attention to the other aspects of the Gospel."[88]

Again, in attempting to appreciate the thoughts, feelings, and decisions of God as depicted in sacred scripture we are fully accustomed to the need to recognize biblical anthropomorphisms and to make allowance for the continuing limitation that all our terms relating to God cannot but have in our own purely human experience and reflection. Thus ascribing human emotions to God is the very stuff of the Hebrew Bible, whether it be God's love, God's wrath, God's forgiveness, or God's frustration, and it is a theological commonplace to allow for and justify such terms when in the end they point to some noble or desirable human trait that can be predicated on God analogically, that is, as partly true and partly false. But the whole idea of sacrifice and its associated terminology that refers to the death of Jesus and to its acceptance by God are not used in the Bible in a metaphorical sense but in a real sense. The switch from viewing the atonement as an early *Star Wars* between good and evil spirits to construing it as a cosmic medieval court of law is described by McGrath as "the transference of the discussion of the salvation of humankind from the *mythological* to the *moral* or *legal* plane."[89] This is well put so long as it is not understood as a transference from the mythological to the *metaphorical* plane. It seems that in respect to the Crucifixion of Jesus, the idea of its being a sacrifice was not seen by his followers as a metaphor or used in a weakened or applied sense. As discussed earlier, it was understood as a real description of what was actually going on under the appearance of a judicial assassination: Jesus was actually offering himself to his father on behalf of his fellow humans and was being actually accepted by God as a real sin offering. As such, this understanding focuses our attention on divine justice and cosmic order and on asking what sort of God this is.

In Anselm's time his theory of the redemption in terms of the divine-human Jesus offering appropriate satisfaction to an offended God on behalf of sinful humanity drew various criticisms, not least from Peter Abelard (1079–1142), who gladly agreed with expelling the devil from the plot, but who also maintained that God did not need to be appeased and who asked the breathtaking question, possibly the most startling suggestion in the whole of Christian theology, "Could God not just have forgiven Adam and Eve?"[90] As Southern paraphrased Lombard, "Why could not God, like any good lord, simply pardon, on whatever condition seemed appropriate, those who repented?"[91] For, as Southern observed, in Abelard's opinion, "the Incarnation was efficacious, not in satisfying the just claims of God or Devil, but in teaching by example the law of love. It left out the whole idea of compensation to God for human sin, and threw the whole emphasis of the Incarnation on its capacity to revive Man's love for God."[92] Such an approach, however, was alien to the thinking of Anselm and of all those who were to follow him. For one thing, Anselm accepted it as historical fact that a redemption really had taken place through Jesus's self-offering to God and that the issue now was to attempt to explain this.[93] Above all, the Norman archbishop argued, was the primacy of justice. It would be an affront to universal justice, and to God's own supreme quality of justice, for any dishonor to God to be left unremedied or to be ignored or deemed not to have happened.[94]

In his study of justification, McGrath makes the point that "the doctrine of the impassibility of God . . . clearly suggests the subordination of a biblical to a philosophical view of God."[95] Perhaps we are witnessing here a similar transference by which the philosophical idea of legal justice is made to dominate and act as a straitjacket on all other considerations relating to God's ways with humanity. Even when the aspects of vengeful justice are removed, not to mention the suspect assurance that the infliction of pain can be justified as cosmically remedial or penally satisfying, the steps described as taken to undo the Fall can still leave one deeply uneasy: The satisfaction theory of the redemption seems to smack too easily of the salving of hurt pride and leaves no room for mercy on the part of God, except after the divine honor has been satisfied. As Portia observed unforgettably, however, mercy

> *is an attribute to God himself*
> *And earthly power doth then show likest God's*
> *When mercy seasons justice.*

It scarcely becomes the Christian believer to insist that as a matter of justice God must have his pound of flesh. In Jesus's parable of the returning profligate son (Lk 15:11–32) it was the father who displayed true prodigality in his eagerness to forgive and more. In other words, the God who emerges from all these elaborations on the Fall and on sacrificial compensation is not a particularly attractive one; they depict a deity scarcely worthy of admiration, far less adoration. In the history of the Christian community, particularly but not only since the Reformation, the central diptych of sin and redemption, the Fall and the cross, has almost dislodged other portraits of the divine being and divine action and has led to a profound imbalance in the portrayal of the Christian Gospel and its God.

It is not surprising, then, that many theologians, sensing this reaction in themselves or becoming aware of it in others, have sought some way of reinterpreting or reexpressing the whole idea of atonement, with its satellite ideas of sacrifice and justification. McGrath observes that in the twentieth century the concept of justification "was seen to be in urgent need of translation out of the legal and forensic language of the sixteenth century into the *lingua franca* of modern western culture," as instanced in the works of Heidegger, Bultmann, Tillich, and others.[96] In a recent, detailed study of some dozen modern theologians, Michael Kirwan classified their views on sacrifice under headings that illustrate how complex and occasionally convoluted contemporary attempts to commend a Christian soteriology can be.[97] He approvingly quotes the comment of Louis-Marie Chauvet that "there is no doubt that the word 'sacrifice' is one of the most treacherous in the Christian vocabulary."[98]

To sum up, the traditional soteriological interpretation of the death of Jesus as related to remedying original sin and the Fall, whether that death is defined as sacrifice or as ransom, redemption, or satisfaction, contains difficulties and incoherencies of which the basic cause may well be the need to connect the Crucifixion of Jesus with the sin of Adam in order to provide both a restitution for the evil done and a reparation of the alienation introduced. It can be something of a theological relief, then, to realize that such a connection between the Crucifixion and the Fall is not theologically required once it is accepted, as I showed in the previous chapter, that there was no original sin and no fall to be compensated for by Christ. The theological challenge, then, becomes one of identifying a positive purpose for the death of Jesus, a purpose that, as I propose, is impressively provided by reflection on modern evolutionary theory.[99]

A POOR ALTERNATIVE

The reservations that I have expressed here about various theories of redemption are not at all original, of course. They figured prominently in the thought of those eighteenth-century Enlightenment figures who took serious human and rational exception to the theological pronouncements that they considered demeaned humanity by tirelessly repeating the rhetoric of redemption continually going on about universal human corruption as a result of the Fall and the reparation that this required through the bloody suffering of Jesus on the cross. Prefacing his study of the Enlightenment critique of orthodox doctrines of justification, McGrath points out, "In that an orthodox theology of justification—whether Lutheran, Reformed or Catholic—presupposed the essential natural alienation of individuals from God (in other words, that individuals enter the world already alienated from God, rather than that they become alienated from God through their subsequent actions), it will be evident that a serious challenge was posed to such theologies by the rise of the moral optimism and rationalism of the Enlightenment."[100]

The European Enlightenment, or *Aufklärung*, which Oman and others have seen as the supreme crisis of Christianity, was a scientific and cultural movement whose temper was reflected by Kant in his famous article that replied to the question "What is Enlightenment?" in which he quoted Horace's exhortation to a young student friend to "wake up" and "dare to know" (*sapere aude*): "Have the courage to use your own understanding; this is the motto of the Enlightenment."[101] An excellent critical survey of Enlightenment attacks on Christianity, and of Christian reactions, is provided by McGrath.[102] As I have written elsewhere, "Enlightenment, Kant explained, was the courageous emergence of humanity from its cultivated immaturity to use its own intelligence without depending on any outside authority. But the experimental ferment and rational excitement of the Enlightenment came up headlong against the immovable revealed dogma of the original human sin of pride reaching above itself to pluck the fruit of knowledge and so rival God himself."[103]

In what we label today as the Age of Reason, G. R. Cragg pointed out, "the authority of the church was challenged in many spheres, but nowhere so seriously as in the intellectual realm . . . and the leaders of enlightened thought grew more outspoken in their criticisms of the church and its faith."[104] Fired by the scientific success of Newton, the Enlightenment mood was one dominated by what Dupré summarizes as "uninhibited critical thinking," and what Byrne calls a desire "for clarity and order," as well as by a persuasion that "if the laws of the universe can be made so clear and intelligible, then there must also be a simple and direct way to understand religion."[105] Such was the thinking, for instance, behind the best-selling apologetic work of John Locke (1632–1704), *The Reasonableness of Christianity*, which studiously avoided all treatment of sacrifice and redemption from sin.[106]

Within the movement deism exercised a powerful intellectual force, postulating "a divine watchmaker who first wound up the celestial mechanism," and was based entirely on mechanistic efficient causality.[107] One view considered deism as a vestige of Christianity, "a rationalistic abstraction of a specifically Christian idea, an undocumented survivor of the rejected revelation."[108] Others claimed to see it as the product of natural theology that provided a rational and intellectually respectable account of creation, and no doubt occasionally provided a cloak for atheism, without making many further demands in terms of religious belief, particularly in terms of biblically revealed Christian beliefs. Such beliefs considered unnecessary clearly included the doctrines about the person and divine nature of Jesus Christ, but they related even more to the fundamental dogmas of original sin that resulted in endemic human depravity, as well as to the solutions elaborated to counter the fallen and benighted state of human nature, these striking, as it were, at the very heart of the new age and its enthusiastic confidence in the analytical and creative power of reason. As Byrne explained, to the philosophes "humanity was characterized by the dignity bestowed by reason and the doctrine of original sin was an affront to this dignity. Thus, to fight *for* reason they felt that they had to fight *against* the doctrine of original sin and what they saw as its attendant pessimistic anthropology."[109] Regarding natural religion, the deists claimed, revelation, which was the source for these dogmas, was "at best superfluous, at worst superstitious."[110]

In particular, in France the twenty-four volume *Encyclopédie* under the directorship of Diderot (1713–84) challenged and denied accepted theological beliefs and dispensed with even deism, motivated above all by a consuming desire "to free the elite from the bondage of authority" and profoundly convinced of the natural goodness of humanity and the absence of any innate propensity to sin.[111] The German scholar Cassirer comments that "the concept of original sin is the common opponent against which all the different trends of the philosophy of the Enlightenment join forces. In this struggle Hume is on the side of English deism, and Rousseau of Voltaire; the unity of the goal seems for a time to outweigh all the differences as to the means of attaining it."[112]

Christian reactions to the strictures of Enlightenment thinkers directed against the traditional Christian dogmas of the Fall and the redemption took a variety of forms, some of them simply reiterating traditional dogmas in defiance of what were condemned as the onslaughts of godless rationalism. Byrne observes disappointedly that "perhaps the tragedy for Christianity is that in its attempts to respond to many of the—often shallow—attacks it endured, its intellectuals too often resorted to condemnation."[113] Others more imaginatively attempted then and since to interpret or express the contested dogmas in ways more congenial to modern thought. So far as concerns the Enlightenment itself, it must be said that, however defensible and justifiable its criticisms of the traditional presentations of the doctrines of original sin and redemption may be considered, what was probably its own most obvious weakness was its reductionist attempts to depict Jesus as nothing more than a moral teacher and exemplar. Even more critical for deism as such, however, in my view, is its mistaken understanding of the divine causality involved in creation. In its totally defective understanding of causality, notably of divine causality, the Enlightenment could not begin to appreciate the view, which is explored later, that divine being must be continually present in all nondivine being of which it is the origin and must be continuously operative as first cause in all the activities of nondivine being.[114] Far from envisaging a god who was a necessary prerequisite to launching the whole enterprise and who has thereafter left it to its own devices, the Christian belief is of a god who created and continues to sustain the whole of creation in its every detail. Not only has God brought everything into existence; God continues to hold everything in existence—"underneath are the everlasting arms" (Dt 33:27)—in the progressive unfolding in history of the divine plan for creation and the divine destiny for humanity in which Jesus has a central role to play. The evolutionary approach to the incarnation and to the achievement of Jesus that I explore respects this approach to divine and created causality and could hardly be further from deism in its stress on the continual dynamic presence of God within all created, secondary causes, particularly as manifested in the mission, role, and work of Jesus himself.

A final reflection on the traditional Christian beliefs in original sin and the redemption is that they depend on the argument that reconciliation presumes estrangement, with the consequence that if there has been no estrangement there is neither need nor scope for reconciliation. It must not be thought, however, that because there was no original sin and fall and therefore no need for redemption, as I have argued, humans do not commit sins and do not require divine forgiveness. On the contrary, as I have made clear, puny moves to divert from God's plan are likely to be as old as human history, as is the need for God's continual forgiveness, but both sin and forgiveness are best understood when viewed within the positive dynamic movement of cosmic evolution.

Moreover, to argue that the incarnation was not undertaken to remedy original sin does not mean that there is no connection between the divine taking on of human existence and the sins of humanity. What is again required, rather, is an understanding of the purpose of the incarnation precisely within the context of evolution. This is why it is interesting to go back, as I began this chapter, to the medieval debate about whether the incarnation would have taken place even without the Fall, since this provided the occasion to explore what other reasons God could have had (and—now, we may say—did have) for deciding to become human. In surveying patristic texts where the incarnation appears independent of the redemption, Michel highlights the argument that all things have been created in Christ, glossing Genesis 1:1 as "In the beginning, *that is,* in *Christ,* God created heaven and earth," and glossing Genesis 1:26–27 that humanity was created in the image of Christ, and of a Christ who was already foreseen before the Fall, his union with the church being mysteriously prefigured in Adam's acceptance of Eve.[115] Moving to the New Testament, Michel cites church fathers who highlighted the fact that Christ as man is the firstborn of creation, echoing Colossians 1:15. It was in Christ also, according to some fathers, that the saints were predestined (Eph 1:4), and it was for him that everything was created (Col 1:16).[116] Subsequently, among the theologians who favored the view of incarnation even without the Fall, a major argument used was based on the consideration that the Word becoming incarnate was the divine work that was most capable of showing the love of God and of manifesting God's goodness in the whole of creation.[117] It appears to be this consideration that underlies Aquinas's recognition as possible justifying reasons for the incarnation without the fall "the exaltation of human nature and the consummation of the whole universe."[118] These in particular happily harmonize with the approach to the incarnation within the context of evolution.

NOTES

1. Aquinas, *Summa Theologiae*, III, q. 1, a. 3.
2. Acker, "Creationism and the *Catechism*," 6.
3. Rahner, "Intellectual Honesty and Christian Faith," 68.
4. Augustine, *Sermones* 174, c. 2 (Migne, *PL* 38: 940).
5. Michel, "Incarnation," cols. 1482–1505.
6. Ibid., col. 1491.
7. Ibid., cols. 1492–93.
8. Ibid., col. 1495. See Migne, *PL* 168, 1628.
9. Ibid., col. 1495.
10. Aquinas, *Scriptum super lib. Sententiarum*, bk. 3, dist. 1, q. 1, art. 3.
11. Michel, "Incarnation," cols. 1495–96.
12. Minges, *Joannis Duns Scoti Doctrina Philosophica et Theologica*, 368.
13. Ibid., 369. See Scotus, Ox. lib. 3, dist.7, q. 3, n. 3.
14. Michel, "Incarnation," col. 1497.
15. Ibid., col. 1498.
16. Ibid., col. 1499.
17. Ibid., col. 1506.
18. Devlin, *Sermons and Devotional Writings of Gerard Manley Hopkins*, xiii.
19. Ibid., 257.
20. Cotter, *Inscape*, 122–25.
21. Teilhard de Chardin, *Christianity and Evolution*, 190.
22. Rideau, *Thought of Teilhard de Chardin*, 537n100.
23. Ibid., 190.
24. Teilhard de Chardin, *Christianity and Evolution*, 45.
25. Ibid., 55n. For further details on his "daring speculations" and the "great trial of faith" that Roman reactions caused him, see King, *Spirit of Fire*, 106–9; and on the modernist context of the episode Speaight, *Teilhard de Chardin*, 136–38, is informative. On these and later sanctions imposed on Teilhard de Chardin by Rome, Küng, *Beginning of All Things*, 98–100, writes feelingly in light of his own experience.
26. Teilhard de Chardin, *Christianity and Evolution*, 40.
27. Teilhard de Chardin, *Activation of Energy*, 259–60.
28. Teilhard de Chardin, *Christianity and Evolution*, 51.
29. Ibid., 198.
30. Ibid., 190.
31. Ibid., 174.
32. O'Malley, *What Happened at Vatican II?*, 258.
33. Teilhard de Chardin, *Christianity and Evolution*, 197.
34. Speight, *Teilhard de Chardin*, 142, see 146–47; Teilhard de Chardin, *Le milieu divin*, 149.
35. Teilhard de Chardin, *Phenomenon of Man*, 339.
36. Mooney, *Teilhard de Chardin and the Mystery of Christ*, 107–45; and 119–23.
37. Ibid., 121–22.
38. Teilhard de Chardin, *Le milieu divin*, 87.
39. Teilhard de Chardin, *Phenomenon of Man*, 340–41.
40. Teilhard de Chardin, *Le milieu divin*, 86.

41. Teilhard de Chardin, *Phenomenon of Man,* 341. On Teilhard de Chardin's evolutionary theology, see also Deane-Drummond, *Christ and Evolution,* 36–40.
42. Daly, *Creation and Redemption,* 197.
43. *Oxford Companion to the Bible,* 667; see 363–66.
44. Wright, *Christian Origins and the Question of God,* vol. 2, *Jesus and the Victory of God,* 109.
45. Ibid., 570; cf. 558.
46. Ibid., 274; see 273–79.
47. Dodd, *Founder of Christianity,* 112–13.
48. Donahue and Harrington, *Gospel of Mark,* 24.
49. Ibid., 315.
50. Ibid.
51. Wright, *Christian Origins and the Question of God,* vol. 2, *Jesus and the Victory of God,* 574.
52. Donahue and Harrington, *Gospel of Mark,* 314.
53. McBrien, *Catholicism,* 1:421.
54. McGrath, *Christian Theology,* 408.
55. Macquarrie, *Principles of Christian Theology,* 314–15.
56. Kelly, *Early Christian Doctrines,* 4.
57. Ibid., 163–64, 168–69, 178, 183–85.
58. Ibid., 166.
59. Ibid., 177.
60. Irenaeus, *Adversus haereses,* III.xviii.1 (Migne, PG VII, 932).
61. Athanasius, *Epistulae Festales,* VII; quoted in McGrath, *Christian Theology,* 411.
62. DS 1513, 1522, 1529, 1738–43, 1751; McGrath, *Christian Theology,* 413–15.
63. Macquarrie, *Principles of Christian Theology,* 318–19.
64. McGrath, *Christian Theology,* 416.
65. Southern, *Saint Anselm,* 207–9.
66. Augustine, *De Trinitate,* XIII, cap. 12, 16 (Migne, PL 42, 1026).
67. Daly, *Creation and Redemption,* 190.
68. Ibid., 186–87; Kelly, *Early Christian Doctrines,* 382–83.
69. Augustine, *Sermon* 130.2 (Migne, PL 38, 726); cf. *Sermon* 263, 1 (Migne, PL 38, 1210). See Kelly, *Early Christian Doctrines,* 391.
70. Daly, *Creation and Redemption,* 171.
71. McBrien, *Catholicism,* 421.
72. Daly, *Creation and Redemption,* 176. See also 186–87.
73. Dillistone, *Christian Understanding of Atonement,* 95. See 96–98.
74. Irenaeus, *Adversus haereses* 5, 1, 1 (Migne, PG 7, 1121). See Kelly, *Early Christian Doctrines,* 173–74.
75. Kelly, *Early Christian Doctrines,* 185–86; McGrath, *Christian Theology,* 415–16.
76. Kelly, *Early Christian Doctrines,* 186.
77. Dillistone, *Christian Understanding of Atonement,* 86.
78. Kelly, *Early Christian Doctrines,* 177.
79. McBrien, *Catholicism,* 447.
80. Southern, *Saint Anselm,* 202–5. See Anselm, *Anselm of Canterbury* (Migne, PL 158, 430).

81. Anselm, *Anselm of Canterbury*, bk. 2, chap. 21, p. 354 (Migne, *PL* 158, 430).
82. Wendel, *Calvin*, 218–19.
83. Calvin, *Institutes of the Christian Religion*, II, 12, 3.
84. Macquarrie, *Principles of Christian Theology*, 315–16. See McGrath, *Christian Theology*, 422–25; Daly, *Creation and Redemption*, 179.
85. Aquinas, *Summa Theologiae*, III, q. 1, a. 2.
86. McGrath, *Christian Theology*, 33.
87. Ibid., 402.
88. Illingworth, "Incarnation in Relation to Development," 182; see chapter 1, this volume.
89. McGrath, *Christian Theology*, 57.
90. Abelard, *Comm. super Pauli Epistolam ad Romanos*, lib. ii, cap. 3 (Migne, *PL* 178, 835); Southern, *Saint Anselm*, 208–9.
91. Southern, *Saint Anselm*, 209.
92. Ibid., 210–11.
93. Ibid.
94. Ibid., 210–16.
95. McGrath, *Christian Theology*, 32.
96. Ibid., 409.
97. Kirwan, "Eucharist and Sacrifice," 214–15.
98. Ibid., 214.
99. See chapter 3, this volume.
100. McGrath, *Justitia Dei*, 360.
101. Oman, *Grace and Personality*, 17; Kant, "Beantwortung der Frage: Was ist Aufklärung?" 169–76. Horace, *Epistles*, I, 2.
102. McGrath, *Christian Theology*.
103. Mahoney, *Ways of Wisdom*, 12.
104. Cragg, *Church and the Age of Reason*, 12.
105. Dupré, *Enlightenment and the Intellectual Foundations of Modern Culture*, 335; Byrne, *Glory, Jest and Riddle*, 29.
106. Locke, *Reasonableness of Christianity*.
107. Hampson, *Enlightenment*, 78; Dupré, *Enlightenment and the Intellectual Foundations of Modern Culture*, 243.
108. Ibid., 248.
109. Byrne, *Glory, Jest and Riddle*, 130.
110. Cragg, *Church and the Age of Reason*, 160.
111. Ibid., 241, 244. See Byrne, *Glory, Jest and Riddle*, 135–43.
112. Cassirer, *Philosophy of the Enlightenment*, 141.
113. Byrne, *Glory, Jest and Riddle*, 26.
114. Aquinas, *Summa Theologiae*, I, q. 8, a. 1. See chapter 5, this volume.
115. Michel, "Incarnation," col. 1492.
116. Ibid., cols. 1493–94.
117. Ibid., col. 1496.
118. Aquinas, *Scriptum super III Sent.* dist. 1, q. 1, art. 3.

CHAPTER FIVE

Seeking a New Paradigm

XAMINING THE TRADITIONAL Christian doctrines of original sin, the fall of humanity, and concupiscence reveals that these beliefs have been heavily influenced by a Jewish culture that was preoccupied in ascribing all human sufferings, including death, to divine punishment for human sins. As the acceptance of evolution and closer theological and historical examination make it unnecessary to continue to subscribe to these traditional beliefs, it becomes apparent that another line of explanation is required to account for human ills and tragedies, and for God's part in these, and this chapter is devoted to exploring what shape such a change of approach might take in an evolutionary context.

PROCESS THEOLOGY AND KENOTIC THEOLOGY

Theologians have proposed various explanations to account for God's permitting natural disasters and catastrophes, or what scholastic theology termed "physical evils," in contrast to the "moral evils" of human sinful acts that I consider later. One such line of explanation of physical evils is to suggest simply that God is unable to control the development and deployment of the natural forces that exist alongside him. The introducing of so-called process theology depicts a view of God that is significantly, even dramatically, different from the portrait of God envisaged in traditional and classical Christian theology. In reaction to a God considered supreme, eternal, omnipotent, omniscient, totally perfect, immutable, and infinite in all the divine attributes, and as such immune to any possibility of change, which was the classical Christian view of God that owed much to Greek reflection as it influenced scholastic philosophy and theology, the process philosophy of Alfred North Whitehead (1861–1947) viewed all of reality as in the process of becoming and in tension between what has been and what could come to be; it envisaged that process as shared in some respects by God too.[1] It is a view of God that many people consider does more justice to the God of love and compassion and to the biblical picture of God and of God's behavior; indeed, it sides with the preference expressed passionately by Pascal for the "God of Abraham, God of Isaac, God of Jacob, not of the philosophers and the scholars." It stresses the immanence of God involved in the continuing process of the world and in loving interaction with creatures, as distinct from the divine omnipotent and timeless transcendence and impassibility of a traditional Hellenistic deity.[2] Norman Pittenger, an English exponent of process theology, insisted that "all that happens in the world, with which [God] is ceaselessly in relationship, has its effect upon him, increasing his joy and providing him with new opportunities for action, or diminishing that joy by denying him such opportunities."[3] Process theology, as so described, with its aim to do justice to the very human attributes of the God of Abraham, Isaac, Jacob, as well as of Jesus, is not without its difficulties and critics, as will be discussed later. For the moment it suffices to quote Daly: "The irony is that we tend not to want a God who is too vulnerable or not sufficiently in control of the world which poses so many problems for us. Such a God appears to fail an essential test of divinity."[4]

Another approach to explain why God appears to permit natural evils to happen is that God does have the power to prevent such occurrences but that he chooses not to use his power. This theodicy, or theological attempt to account for evil, is commonly referred to as kenotic, or emptying, theology, which draws on Paul's description of how Jesus "did not regard equality with God as something to be exploited, but emptied (Greek *ekenosen*) himself, taking the form of a slave, being born in human likeness" (Phil 6–7). Paul is referring here to God choosing freely in the incarnation to divest himself of his divine power in taking on human existence, but in kenotic theology the idea of God's freely choosing to limit himself is expanded from the incarnation to the larger canvas of creation in the suggestion that God freely restricted his omnipotence in choosing to create and sustain the world, a choice that would find its logical culmination in God's later choosing to enter into that world and its destiny and freely accepting the limitations of creaturehood.

The feeling of theological outrage experienced by many at physical evils is not so much directed at the inexorable collision of physical forces that often occur on such occasions and that can take the form of awe-inspiring cosmic firework displays as it is at the deaths of human beings who happen to be helplessly caught up in such colliding forces. Viewed in evolutionary terms, this approach to the occurrence of natural evils postulates that in choosing to create a world subject to the laws or conditions of evolutionary development God has freely chosen to restrict himself and the further exercise of his power. The kenotic explanation offered for such phenomena is twofold: that God has limited himself to accepting the qualities and characteristics of the matter that he created in making the original universe and that he has decided not to intervene subsequently and decide miraculously to suspend the laws of matter, saving people who may happen to be unwittingly at risk from the effects of relentless natural forces.

One advocate of this self-denying ordinance on the part of God in creation, John Macquarrie, sympathizes with process theology in drawing a contrast between, on the one hand, the imagery of the religious monotheism of the Bible that feeds a sense of personal affinity with God and, on the other hand, the concepts deployed in philosophical monotheism that are aimed, and found, to provide more intellectual satisfaction.[5] He warns of the danger of process theology's reducing God to becoming a "puny godling," the classical divine attributes being reduced to ineffectiveness.[6] He proposes instead an approach by way of "dialectical theism," arguing that, in dealing with the sheer mystery of the godhead, there must always remain for us a tension, or a dialectic, between biblical images and rational concepts.[7] He considers such classical divine attributes as impassibility, immutability, eternity, and perfection to be too one-sided and to be in need of some dialectical balance, or corrective, in order to be both "religiously and intellectually satisfying."[8] He stresses that his proposed "dialectical theism does not deny the transcendence of God or most of the attributes which he had in classical theism, but simply asks that the properties ascribed to him should be understood dialectically, that is to say, each property is qualified by its opposite, and God himself, in accordance with the logic of the infinite, is understood as *coincidentia oppositorum* [the coming together of opposites]."[9]

It might be objected that Macquarrie, in reacting to the limitations of both classical theism and process theology, has settled for drawing up a list of the classic divine attributes and a parallel list of biblical correctives and simply called for the two to be juxtaposed in dialectical tension, a move that does not take one very far. In addition, however, there is a particular concept that runs as a refrain through Macquarrie's exposition of his dialectical theism. This is the difficult concept of divine risk, which he considers is involved in creation and which may carry within it the topics of vulnerability and lack of completeness on the part of God that process theology aimed to emphasize and that Macquarrie himself appears to find necessary as a complement to the classic divine attributes. As he explains,

God's essence is Being .... [A]s Being moves out to manifest itself in the world of beings, it involves itself in what can only be called "risk." . . . [I]t goes out into the openness of a world of beings, a world of change and multiplicity and possibility. We talk of "risk" because in this process Being could become split, fragmented, and torn within itself. The risk becomes acute when the universe brings forth beings, such as man, who have responsibility and a limited freedom that empowers them up to a point to manage their own lives and even to manipulate nature.[10]

Elsewhere Macquarrie spells out these implications of godly risk when he observes that "God is affected by the world as well as affecting it, for creation entails risk and vulnerability; God is in time and history, as well as above them."[11] "The risk," he explains, "is that beings may get lost in nothing—the potentialities for worldhood may not be attained."[12]

In other words it appears that, for Macquarrie, in the enterprise of creation God accepts the risk of failure, of something going wrong with his designs, if only in particular instances, not unlike the way in which process theology views God as himself limited and progressing in his relations with the world. This is why he is able, in referring to the divine immanence in what he calls "the world process," to claim that God "takes upon himself the suffering of the world and shares it with his creatures," and that this "eases the whole question" of the problem of evil. For, he goes on, "it is easier to reconcile ourselves to the presence of evil in the world if we know that it causes pain even to God, and that in his temporal aspect, he too has to face and overcome it."[13] However, in referring to "the risk involved in Being's going forth," Macquarrie differs from process theology in viewing such risk as a contingency freely chosen by God, explaining the need to "visualize this as constituting a self-imposed limitation on God's power."[14] Indeed, Macquarrie views God's freely accepting such a risk as an expression not simply of divine self-limitation but as an important instance of divine "self-emptying," or what we have seen referred to by Paul as *kenosis* (Phil 2:6–7). Daly explains that for Macquarrie "there is a self-emptying, or *kenosis*, of God as he pours out Being," a claim that enables Daly to comment that "Macquarrie puts forward a theory of theistic *kenosis* whereby God freely chooses to create and, having done so, accepts the inevitable consequences of his creative act," and to observe further that this shows "how an all-powerful being can exercise his power without logical incoherence by choosing to take into himself a vulnerability which, precisely because it is freely chosen, is a strength rather than a weakness."[15]

The eloquent appeal to kenotic theology, with its implications of divine emptying out and generous self-limitation, is a popular one in some accounts of evolutionary theology. The American theologian John F. Haught, for instance, envisaged a theology of evolution based on a kenotic understanding of God as humble, self-giving love. In fact, Haught has grand claims to make for such a kenotic conception of the creating God—not just of the Word incarnate—which he considers crucial to an evolutionary theology.[16] "The image of a self-effacing God, although always resident implicitly in Christology, is now—at least in the best of our theologies—beginning to supplant the image of an invulnerable, immobile, and essentially nonrelational God that seemed so antithetical to the world's evolutionary becoming and self-creativity."[17] It does appear, however, that Haught is almost fancifully ascribing too much to what he considers the world's capacity for self-directing action and its apparent problematic responsiveness to the divine invitations when he writes that "in the presence of the self-restraint befitting an absolutely self-giving love, the world would unfold by responding to the divine allurement at its own pace and in its own particular way."[18]

On the application of kenosis to the divine activity of creation by a God who freely accepts the limits of loving finite and created beings, as distinct from its Christological relevance, Edwards has this to say: "The theology of incarnation and the theology of the cross point to a God of unthinkable vulnerability and self-limitation. It is this concept of God, I believe, which needs to be brought into relation with natural selection."[19] In a somewhat similar vein, Arthur Peacocke argues from an evolutionary perspective to divine self-limitation in the sense that "God has so made the world that there are certain areas over which he has chosen not to have power," to such a degree that God submits his design to the element of chance, to the operation of random events, and to a limited knowledge of future states of affairs.[20] The difference, however, that this kenotic explanation introduces from any godly inability to control evil as is found in process theology is that such inability is now freely chosen. Given this, however, one unwelcome consequence that follows is that the question of how to account for natural evils returns in a new form, now asking precisely why God should have freely chosen to limit himself in their regard.

ACCEPTING THE UNAVOIDABLE

Apart from the difficulties involved in accepting process theology or kenotic theology, it appears possible, moreover, to avoid taking on board so massive a systematic alternative to traditional classical theology just in order to account for the world's natural evils that the Hebrew Bible ascribed invariably to human sinfulness being divinely punished. A simpler possibility, I suggest, can be found, not by way of suggesting that God shares in the limitations of being as this continues in process, nor by proposing that God has freely constrained himself to accept the characteristics of the universe he created, but by way of considering that, once God had decided to draw nondivine being into existence in the first place, he could not do other than accept the essential characteristics of such being. Macquarrie appears to hint at this approach when he suggests that God's governance of the world in his providence "must be such that he leaves to the world a certain openness and autonomy appropriate to the measure of reality and independence which it possesses."[21] The question, then, is not one of divine limitation in the handling of non–divine being but one of such non–divine being not being capable of being treated otherwise, once it exists. In other words, the point is not that there are some things that God cannot do or chooses not to do, but that there are some things that cannot be done, such as undoing past events or, as discussed later, causing a human being to choose freely.

The basic divine freedom is whether to create or not; the basic puzzlement then for us concerns just what it is that God creates. Peacocke draws attention to the mystery of scientific matter: "There is a genuine limitation in the ability of our minds to depict the nature of matter at this fundamental level; there is a mystery about what matter is 'in itself', for at the deepest level to which human beings can penetrate they are faced with a mode of existence describable only in terms of abstract, mathematical concepts that are the product of human ratiocination."[22] What is being considered here is even deeper than such material of scientific probing and observation. Just what is this non–divine being that God has freely chosen to bring into existence?

Searching for the characteristics of nondivine being, which, I am suggesting, cannot but be respected by God once he has created it, can be seen as seeking its intrinsic consistency or inner laws of being, yet such language raises numerous problems. Conceiving created being as operating in accordance with some intrinsic laws prompts the question of why a loving God should not on occasion be able to intervene to suspend those laws—the characteristic behavior of matter—when he so wills for his own good reasons, which is the traditional way of describing miracles. In addition, introducing the notion of scientific law supposes a regularity of behavior and implies the possibility of divine intervention that is seen as an exceptional interruption of such regularity. This idea of divine intervention, however, raises many problems of its own that lead off even further into the ocean of divine mystery. One problem is that using the language of laws and exceptions and interventions tends to depict a deist God who launches the world into existence and then lets it proceed on its own for the most part, but who seems prepared on occasion to change his mind and intervene directly to change the world's behavior. Yet the immediacy and intimacy of divine creative causality does not seem capable of being differentiated in such a way: as I examine in more detail in chapter 6, absolutely every event in creation is permeated by the divine presence, energy, and purpose.

An additional difficulty raised by the idea of occasional divine intervention is that it is a temporal concept, which implies the idea of time. It involves an interruption of a sequence, of a temporal succession, which is an idea which makes sense when applied to humans, but not when applied to God, whose existence is above and beyond time. I remember my metaphysics professor once pointing out that eternity should not be thought of as time open at both ends; it is time-less, because it does not proceed through stages. As defined by the sixth-century Christian philosopher Boethius, "eternity is the complete and perfect simultaneous possession of unending life" (*aeternitas igitur est interminabilis vitae tota simul et perfecta possessio*).[23] The chain of temporal events in world and human history is integral to our existence as physical creatures that exist and operate in a context of before and after. But in some utterly mysterious way, such events are all simultaneously in the present to God with whom there is no succession, no before, and no after. Likewise, the knowledge that God himself has of created things and events has no before or after: Strictly speaking, there can be no such thing as divine foreknowledge, the idea of divine prescience being one that can make sense only to us historical beings, and extremely complicated and confusing sense at that. If it makes any sense, the least inadequate scenario of the world's and humanity's history is that it is contained in a single divine idea that exists in divine eternity and works itself out progressively in evolutionary history. Something like this thought seems to lie behind Augustine's reflection in *The Confessions*, "O truth, everywhere you preside over all who ask counsel of you. You respond at one and the same time to all, even though they are consulting you on different subjects" (*veritas, ubique praesides omnibus consulentibus te simulque respondes omnibus diversa consulentibus*).[24]

Returning to the question of how God can allow the occurrence of natural evils in which innocents are harmed or destroyed by the ineluctable force of physical phenomena, we might conjecture that the explanation that I have offered, that God could not do other than accept the intrinsic characteristics of matter once he has decided to create it in the first place, can apply with fewer difficulties than the explanations offered by biblical sin and punishment, or by kenotic theology or process theology. Gerard J. Hughes emphasizes the incredible complexity and interdependence of reality in various situations in which the slightest variation can result in a totally different situation:

> A universe like ours, so far as we can tell on the basis of the scientific knowledge we have, comes as a package. The various aspects of our world are very tightly interlocked, simply because the things in our world interact with one another in ways determined by their various natures. Not, of course, that the laws of nature force things to behave in a fixed way: the laws of nature are not in any sense causal agents; rather they describe the fixed ways in which things of themselves of necessity interact. The more we learn, the more we appreciate how tight the limits of our universe are. If the fundamental forces in our universe were even very slightly different, the substances and materials to which we are accustomed simply would not exist at all. So far as we can tell, it is absolutely not possible to make small-scale changes in the laws of physics which will leave most things much the same, with only selected differences. A radically different creation might well be possible, for all we know; but a very slightly different one seems to be highly unlikely. . . . [I]n creating anything physical, as we understand that term, God inevitably creates limited, finite things which have the natures they do, rather than different things altogether. A world containing such limited things is a world in which not everything is still possible. To create is inevitably to decide. The laws of physics do not limit God's power: they are simply a way of describing the limitations of the universe which God has chosen to create.[25]

In a line of reflection similar to that considering God's acceptance of the unavoidable implied in his decree to create, Edwards observes that "scientists point out that, for example, the universe needs to be as old as it is and as big as it is, if all the processes necessary for the emergence of life on Earth are to take place."[26]

MORAL EVILS AND HUMAN FREEDOM

Interestingly, if the suggestion that God cannot but respect the inner integrity of the nondivine being that he has chosen to create carries weight, it seems clearer to grasp when we turn from physical disasters to consider moral evils, or the morally wrong harm that human beings deliberately and knowingly cause to their fellows. If material nondivine being, once it is created, may possess characteristics that due to their nature cannot then be restricted or contradicted by divine being on pain of that nondivine being's annihilation, it appears that this is more obviously the case when we consider spiritual beings and the freedom with which God has necessarily endowed his human creatures. John Hick highlighted the significance of human freedom when he wrote, "Having created man through the long evolution of the forms of life on this earth, God is now, through our free responses, fashioning 'children of God' out of human animals."[27] As I once expressed it elsewhere, "the artistic medium in which God is fashioning and crafting his human creatures is the medium of their personal freedom."[28] And this medium is possessed of such a nature, it appears, that the human creature's intrinsic power of initiative must be respected even by God, on pain of that freedom—and therefore that creature—being destroyed.

Here again we are wandering into the foothills of divine mystery—now the mystery and the challenge of how to accept the idea of an all-powerful God bringing a cosmic design to fulfillment while respecting the freedom and initiative for action of his created human creatures. Ultimately it is the mystery of predestination, recalling for students of theological history the controversy *de auxiliis* (on divine helps) between sixteenth- and seventeenth-century Jesuits and Dominicans at loggerheads over the relationship between divine and human action, where Jesuits were determined to protect human freedom and Dominicans were at pains to preserve the divine omnipotence. With the parties at length suffering from disputation fatigue, a wearied Pope Paul V sent all the contestants home in 1607 and ordered both orders to stop condemning each other as Pelagians and Calvinists, respectively, until the papacy could resolve the issue, which it never did. A lively account of the controversy is provided by the Jesuit historian James Brodrick, in *Robert Bellarmine: Saint and Scholar*, in his chapter on "The Controversy about Efficacious Grace," whose concluding challenge remains pertinent: "Every problem in which God is concerned ends in mystery, and the difficulty facing the theologian is not to admit this but to admit it too soon."[29]

Part of the mystery here appears to be how to understand the apparent fact that when divine freedom creates human freedom, just as when divine love creates human love, the created expression must genuinely share in its own right some of the essential characteristics of the originating divine attribute. The whole of Browning's lines partly quoted by Tennant recognize the need for the God who is all nevertheless to stand back "as it were a handbreadth off" and leave his human creature moral space for maneuver:

> *You know what I mean: God's all, man's nought:*
> *But also, God, whose pleasure brought*
> *Man into being, stands away*
> *As it were a handbreadth off, to give*
> *Room for the newly-made to live,*
> *And look at Him from a place apart,*
> *And use his gifts of brain and heart,*
> *Given, indeed, but to keep for ever.*[30]

What Browning expressed poetically as a paradox of divine omnipotence and human initiative Aquinas had tried to explain more metaphysically. In writing of providence, or planning, he observed that every creature is subject to God's providence but that this applies to the human creature "in a more excellent manner, insofar as he is also made a sharer in providence, by taking foresight for himself and for others" (*Inter cetera autem, rationalis creatura excellentiori quodam modo divinae providentiae subiacet, inquantum et ipsa fit providentiae particeps, sibi ipsi et aliis providens*).[31] It was Aquinas also who was able to throw some light on the perplexity that Augustine earlier experienced as he tried to reconcile divine agency with human agency in commenting on Paul's statement that the children of God are "driven," or acted upon (Latin *aguntur*, Greek *agontai*: Rom 8:14), by God's spirit. If God's children are driven, or are actuated, by God's spirit, Augustine asked in his puzzlement, how can they themselves be active?[32] Augustine's mistake, as was that of the Jesuits and Dominicans, was surely to put divine and human activity on the same level of being and to view them as therefore in rivalry or in competition; or, as in the opposing scales of a balance, so that what is given to one is thereby taken from the other. The same error can be seen at work in the rhetoric of Augustine and Calvin and, indeed, as I have written elsewhere, in the thought of all those who view humanity's relationship with God "as a continual border dispute" who conclude that "what is gained by mankind is snatched from God in a Promethean rewriting of the gospel of creation," and that the more, for instance, one degrades sinful humanity the more one is glorifying a merciful God.[33] Southern wrote perceptively of Anselm's theory of atonement that "he magnified the debt in order to glorify God."[34]

Part of the answer, then, appears to be a theology of the analogy of being and of analogical causality. The theology of the analogy of being does not posit created being as a threat to, or a subtraction from, uncreated being in some form of demarcation dispute, like tectonic plates jostling against each other. It sees created beings as sharing in, or participating in, uncreated being to a derived degree. As applied to causation, the analogy of being views human causality as a genuine sharing in God's own causality, but at a different, lower level of being. These theologies appear to underlie, or at least can help to illuminate, the teaching of the Second Vatican Council that "far from thinking, then, that the achievements of human enterprise and ability are in opposition to the power of God, or that the rational creature is a rival to God, Christians are of the view that the successes of the human race are a sign of God's greatness and a result of God's marvellous design."[35]

In particular, the idea of primary and secondary causalities that are found in Aristotle and richly applied by Aquinas to Christian theology can to some degree throw light on the mystery of God respecting human freedom, when God is viewed as the principal agent working through an intelligent instrument, and at the same time the human is viewed as God's free instrument with its own subordinate, yet real, contribution to make to decisions and events, "acting in such a way that it is also acted upon," as Aquinas expresses it.[36] One attractive comparison, imperfect though it obviously must be, is to see the human person as being carried along in a boat whose sail is filled with the spirit of God, yet with a human hand lightly on the tiller: totally driven, yet directing. Korsmeyer's equally faltering attempt to connect divine with human love in a similar manner is appealing. As he wrote,

A little reflection about love makes clear that there is nothing worthwhile that can occur between lovers that is coerced. In our neoclassical model, God's power is solely persuasive. God persuades creatures into being, granting them some power of creativity, but not just because God decides it would be nice to do so. It is the divine nature to create, because it is the divine nature to love. Love must share, love requires others. And, as Thomas Aquinas said, nothing can act contrary to its nature [CG 1, 84, 3]. As a result, God doesn't have all the power in the universe. It is shared by creatures. But God has all the power that a God could have who created a world with creatures who are really free.[37]

Before leaving the topic of process theology as developed by many modern theologians, which I have argued is not required in an evolutionary approach, it might be worth commenting that the god from which White-head, Pittenger, and others proceed and with which they express dissat-isfaction is not the Christian god. It is a remote philosophical construct based on Aristotelian metaphysics and totally divorced from the ideas of trinity and of incarnation. As I comment in chapter 2, Grant's study on altruism and Christian ethics is theologically thin in its lack of a Trinitar-ian as well as a Christological dimension. If he, and others, took into effect what I suggest in my chapter on altruism about the nature of the Christian God as being essentially interpersonal in its love and as fully embracing human creaturehood into its intimacy, there would be less need to seek a corrective of the theology of an impersonal, remote, and unaffected divin-ity.[38] An analogy with the sun might help. As we view the sun, it appears distant and completely self-absorbed, whereas in reality it is a furnace of blazing energy on which the world is totally dependent for its light and its warmth. Likewise, so far as created reality is concerned, and as mystics like Saint John of the Cross maintain, the God who is its source and origin is a furnace of love and as such is committed to preserve and sustain created reality within its all-embracing ambit.

NOTES

1. Whitehead, *Process and Reality.*
2. Cobb and Griffin, *Process Theology.*
3. Pittenger, *Catholic Faith in a Process Perspective,* 46.
4. Daly, "Creation and Original Sin," 22.
5. Macquarrie, *In Search of Deity,* 23.
6. Ibid., 180.
7. Ibid., 26.
8. Ibid., 54.
9. Ibid., 228.
10. Macquarrie, *Principles of Christian Theology,* 200.
11. Ibid., 121.
12. Ibid., 215–16.
13. Macquarrie, *In Search of Deity,* 183.
14. Macquarrie, *Principles of Christian Theology,* 206.
15. Ibid., 302; Daly, *Origins of the Christian Doctrine of Sacrifice,* 24.
16. Haught, *God after Darwin,* 117–22.
17. Ibid., 52.
18. Ibid., 57.
19. Edwards, *God of Evolution,* 44. See 40–44.
20. Peacocke, *Theology for a Scientific Age,* 119–22.

21. Macquarrie, *In Search of Deity*, 37.
22. Peacocke, *Theology for a Scientific Age*, 34.
23. Boethius, *De Consolatione Philosophiae*, 159.
24. Augustine, *Confessions*, 201.
25. Hughes, *Is God to Blame?*, 47–48.
26. Edwards, *God of Evolution*, 48.
27. Hick, "Evil and Incarnation," 80.
28. Mahoney, *Making of Moral Theology*, 340.
29. Brodrick, *Robert Bellarmine*, 216n1.
30. Browning, "Christmas Eve," in *Poetical Works*, 1:483. Quoted in Tennant, *Origin and Propagation of Sin*, 127.
31. Aquinas, *Summa Theologiae*, Ia IIae, q. 92, a. 2.
32. Augustine, *Sermones* 156:10–11 (Migne, *PL* 38, 855–56).
33. Mahoney, "Sin of Pride," 284.
34. Southern, *Saint Anselm*, 211.
35. Vatican Council II, Pastoral Constitution on the Church in the World of Today, par. 34, in Tanner, *Decrees of the Ecumenical Councils*, 2:*1089.
36. Mahoney, *Making of Moral Theology*, 247.
37. Korsmeyer, *Evolution and Eden*, 96–97.
38. See chapter 2, this volume.

CHAPTER SIX

The Church and the Eucharist in Evolution

A S THE PREVIOUS chapters have examined, acknowledging the findings of evolutionary science can highlight and clarify the evolutionary achievement that Jesus brought about for the human race through his leading it through death to a richer life with an altruistic God. It can also enable us to dispense with the traditional beliefs in original sin, the Fall, and redemptive atonement, or propitiatory sacrifice, along with the inherent historical and intellectual difficulties that have been raised by these beliefs. Is it possible that such an exploration of Christian belief in reference to evolution, as this chapter is titled, can expand to throw light on other traditional doctrines, including the extent of salvation and the nature of the church and of the Eucharist? That is the purpose of this chapter.

WHO SHALL BE SAVED?

A preliminary question that arises in exploring the impact of Christ's evolutionary work for the human species must ask how members of the species will benefit from this achievement; or, in terms of the traditional doctrine, who will be saved, and who condemned, within an evolutionary context. To begin with the latter, the possibility of being consigned to eternal suffering by a just God is not a tenet—or a prospect—that all Christian believers have found it easy to live with (Darwin thought everlasting punishment for nonbelievers "a damnable doctrine").[1] Yet we appear to have the incontrovertible teaching of Jesus on the subject in Matthew 25:41–46 that when the Son of Man returns in judgment, the good and the bad will separately be consigned to what Kelly calls "their eternal destinies."[2] Origen, and under his influence other Greek authorities, were disposed to question the eternity of the divine condemnatory sentence, arguing that

God's power would finally triumph, although the sixth-century Synod of Constantinople anathematized such a view (DS 411), while among the Latins, Ambrosiaster, Jerome, and Ambrose were disposed to mitigate the sentence for some of the condemned.[3] Augustine, however, considered at length and adamantly rejected what he considered "the error, promoted by tenderness of heart and human compassion, that the miseries of the condemned would come to an end." Would this, he asked rhetorically, even indignantly, extend as far as the evil angels and the Devil himself?![4] (Origen thought this not impossible.)[5] Even though some people might argue for eventual divine clemency from Paul's assertion in Romans 11:32 that "God has imprisoned all in disobedience so that he may be merciful to all," in point of fact, Augustine retorted, "they are pleading their own cause, promising themselves a delusive impunity for their own disreputable lives by supposing an all-embracing mercy of God towards the human race."[6]

It has always been generally understood by Christians that no human individual is considered as definitively sent to hell, but it was considered a very distinct and alarming possibility, as many graphic church murals and windows that depict the final judgment and damnation relished portraying in the Middle Ages, even up to Michelangelo's Sistine Chapel, where popes are elected.[7] The Council of Florence in 1442 was in no doubt as to what classes of people merited eternal damnation, being firmly of the view that "no one outside the Catholic Church, not only pagans but also Jews, heretics and schismatics, can become sharers in eternal life, but are headed for the eternal fire which has been prepared for the devil and his angels [Mt 25:41] unless they join the church before they die" (DS 1351). And not just the dead, but also the eternally damned, would be in the great majority, for, as Matthew recorded, "few are chosen" (Mt 22:14). As A. T. Hanson observed, "Whether we turn to Augustine or Aquinas or Calvin, we can scarcely avoid the conclusion that in their view only some are predestined to eternal life, and that the rest are predestined to eternal loss."[8] Both Catholics and Reformers followed Augustine in this gloomy prediction, but with the beginning of the questioning of the verbal inspiration of scripture, Hastings noted, Protestant theologians began to divide ranks on the eternity of hell, although it was not until the middle of the twentieth century that Catholics too began to question the biblical and church teaching that those condemned to hell would suffer for eternity.[9]

The opposing theological view, universalism, holds that everyone will go to heaven, even if only eventually, and this was embraced by some Protestants and developed into a sect teaching "a gospel of gratuitous salvation."[10] Recent and modern universalists include Friedrich Schleiermacher and F. D. Maurice, the latter being expelled from his professorial chair at the Anglican King's College London on the grounds that he denied the eternity of hell's punishment (although his daring espousal of Christian socialism is more likely to have been the real reason). Barth and Rahner are modern theological giants commonly considered to be inclined to universalism.[11]

The dilemma of eternal damnation seems clear from the forthright biblical teaching of Matthew 25:31–33, 41–46 ("Depart from me you cursed . . ."), which seems more redolent of the moral teaching of the Baptist (Mt 3:7–12) and of the tradition of Jewish apocalypse than of the mind of Jesus. In fact, the passage appears only in Matthew's gospel, which is widely recognized for its Jewish editorial preoccupations, as we shall have occasion to see again later, and the *New Jerome Biblical Commentary* recognizes wide discomfort about the provenance of these verses, asking whether they stem "from Jesus, from Matthew, from the early church, or, as Bultmann has suggested, from Judaism."[12] In an attempt to soften the apparent harshness of the belief, agreement grew among theologians on the refinement that it is not so much a matter of one being consigned to hell for one's misdeeds by a vengeful God than it is a matter that one chooses hell for oneself, electing freely to reject the choice of moral good with all that implies in terms of separating oneself definitively from the source of good. Yet, as Hastings counters to even this version, "in the light of divine goodness, is it plausible to think that God could allow anyone an eternity of misery on account of decisions taken in one brief life?"[13] Moreover, as discussed earlier in considering Anselm's theology of the atonement, what possible limits can one possibly put on divine forgiveness?[14] Conversely, it can be, and is, argued that, if God eventually in his unbounded mercy will forgive even the most serious sinners for their heinous behavior in this life, not excluding the most murderous tyrants in history, will this not inevitably reduce human choice and moral responsibility to eventual insignificance and degrade God's vaunted respect for the autonomy of his creatures into a specious and temporary make-believe?

Possibly the acceptance of an evolutionary approach to creation and human life opens up a third line of solution to this apparent dilemma of either heaven or hell as the destiny for every human being after his or her death: namely, the possibility for some people of not surviving death, but of simply ceasing to exist once they die. In effect, as noted already, death and dissolution is the universal evolutionary presupposition for all living things as a condition for genetic mutations to occur in their replacements. And the achievement of Jesus in struggling loyally through death to an afterlife, and his offer to communicate this to others, can be recognized as a new phase of existence for humans that cannot necessarily be presumed to be applied to every one of these automatically. Indeed, the extinction of some humans at death could be seen as almost the normal evolutionary expectation implied in the idea of the survival only of those who are equipped for that purpose. Moreover, it would be much more in accord with divine mercy to allow condemned sinners to slip into annihilation than have them live in torment for eternity.

One consideration that can be raised against this possibility, however, is the common Catholic, if not Christian, persuasion, which derives more from Greek and scholastic philosophy than from faith, that every human being is directly created by God with an immortal soul: It will naturally survive death and eventually be reunited with its body, being logically destined thereafter to spend an eternity in either eternal happiness or eternal suffering. This strict dichotomy between body and soul, as between destructible matter and a naturally indestructible spirit, was maintained tenaciously by the church's magisterium against the fear that otherwise total materialism—and atheism—would prevail, and it was conviction of such a clear difference between soul and body that led Pope Pius XII to express serious misgivings in his 1950 encyclical letter *Humani generis* about the novel scientific theory of human evolution.[15] As he explained, the teaching authority of the church does not forbid responsible research and discussion "with regard to the doctrine of evolution, in as far as it inquires into the origin of the human body as coming from pre-existent and living matter—for the Catholic faith obliges us to hold that souls are immediately created by God" (DS 3896).

However, this traditionally held Catholic disjunction between body and soul as between matter and spirit insofar as these are quite contrary, indeed, contrasting, ways of being is more a matter of early Greek and scholastic philosophy than an element of biblical teaching, and it is not an easy one to maintain, especially in light of evolutionary thinking. Commenting on papal toleration of the evolution of the human body but not of the soul, as quoted earlier, Daly judges, "this attitude is a throwback to the old hellenistic dualism. In effect it refuses to recognize the potential spirituality of physical evolution."[16] Karl Rahner observes, by contrast, that "body and soul are two *meta*-physical principles of one single being, and not two beings, each of which could be met with experimentally."[17] Moreover, he is prepared to consider "a certain homogeneity between matter and spirit." Indeed, he is prepared to "try to see man as the being in whom the basic tendency of matter to find itself in the spirit by self-transcendence" can arrive "at the point where it definitively breaks through."[18] In other words, Rahner argues that the one God has created a single world in which the most varied things have "an inner similarity and community," and from this he concludes "that it would be quite wrong and unchristian to conceive matter and spirit as realities simply existing side by side in the actual order of things while being really quite unrelated to each other, the spirit in its human form having—unfortunately—to utilize the material world as a kind of external stage. A Christian theology and philosophy deems it self-evident that spirit and matter have more things in common (to put it this way) than things dividing them."[19] So much so that "it may be said without scruple that matter develops out of its inner being in the direction of spirit."[20]

Rahner's reference here to matter as having a basic tendency to transcend itself in terms of the spirit highlights the significance in his thought of the whole idea of self-transcendence—he goes so far as to claim that "man is thus the self-transcendence of living matter."[21] The idea of something "becoming," he reflects, does not mean becoming other; "true 'becoming' must be conceived as something 'becoming *more*,' as the coming into being of more reality, as an effective attainment of a greater fullness of being." This "more" is not simply an add-on; it "must be the inner increase of being proper to the previously existing reality." In other words, "'becoming' must be understood as a real self-transcendence, a surpassing of self or active filling up of the empty."[22] Moreover, importantly for Rahner, as he expounded elsewhere in considerable detail, God is forever at work in all such self-transcendence on the part of created being.[23] The actual source of active self-transcendence, "by which an existing and acting being actively approaches to the higher perfection still lacking to it," can only be "the power of the absolute fullness of being," which must be thought of as "so interior to the finite being moving towards its fulfilment that the finite being is empowered by it to achieve a really *active self*-transcendence and does not merely receive this new reality passively as something effected by God."[24] Moreover, such self-transcendence can include transcendence into what is substantially new, that is, "the leap to a higher *nature*," such that "there is no necessary reason for disputing the fact that matter has evolved in the direction of life and of man." Such metaphysical reasoning, he concludes, acknowledging that matter, life, consciousness, and spirit are not at all the same thing and yet are capable of developing, or proceeding through, essential self-transcendence, is borne out by the known history of the cosmos, which "is seen more and more as one homogeneous history of matter, life and man."[25] As Pope concluded, "Rahner believed that the emergence of the human soul is part of the larger dynamism of an evolving universe that gives rise to beings who become capable of freely accepting God's self-gift."[26]

In light of these considerations, several conclusions begin to emerge. For one thing, most relevant to our current consideration of the eternity of hell, it is difficult to continue to argue that there is an intrinsic disjunction between matter and spirit, body and soul, such that (as Greek and scholastic philosophy conceived it), on the one hand, matter and the body are composite, divisible, and therefore perishable, while on the other hand, spirit, the soul, and form is simple and naturally indivisible and consequently immortal and must therefore live forever (with a resurrected body) logically in either heaven or hell. The common experience of death as the prospect of annihilation, without any comforting Hellenistic presumption of the soul's natural survival after death, can now exercise its full devastating impact while also creating a space for a religious hope that entry into a new form of human life may be accessible at least to some through the evolutionary achievement of Jesus in himself conquering death. This acknowledges that being associated with the altruistic death of Jesus saves one from one's own death and ushers one into sharing the new risen life of Christ and suggests tentatively that those who are not so associated may cease to exist at death.

A second conclusion that emerges from considering Rahner's evolutionary metaphysics is the recognition that the inherent potential of all non–divine being for self-transcendence, which starts in its most rudimentary form and progressively transcends itself as a result of interior divine impulsion through the stages of matter, life, spirit, intelligence, and self-consciousness, can be considered in principle to open the way for yet further human self-transcendence. Indeed, Rahner's reflection can even be seen as providing a metaphysical definition of evolution as the process of progressive stages of self-transcendence that created being experiences and achieves under the immanent urge and empowering activity of uncreated being. This points, I suggest, to a transcendence achieved by the human species as a whole in the achievement of Jesus as he experienced and overcame death to introduce the culminating stage of God's altruistic enterprise of creation that is to be shared by those who are in some way associated with the risen Jesus.

A third conclusion is that what, following Rahner, I have called this immanent urge of uncreated being suggests a view of divine causality that is different from, and richer than, the view more commonly encountered in Christian theology, namely, the view that inclines to a sort of container view of causality, making much of the idea of infusion, or of pouring in of being. We speak regularly of God at creation infusing, or pouring, the soul into the human body, as into a material container (which Aristotle and others, including Aquinas, thought required time to prepare), and we have a whole tradition stemming at least from Aquinas, of some human capacities, or virtues, being divinely "infused" or poured directly by God into the soul, as distinct from those virtues actively acquired through human exercise. Likewise, in spiritual theology we are accustomed to refer to infused contemplation as a type of passive prayer directly imparted by God contrasted with acquired contemplative prayer. In all of these the half-conscious image is one of a God separate from us and pouring into us as into distinct containers the created expressions of divine causal energy. In contrast, the view of divine communication that emerges from the evolutionary approach of self-transcendence under divine impulse implies a more immediate and intimate communion between divine cause and created effect. It partakes more of the idea of a fountain welling up from inside rather than of something being poured in from the outside. In the evolutionary approach, the creative energy of divine being is viewed as entirely immanent within all nondivine being, welling up within it like a spring of water, in the process impelling noncreated being to transcend itself progressively in a variety of ways in the course of the onward evolutionary march of God's creative purpose. So much so that it is possible to consider that in one instance the divine presence and immanence in created being reached such a peak of intensity that God actually became a human being, Jesus of Nazareth.

THE EVOLVING CHURCH

A further development that can be regarded as intrinsic to the evolutionary achievement of Jesus concerns the body of the faithful whom he is actually introducing to a new phase of existence after death, that is, the church, which we can now consider. As it was helpful in a previous chapter that examined Jesus's role in evolutionary ethics to examine what Darwin had to say on the birth of ethics in turning to consider the community dimension of evolutionary theology it can be enlightening to look at what Darwin and others might have said about the birth of religion.

Darwin was not of the view that early man possessed an innate belief in an omnipotent God, and indeed he was of the belief that numerous races had had no idea that one or more gods existed. However, he was convinced that a belief in "unseen or spiritual agencies" seemed universal "with the less civilised races" and that "with savages the belief in bad spirits is far more common than that in good ones."[27] In general, he conjectured that "as soon as the important faculties of the imagination, wonder, and curiosity, together with some power of reasoning, had become partially developed, man would naturally crave to understand what was passing around him, and would have vaguely speculated on his own existence."[28] In fact, he considered that in the course of human evolution a process of religious development had taken place in which humans, once they had acquired mental faculties, had progressed from belief in spirits through fetishism and polytheism ultimately to monotheism. The more sophisticated feeling of religious devotion Darwin considered was one that would require a fairly high level of "intellectual and moral faculties," as it would include elements of "love, complete submission to an exalted and mysterious superior, a strong sense of dependence, fear, reverence, gratitude, hope for the future, and perhaps other elements."[29]

The leading modern authority on the study of religion, Ninian Smart, has observed the popularity in late Victorian times of attempting to develop theories explaining the rise of religion in the human mind. These included the theory of evolutionary development proposed by Fraser's highly popular *The Golden Bough*, which starts with recognition of *mana*, or sacred phenomena and powers, and proceeds, like Darwin, through animism, or belief in the existence and activity of spirits, to a plurality of gods in polytheism and culminating in monotheism, or the worship of one supreme god. Smart opines that "there must have been very divergent patterns of ritual and belief through the varied cultures that were developing" but makes his view quite clear that "questions about the origin of religion are guesswork."[30] Indeed, we can conjecture that many aspects of prehistoric human life are likely to have contributed to the evolution of religious sensitivity and belief among early men and women over a very long period of time. These would include the emergence of intelligence and the physiological attributes necessary to permit the development of spoken language and communication; shared life in community to facilitate group and intergenerational social activities; rational attempts to explain and make sense of recurrent cosmic and other phenomena that aroused fear, admiration, and wonder; the development, embellishment, and transmission of explanatory storytelling and of symbolic ritual and ceremonial actions that were aimed at respecting, placating, and manipulating what were perceived as superhuman entities; and, probably most intriguing of all, coming to terms with the unavoidable experience of death and vesting it with beliefs and rites that depicted death as a mysterious threshold to some form of human afterlife.

Once writing was developed, cultures began to take firmer shape and oral traditions became recorded history. So, parallel to developments in other cultures, in the case of the Israelite people, out of religious insights and reflections sacred narratives emerged and were recorded and gradually embellished and developed. These claimed to make known the God who it was believed had revealed himself progressively to Abraham, Isaac, Jacob, and Moses, the special deity who chose to create his own people out of Egyptian slaves and who led them triumphantly out of bondage into a land "flowing with milk and honey" (Ex 3:8) that this God had destined should be theirs.

"THROUGH CHRIST OUR LORD"

An interesting parallel to the evolutionary emergence of the sense of religion sketched here is found in the work of the pioneering Protestant theologian Friedrich Schleiermacher (1768–1834), who sought to develop Christian thinking in a new manner that would get round the apparent cul-de-sac into which Enlightenment rationalism had led it. Hitherto, Christian theologians had chosen to begin their reflections with the documents of scripture and to draw upon what was considered divine revelation in order to discern the nature and implications of Christian beliefs. By contrast, and thus appropriately seen as "the father of modern theology," Schleiermacher focused his attention on inner subjective experience as the locus of religious reflection rather than on objective textual sources, so that with him religious feeling became the stuff of theology, and dogmas became the communal expressions of such feeling. As B. A. Gerrish explains, "Schleiermacher began on the inside: not with the outward trappings of dogma and usages . . . , but with what he took to be a universal, if elusive, element in every human consciousness, what he famously termed the 'feeling of absolute dependence.'"[31] Commenting on this, McGrath explains that "the general human consciousness of being dependent on something undefined is, according to Schleiermacher, recognized and interpreted within the context of the Christian faith as a sense of total dependence upon God."[32]

Thus, in an interesting parallel with Darwin's reconstruction of the evolutionary development of human religious awareness, Schleiermacher spent a major part of his work in conjecturing on the gradual historical origin of the human sense of religion, and—what is of particular significance for my purpose—within that in exploring the nature of the Christian community as composed of those people who come to share Christ's own highly developed human consciousness of God. McGrath describes this process of incorporation into Christ as follows:

Schleiermacher attributes to Christ an "absolutely powerful God-consciousness" charged with such assimilative power that it is able to effect the redemption of mankind. The essence of redemption is that the God-consciousness already present in human nature, although feeble and repressed, becomes stimulated and elevated through the "entrance of the living influence of Christ." As the redeemer (*Erlöser* [liberator]), Christ is distinguished from all other men both in degree and kind by the uninterrupted power of his God-consciousness. *The redemptive activity of Christ consists in his assuming individuals into the power of his God-consciousness.*[33]

For Schleiermacher the implicit consciousness of God that he considered part of the human condition was supremely the case in Christ, to such an extent that Christ's role is to communicate his profound awareness of God to his fellows and thus to attract them into the community that he founded as his church. In Macquarrie's words, for Schleiermacher, "Christ himself is to be understood not just as the individual Jesus of Nazareth but already as the beginning of a new community into which individuals are constantly incorporated."[34]

Such a view of the church as expounded by Schleiermacher is obviously congenial to the approach I am outlining, that the achievement of Jesus in breaking through death to a new phase of life is shared by all those who accept his message of universal altruism and are thus accepted into his evolutionary fellowship. The approach raises a question, however, about the extent of those traditionally regarded as redeemed and to what extent they are required to be committed to consciously sharing in the work of Christ. This is a long-standing difficulty that has been associated with the traditional theology of salvation: how Christ's atoning sacrifice can be applied to those who have never heard of him or, in the more formal phrase, how to account for "the salvation of the unbeliever." The belief that "outside the Church there is no salvation" had a long run in Christian theology, extending from an early polemical exclusivist interpretation to a much more accommodating subjective, modern interpretation of the phrase, in practice almost tantamount to its abandonment.[35] As the Second Vatican Council declared confidently, "divine Providence does not deny the aids needed for salvation to those who through no fault of their own have not yet arrived at an express acknowledgement of God, but who by the help of his grace try to lead a good life" (*rectam vitam non sine divina gratia assequi nituntur*).[36]

What traditional theology viewed as the problem (for Christians, but not for anyone else) of how entry into heaven can be conceded to the unbeliever who did not recognize God, far less know Christ as savior, was thus eventually solved in general ethical terms, making individual salvation dependent on "trying to lead a good life," as Vatican II expressed it. Significantly, within the evolutionary context, in which there is no longer a need or place for the doctrine of original sin or the Fall, there is no longer an identifiable barrier that threatens to keep such individuals out of heaven unless, as it is expressed in traditional terms, they become associated with the redeeming blood of Christ. The focus thus moves to an ethical approach to salvation and enables us to highlight the enrichment that can be added to this by introducing the idea of altruism. As argued in chapter 2, this other-centeredness, or neighbor love, is not just one expression of trying to lead a good life; it is the common element of what constitutes a good life, to be found also in God's creative enterprise and in the self-giving achievement of Jesus.

There, indeed, appears to be a certain attractiveness in viewing altruism, or agape, as characterizing the divine initiative in creating an evolutionary world as well as providing a concentrating and transforming focus for all human ethical behavior, including that of Jesus. We can find the defining shape of Christian ethics as a response of wholehearted generosity in which altruism, agape, and love are synonymous, which can therefore be seen from an evolutionary point of view as the core ethical attitude to be inculcated and expressed in all human behavior in an infinite variety of ways, leading individuals into community, or fellowship (*koinonia*), with the risen Christ. In understanding the significance of this mysterious—and mystical—association of the altruistic with the risen Christ, we can be helped by the insight of Schleiermacher in seeing the church as the community of those who have come to share the supreme God consciousness that Christ brought into existence as "a new corporate life."[37] Altruism is seen, then, as the cosmic, connecting link between the initiative of God, the self-surrender of Christ, and the ethical call to evolving humanity to transcend itself in imitation of both God and Christ and, as the church, to enter into fuller communion with both.

THE EUCHARIST IN EVOLUTION

A focus on the nature of the church within an evolutionary perspective draws unavoidable attention to the connected question of how the Eucharist can be understood within the same perspective, since, as Pope John Paul II pointed out, there is an intimate symbiosis between the Eucharist and the church.[38] In fact, how to understand and interpret the Christian

Eucharist in the evolutionary mode that I am developing here is probably the most sensitive, and delicate, part of this whole exploration. Can what has for centuries been considered by Roman Catholics the redemptive sacrifice of the Mass be transposed into a liturgical celebration consonant and congenial with human evolution and remain the central daily life-giving mystery of Christian worship and life? It should be noted that this is very far from attempting a sort of theological legerdemain to suggest that the Mass is implicitly or latently evolutionary. It is basically asking, rather, whether the Mass is essentially, or, indeed, exclusively, sacrificial as a ritual participation in Christ's offering of his suffering and death to his father for the purpose of reconciling alienated humanity, or whether it is capable of ritually recalling and celebrating the freely accepted suffering and death of Christ as the divinely chosen means of having the human species transcend death and live together as a community participating fully in the life of God. The first step, then, is to examine the question of whether the Mass is essentially, even—dare one say it—irremediably, sacrificial, and for this we can best begin with the New Testament accounts of the Last Supper and the founding of the Eucharist by Jesus. It is worth noting that since the Reformation the Protestant churches in general consider their Eucharistic service to be the central act of Christian worship in spite of the fact that they have resolutely refused to consider it as sacrificial in any way, and this is not because they are opposed to the idea of Christ's offering himself to the father in atoning sacrifice for sins (far from it), but because they insist that this offering took place on the cross (see Heb 10:10) and cannot in any way be repeated in the Mass.[39]

The Nature of the Last Supper

In his impressively detailed and classic study, *The Eucharistic Words of Jesus*, Joachim Jeremias argues that the Last Supper that Jesus celebrated with his disciples was the Jewish Passover meal, at which, he writes, "the people of God remember the merciful immunity granted to the houses marked with the blood of the paschal lamb and the deliverance from the Egyptian servitude" as well as "a looking forward to the coming deliverance of which the deliverance from Egypt is the prototype."[40] Jeremias recognizes in the New Testament accounts of Paul, Mark, Matthew, and Luke parallel versions of Jesus's words of institution at the Last Supper based on original versions in both Aramaic and Hebrew.[41] In addition, he views the differing words of Jesus in the four versions that we now possess as reproducing different liturgical texts that had developed independently in various local communities for the Eucharistic rite, or the breaking of the bread, a view that Joseph Jungmann confirms in observing that the differences in the words of institution "must arise from the differences in the liturgical practice from which the accounts sprang."[42] In subsequent church life, out of respect for the perceived words of Jesus all four passages were coalesced into one institution narrative, losing their distinctive differences.

Jeremias also considers it very important for our understanding of the institution narratives which we possess that we realize that "Jesus said more at the last supper than the few words preserved in the liturgical formulae."[43] In the course of the supper, Jeremias argues, Jesus would have formally provided a Passover *haggadah*, a series of reflections on the events of the exodus that was being celebrated, and these reflections would have provided the participants with an explanatory context of what was going on. As he further comments on the Passover meditation that Jesus would thus have delivered, "This is an important observation because it justifies the conclusion that the disciples were thereby prepared for the words of interpretation," or institution, which Jeremias describes as "in themselves puzzling."[44] Indeed, the absence from the New Testament accounts of the supper of such a meditation by Jesus as postulated by Jeremias leaves us also with the puzzling situation of how to understand the terse liturgical phrases that are all we possess:

1 Cor 11	Mk 14	Mt 26	Lk 22
23 For I received from the Lord what I also handed on to you, that the Lord Jesus on the night when he was betrayed took a loaf of bread, 24 and when he had given thanks, he broke it and said, "This is my body that is for you.	22 While they were eating, he took a loaf of bread, and after blessing it he broke it, gave it to them, and said, "Take; this is my body."	26 While they were eating, Jesus took a loaf of bread, and after blessing it he broke it, gave it to the disciples, and said, "Take, eat; this is my body."	19.a Then he took a loaf of bread, and when he had given thanks, he broke it and gave it to them, saying, "This is my body [Long Form: b which is given for you.]
Do this in remembrance of me."			Do this in remembrance of me."

(continues)

1 Cor 11	Mk 14	Mt 26	Lk 22
25 In the same way he took the cup also, after supper, saying,	23 Then he took a cup, and after giving thanks he gave it to them,· and all of them drank from it.	27 Then he took a cup, and after giving thanks he gave it to them, saying, "Drink from it, all of you;	20 And he did the same with the cup after supper, saying,
"This cup is the new covenant in my blood.	24 He said to them, "This is my blood of the covenant, which is poured out for many."	28 for this is my blood of the covenant, which is poured out for many for the forgiveness of sins."	"This cup that is poured out for you is the new covenant in my blood."
Do this, as often as you drink it, in remembrance of me. 26 For as often as you eat this bread and drink the cup, you proclaim the Lord's death until he comes."			

Thus, on Jesus's words over the bread, Mark and Matthew record simply "this is my body," and Paul adds the clause "which is for you," which Luke in the alternative long form qualifies "which is given for you." It seems clear that the Pauline and Lucan words "for you," literally, "on behalf of (*huper*) you," are an attempt to clarify the clause "this is my body," although it is not made clear what being "for" you means. To try to add further light, Luke adds the word "given (for you)," but it is not clear from the text who it is to whom Jesus's body is being "given" (*dedomenon*). The word could have the sacrificial meaning of being given, or offered, to the father on behalf of humankind, which is the usual interpretation, but it might equally mean that the body is about to be surrendered, or given over, by Christ to his enemies on behalf of his disciples, although for this "handed over" (*paradidonai*, cf. Mt 26:2) would have been clearer. A further, and attractive, possibility is to understand that the body is being given *to* the disciples (and referring also to later congregations?) in the sense, "Take. Eat; this is my body which I am giving you," in a sense reminiscent of John 6:51: "The

bread that I will give (*doso*) for the life of the world is my flesh," a passage
that Jeremias suggests originally formed a Eucharistic homily.[45]

The passage referring to the bread concludes in Paul and Luke with
the injunction, "Do this in remembrance of me." Jungmann sees the early
community as fulfilling Jesus's command, as it extracted from the narratives the formulas relating to the bread and wine, and brought these
together under the title of "the breaking of bread" (Acts 2:42, 46; 20:7.
Cf. Lk 24:35) while dropping all the other Passover details, as indeed do
the New Testament texts.[46] Jeremias explains that the subsequent repeti-
tions performed by the disciples have the commemorative role of reminding God of the purpose of Jesus's death and "of the unfulfilled climax of the
work of salvation."[47] This last suggestion, that repeating the rite is so that
God should be prayerfully reminded, seems strained to me, but Jeremias is
driven to it by finding it strange, as he put it, that it was the disciples who
would need to be reminded of Jesus.[48] Alternatively, it may be, as Jeremias
also considers acceptable, a phrase written back into the institution narrative to legitimate the growing practice of the rite of breaking of bread in
the Christian assemblies.[49] Interestingly, Paul provides another reason for
repeating the rites concerning the bread and wine in memory of Jesus by
explaining that "for as often as you eat this bread and drink the cup, you
proclaim the Lord's death until he comes," although it is not obvious what
purpose such a proclamation serves.[50]

The meal continued with Jesus pronouncing formally over the cup
of wine, which he identified with his blood, and it is here that the note
of sacrifice may appear most evident. In all four versions Jesus describes
this as "the blood of the covenant," which Paul and Luke qualify as "the
new covenant." Mark and Matthew describe the blood as "poured out for
many," while Luke describes it as "poured out for you," and Matthew, alone
of all four accounts, it is worth noting, adds "for the forgiveness of sins."
Jeremias notes that the "many" in Mark and Matthew is a Semitism for
"all," indicating an older form of the formula than the "you" in Luke.[51] He
also identifies the (new) covenant referred to as the one described by Jer-
emiah 31:31–34 and rejects the suggestion that the phrase "the blood of the
covenant," which occurs substantially in all four versions, may be "an old
theological interpretation."[52] He maintains that "the possibility that Jesus
spoke of the covenant at the Last Supper cannot be disputed," and he adds
that "the thought of the new covenant was not far from his thoughts, even
when it is not otherwise attested expressly in the tradition of his words."[53]
As Wright comments, the reference is both to the old covenant and to the
new, or renewed, covenant, echoing Exodus 24:5–8 of the Mosaic covenant

and Zechariah 9:11 ("the blood of my covenant with you"). Behind the four versions over the cup, Wright observes, "there is a common meaning . . . that Jesus' coming death will effect the renewal of the covenant, that is, the great return from exile for which Israel had longed."[54]

In describing the wine as his blood being poured out, as well as in separating his actions over the bread identified as his body and then over the wine identified as his blood, Jesus, according to Jeremias, is evidently using the language of sacrifice. What is presupposed, he observes, is "a slaying that has separated flesh and blood. In other words, *Jesus speaks of himself as a sacrifice.*"[55] Furthermore, he considers it a likely assumption that in the more extensive commentary and allegorical application that Jesus, Jeremias postulates, will have traditionally given on the paschal supper ritual he would identify himself with the paschal lamb, as Paul was later to do in declaring that "our paschal lamb, Christ, has been sacrificed"(1 Cor 5:7).[56] Indeed, Jeremias proposes that by referring to his sacrificial flesh and his sacrificial blood, Jesus is "most probably speaking of himself as the paschal lamb. He is *the eschatological paschal lamb*, representing the fulfillment of all that of which the Egyptian paschal lamb and all the subsequent sacrificial paschal lambs were the prototype."[57]

However, this suggested development by Jeremias of the sacrificial nature of the Last Supper raises difficulties. The details of the institution may very well point to the impending violent death of Jesus that he foresees, and this might be symbolically anticipated in the separate references to his body and his blood, but this is not self-evident. Moreover, as I have argued earlier, the sacrificial interpretation of Jesus's death seems to have been something that emerged on reflection after his death took place, in which case it would follow that Jesus would not in anticipation have portrayed his death as a sacrifice, that is, what Jeremias calls "a saving death," something to be offered by him to God to atone for sins.[58]

Nor does the idea of sacrifice appear central or essential to the Jewish traditions of the Passover and the Exodus. In Exodus 12:27 Moses does refer to the whole future annual ceremony commemorating the Exodus preparations as "the Passover sacrifice to the Lord," but there is no reference whatever in the Exodus narrative to the paschal lamb itself being sacrificed; it was slaughtered so that its flesh could be eaten in haste by each household, along with unleavened bread, on the eve of departure from Egypt, and mainly, it appears, so that its blood could be smeared on the Jewish doors as a distinctive sign ensuring that their houses would be "passed over" and preserved from divine destruction (Ex 12:1–13, 21). Mark's account of the Last Supper does refer to the previous day as the day "when the Passover lamb is sacrificed" (Mk 14:12), but this seems to be almost a comprehensive synonym for the temple slaughtering of hundreds of lambs to provide meat for the meal, just as Moses had his young men slaughter and sacrifice oxen (Ex 24:5) purely to provide blood in preparation for the covenant ceremony, as is discussed later. It seems to be concluding too much, if not outright fanciful, theologically for Jeremias to write that "the blood of the lambs slaughtered at the exodus from Egypt had *redemptive power* and made God's covenant with Abraham operative."[59] He may well be correct in proposing that "Jesus made the broken bread a simile of the fate of his body, the blood of the grapes a simile of his outpoured blood," but it does not automatically follow that in doing so he interpreted his death as a sacrifice, far less as a paschal sacrifice that he would offer to God in order to liberate humanity from a state of alienation from God, as the later Christian community would come to believe.[60]

Moreover, Jeremias does not appear to do full justice to the significance of the poured out "blood of the covenant" with which Jesus identifies the wine, a passage that Jeremias insists is authentic but which strictly has no connection with sacrifice, for the striking of the original covenant between God and Israel that Moses negotiated did not include sacrifice as an integral part. When the people of Israel were led to meet God at Mount Sinai, it almost appears from the narrative that they were too terrified to offer sacrifice (Ex 20:18–21). There is no reference to any sacrifice except the preparatory occasion when Moses sent out young men to offer oxen in sacrifice (Ex 24:5), but, as I have just suggested, this was for the evident purpose of obtaining the large amount of blood that he was going to use in inaugurating the covenant.

As Michael McGuckian observes of Old Testament animal sacrifices, apart from their making the animals' flesh available as food, "the death of the animal has a second effect that is of great importance in the sacrifices of Israel, the release of the blood. There is a great mystique about blood in the Bible. For us the blood is an essential principle of life, but for the Hebrews it was more, it was *the actual life itself*: 'The blood is the life" (Dt 12:23).'"[61] In this case the blood obtained was, as Exodus describes it, "the blood of the covenant," half of which Moses "dashed against the altar" and the other half of which he dashed on the people, and said, 'See the blood of the covenant that the Lord has made with you'" (Ex 24:5–8). If this, then, is "the blood of the [new] covenant" with which Jesus identified the wine at the Last Supper, it is distorting the significance of the event to consider it sacrificial. Its purpose here was not sacrificial, but it was directed in a life-sharing ritual to unite the two parties to the covenant, God and his new people, as Moses achieved in Exodus with the people of Israel. Michael O'Carroll writes of Jesus's reference to the (blood of the) covenant that this is "the only occasion on which Jesus uses the word. The uniqueness is eloquent, as is the echo of Ex 24 on the mention of blood. But here the author of the new covenant makes his own blood the pledge of its efficacy and endurance."[62] The point is made in Hebrews 12:24, in its reference to Christians coming "to Jesus, the mediator of a new covenant, and to the sprinkled blood that speaks a better word than the blood of Abel."

In fact, it can be concluded that in the New Testament institution narratives of the Eucharist that we possess containing the authentic words of Jesus, as contrasted with later community or editorial elaborations, there is no direct reference, far less allusion, to Jesus's death as being a sacrifice offered to God. The sole exception appears to be the clause peculiar to Matthew's account that describes Jesus's blood as poured out for many "for the forgiveness of sins." McGuckian notes the sacrificial significance of this phrase, which he accepts as the words of Jesus, in arguing that "the Eucharist is not simply a New Passover, but a sin offering as well. Our Lord said as much."[63] Against this ascribing of the phrase to Jesus himself, however, it can be noted that Matthew's gospel is generally recognized as emerging from a community with its own Jewish-Christian preoccupations, and in view of what I have argued earlier about the Jewish cultural predisposition to stress the ideas and theologies of sin and sacrifice, it is not at all surprising to find that Jeremias considers that Matthew's ascribing of "the forgiveness of sins" here as the motive for Jesus's blood being poured out is "probably an addition."[64] In this Matthew is in fact echoing toward the end of his gospel its Jewish preoccupations with sin and repeating the particular focus that he alone gave at its opening to the significance of the name of Jesus as referring to one "who will save his people from their sins" (Mt 1:21). On the addition in Matthew of the reference to the forgiveness of sins, Wright stresses that this does not envisage individual sins being forgiven in the normal sense of the term; it refers to Israel's being brought back from the exile that had resulted from the people's sins. As he explains, "In its first-century Jewish context, this denotes, not an abstract transaction between human beings and their god, but the very concrete expectation of Israel, namely that the nation would at last be rescued from the 'exile' which had come about because of her sins. Matthew is not suggesting that Jesus' death will accomplish an abstract atonement, but that it will be the means of rescuing YHWH's people from their exilic plight."[65]

We can conclude, then, that the New Testament narrative of the institution of the Eucharist by Jesus at the Last Supper need not be considered as depicting the Eucharist as intrinsically sacrificial. This is the case even if the Last Supper was a Passover meal, the annual celebration of the Jewish pasch, as Jeremias strongly argues. Indeed, it is from the alleged Passover character of Jesus's Last Supper that Jeremias is mainly able to argue that the Eucharist has a sacrificial dimension. As John P. Meier points out critically, "One reason why Jeremias is such a passionate champion of the Passover nature of the meal is that otherwise his whole approach to the Eucharistic words of Jesus is undermined."[66] Jeremias himself acknowledges the strong scholarly support that exists for the alternative view that the Last Supper was not a Passover celebration, support that is based on the chronology of John's gospel, and he spends his whole first chapter attempting to discredit this view. Meier's case against the Passover nature of the Last Supper, apart from his criticisms of Jeremias's argumentation, depends on questioning the originality of two phrases in Mark, namely, Mark 14:1a ("two days before the Passover") and Mark 14:12–16, which refers to the disciples making arrangements "to eat the Passover." It is ironic that the popularly held general view is that according to the New Testament evidence Jesus died on the feast day of the Jewish Passover, apart from the embarrassing implication in John's gospel that he died on the day before the feast (Jn 18:28). On the contrary, Meier comments that "the intriguing fact is that, if Mark's Passion Narrative is shorn of [the above] two passages that probably come from either a secondary level of the tradition or from Mark's own redactional activity, the remaining Passion Narrative contains no clear indication that the Last Supper was a Passover meal or that Jesus died on Passover Day."[67]

Meier's own preferred view is attractive in its own right as well as being compatible with, and even lending itself more to, the proposal that I am exploring about the Last Supper in the context of evolution. It depends on Meier's judging that Jeremias unduly limited himself to considering only two possibilities, either the Last Supper was a fully blown Passover celebration or it was just an ordinary meal. As Meier observes persuasively, however,

> there is another possible scenario, one that is quite plausible on any reading of the Gospel tradition: sensing or suspecting that his enemies were closing in for an imminent, final attack, and therefore taking into account that he might not be able to celebrate the coming Passover meal with his disciples, Jesus instead arranged a solemn farewell meal with his inner circle of disciples just before Passover. Wanting privacy, and having his days taken up with teaching in the Jerusalem temple, Jesus

chose to have an evening meal with his closest followers in the house of some affluent Jerusalem supporter on a Thursday around sunset, as the fourteenth of Nisan was beginning. The supper, though not a Passover meal and not celebrated as a substitute Passover meal, was nevertheless anything but an ordinary meal. With Jesus bidding farewell to his closest disciples as he prepared himself for the possibility of an imminent and violent death, the tone of the meal would naturally be both solemn and religious.[68]

Besides solving the chronological problem, this alternative explanation of the Last Supper offered by Meier has many attractions, notably the advantage of dispensing with the problems raised by Jesus's silence about what should be the central element of any Passover meal, namely, the Passover lamb, as well as the fact that Jesus connected his blood with the Mosaic covenant rather than with the Passover event. Wright opined that the Last Supper was "*some kind of* Passover meal," although he does not refer to Meier's arguments or the latter's criticism of Jeremias.[69] This view enables Wright to point out that there was scriptural warrant for choosing the day before (Num 9:10–11) and to observe that "this, of course, would have meant doing without a lamb (since the priests would not be killing them for Passover until the following day); that would be no bar to treating the meal as a proper Passover, since it was what happened after all in the Diaspora (and, of course, what was to happen throughout the Jewish world after AD 70)."[70] In effect, Wright claims, Jesus himself was now the Passover lamb and he was giving a new meaning to the old meal, "intending it to symbolize the new exodus, the arrival of the kingdom through his own fate. The meal, focused on Jesus' actions with the bread and the cup, told the Passover story, and Jesus' own story, and wove these two into one."[71] In this scenario there is no occurrence of sacrifice.

However, serious difficulties also exist concerning the non-Passover interpretation of the Last Supper, as Albright and Mann note, including the arguably authentic Markan verses mentioned earlier and their Lucan parallel (Lk 22:7–13), together with Luke 22:15: "I have eagerly desired to eat this Passover with you before I suffer."[72] It is therefore a relief to recognize that my proposal on the compatibility of the founding of the Eucharist with an evolutionary theology is not dependent on any one view of the Last Supper, but is compatible with the various possible views. There seems to be no doubt that the institution of the Eucharist was built around the impending death of Jesus, and until modern times any attempt to screen out the apparent connections with sacrifice would for Roman Catholics have left a theological vacuum: What theological reason could there be for Jesus establishing the Eucharist, or equivalently, what theological purpose for the death of Jesus on Calvary can be advanced, other than both relating to his redemptive sacrifice to restore the relationship between God and an alienated humanity?

With the development of evolutionary theory, however, an alternative purpose has appeared on the scene that can serve to explain the fundamental question of why at his final meal with his disciples Jesus decided to institute what became the Christian Eucharist. In his final weeks Jesus saw resistance mounting to his provocative evangelizing, with the determination forming among his enemies to eliminate him. He was no doubt unaware of what the future had in store for him apart from his coming death, "which he accepted as part of God's mysterious will for bringing in the kingdom."[73] He decided to ritualize his rejection and death—which would also be his supreme achievement of altruism—in a meal for his future followers to share regularly in his memory and to keep him and his work alive and operative in their minds and lives after he had physically left them—in other words, for building up his church. His achievement would not be to reconcile humanity with God through sacrificially offering himself in atonement for the Fall, but to lead the human species through death to the new evolutionary stage, that is, in theological terms, the new covenant, of sharing more fully in the life of God. In that sense it is now possible to provide a rich evolutionary dimension to his words, "I came that they may have life" (Jn 10:10), with which I have prefaced this work. However one interprets the New Testament accounts of the Last Supper, the final comment of Meier in the *New Jerome Biblical Commentary* is appealing: "This last meal was a pledge that, despite the apparent failure of his mission, God would vindicate Jesus even beyond death and bring him and his followers to the eschatological banquet."[74]

The Mass as Sacrifice

This examination of the Last Supper has thus led to the conclusions that the New Testament narrative need not be considered as depicting the Eucharist instituted by Jesus as intrinsically sacrificial and that the few textual references to its having a sacrificial aspect can be understood as later elaborations that arose from the belief that emerged after the Crucifixion that the death of Jesus on Calvary that was foreseen at the supper was a propitiatory sacrifice offered to an offended God. Under those circumstances it becomes even more relevant to look at the way in which the Eucharist itself has developed historically as a sacrifice. It emerges that this has been determined from the very start by two verses regularly taken from the Old Testament, the first being Malachi 1:11, "in every place incense is offered to my name, and a pure offering," which the Septuagint Greek version rendered as "a clean sacrifice" (θυσία καθαρά), and the second being Psalm 110:4, "You are a priest for ever according to the order of Melchizedek."

The early Christian document that claimed to be the teaching (*didache*) of the twelve apostles and is widely considered to date from the end of the first century shows evidence in the early community of a developed Eucharistic rite that, according to Aaron Milavec, "presents the oldest explicit instance of the community understanding the eucharist as a sacrifice." The *Didache* bases this on Malachi 1:11 and enjoins that on the Lord's day the disciples should gather and break bread and give thanks, first confessing their sins, "so that your sacrifice may be pure" (καθαρὰ ἡ θυσία ὑμῶν) and so that they would obey the divine command, namely "in every place and time, offer to me a pure sacrifice" (Ἐν παντὶ τόπῳ καὶ χρόνῳ προσφέρειν μοι θυσίαν καθαράν).[75] In this way the *Didache* exemplified the comment of Raymond Brown that "by the end of the 1st century the Eucharist was beginning to take the place of the sacrifices of Israel," and also, in my view, witnessed to the regular drawing by the developing Christian church on the religion and culture of ancient Israel for precedent and enlightenment.[76] The same injunction of Malachi 1:11 became an Old Testament proof text regularly repeated in subsequent Christian sources in the patristic era to create and confirm the belief in the sacrificial character of the Eucharist or Holy Mass. R. J. Halliburton puts the matter clearly: "For the Fathers, the Eucharist was the Christian sacrifice. This is a term that may have been avoided during the sub-apostolic age, but that from the second century onwards is commonly used to refer to the principal act of worship of the Christian Church.... By the end of the fourth century, there is a strong sense in some writers that the worshipper at the Eucharist stands in the presence of Christ sacrificed."[77]

In his study significantly titled *The Eucharistic Sacrifice and the Reformation*, Francis Clark attempted to vindicate this traditional sacrificial nature of the Christian Eucharist against the onslaught of Martin Luther and his fellow Reformers. In his second edition, revised in light of the teaching of the Second Vatican Council, Clark showed not only how emphatically the Council of Trent defined the sacrificial nature of the Eucharist but also how "more insistently even than the Council of Trent, the Second Council of the Vatican declares the essential unity and identity of the sacrifice of the Mass with the one saving sacrifice of the cross: 'At the Last Supper, in the night in which he was betrayed, our Saviour instituted the Eucharistic sacrifice of his body and blood, by which he would perpetuate the sacrifice of the cross through all the ages until his coming, and thereto entrust to his beloved spouse, the Church, a memorial of his death and resurrection.'"[78]

Over the course of centuries, celebrations of Holy Mass had become subject to a variety of abuses and corruptions giving rise to frequent complaints that culminated in the strong protests of Luther and his fellow Reformers. The objections of Luther and his fellows were not, however, limited to these aberrations of orthodox belief and practice, as Clark shows clearly. They had much deeper theological roots in taking offense precisely at belief in the doctrine of the Mass as a propitiatory sacrifice. "To this Catholic belief the Protestant Reformers, with their watchword 'faith alone' and their rejection of any instrumental 'work' in the economy of salvation, were from the first inflexibly opposed."[79] Thus, as can be seen in Luther's early diatribe on "the Babylonian Captivity of the Church" in which he attacked the sacramental system of Catholicism as so many good works, the Protestant leader dismissed as erroneous the idea that the Mass is a good work and even more that it is "a sacrifice offered to God."[80] Depending not only on his principle of "faith alone" and not good works, but also on the other Reformation maxim of "Scripture alone" and not tradition, he rejected the "many sayings of the holy Fathers, and the whole custom of the church as observed throughout the world," which supported "the common belief that the mass is a sacrifice offered to God." He appealed rather to "the words and example of Christ" at the Last Supper and proclaimed that "those words contain nothing about a good work or a sacrifice."[81] In brief, for Luther "the gospel offers no warrant for calling the mass a sacrifice," on which Jungmann commented, "Taking as his principle the Bible alone, Luther denied the sacrificial character of the Mass and thought in this way to have reached the root of the trouble."[82] Clark is surely correct, therefore, in concluding that "the abuses which had grown up around the altar were real evils crying for reform, but the root of the conflict lay deeper—in the cardinal principles of the Reformation."[83]

It was not just to introduce a program of liturgical reform, then, but above all to defend the traditional Catholic belief in the Mass that the church's bishops at the Council of Trent devoted its twenty-second session in September 1562 to the subject of "the teaching on the most holy sacrifice of the Mass" and declared its belief, which should be preached to the faithful, that the Eucharist is "a true and unique sacrifice" (DS 1738). The tortuous conciliar text, with its collage of subordinate clauses, merits care-ful reading in the literal translation I offer, in which I have italicized the key theological argument:

Since, as Paul testifies [Heb 7:11, 19], there was no perfection attainable under the previous covenant because of the powerlessness of the levitical priesthood, *another priest had to "arise according to the order of Melchisedech"* [Heb 7:11], as ordained by God the Father of mercies, our Lord Jesus Christ, who would be able to complete and bring to perfection all those who were to be sanctified [Heb 10:14]. Therefore that God and Lord of ours, even although he was about to offer himself to God the Father by the intervention of death on the altar of the cross to effect an everlasting redemption for them, yet *because his priesthood was not to be ended by death* [Heb 7:24, 27], at the last supper "on the night he was betrayed" [1 Cor 11:13], in order to leave to his beloved spouse the church a sacrifice that was visible (as human nature requires), by means of which the bloody one about to take place once on the cross would be represented and its memory would remain to the end of the world, and its saving power would be applied for the forgiveness of our daily sins: *declaring himself "a priest for ever according to the order of Melchisedech"* [Ps 110:4] offered his body and blood to God the Father under the appearances of bread and wine, and under the same symbols offered the same objects to the apostles (whom he then made priest of the new testament) to take, and *ordered them and their successors in the priesthood* to offer with these words: Do this in remembrance of me, etc. [Lk 22:19], as the Catholic Church has always understood and taught. For having celebrated the old Pass-over which the multitude of the children of Israel sacrificed in memory of their departure from Egypt [Ex 12], he instituted a new Passover, himself, *to be sacrificed under visible signs by the church through priests* in memory of his passage from this world to the Father, when he redeemed us through the shedding of his blood and snatched us from the power of darkness and transferred us to his kingdom [Col 1:3]. This is that clean oblation which cannot be soiled by any unworthiness or evil of those offering it which *the Lord foretold through Malachy* [1:11] *was to be offered cleanly to his name....* And since in this divine sacrifice which is performed in the mass that same Christ is contained and sacrificed unbloodily who "offered him-self once on the cross bloodily" [Heb 9:14, 27], the holy council teaches that it is a truly propitiatory sacrifice" (DS 1738–43).

By contrast with the Council of Trent, which was focused in the six-teenth century on expounding and defending the doctrines of the church against attack, the Second Vatican Council was more concerned as a twen-tieth-century pastoral council with the ways in which the church's doc-trines should be understood in contemporary terms and be appropriately applied and communicated. The Vatican II decree on the liturgy was there-fore much less defensive than Trent's decree on the Mass and more con-cerned with encouraging liturgical reform. Hence, as Jungmann observes in his commentary on the Vatican decree, the prooemium in the section on the Eucharist "was to present, as briefly as possible, the theological and pastoral basis of the stipulations to follow."[84] As noted earlier, in the quota-tion offered by Clark, it did so with a simplicity and elegance far different from the cumbersome Tridentine statement, yet retained the theological basis of sacrifice. Indeed, Jungmann notes, "it was insisted upon by theo-logians that the concept of sacrifice—that is, the concept of Eucharistic sacrifice—must be given top priority." He adds that the proposal to refer to the sacrifice as propitiatory was not taken up from Trent at Vatican II on the grounds that a full dogmatic statement was not intended and "that, in particular, those doctrinal aspects at which the separated brethren took offence should not unnecessarily be stressed."[85] This had the added advan-tage of avoiding debate on the various possible meanings of "propitiatory" that are listed by Clark.[86]

Some observations seem called for on the Tridentine teaching on the sacrifice of the Mass as faithfully followed by Vatican II, particularly regarding the structure of the argument. As providing a context to inter-pret the sparse New Testament data on the Last Supper, Trent relied heav-ily on the sacrifice-centered culture of ancient Israel, for much of its force drawing not only on the church's tradition through the centuries but also and primarily on the letter to the Hebrews, which, as explained by Burke, "wishes to show that the sacrifice of Jesus has replaced the OT sacrificial worship."[87] Central to the Council's argument is the second Old Testa-ment text that I have highlighted, Psalm 110:4, "You are a priest for ever according to the order of Melchizedek." Taking this up as a prophetic ref-erence to Jesus, the letter to the Hebrews had argued that "if perfection had been attainable through the levitical priesthood . . . what further need would there have been to speak of another priest arising according to the order of Melchisedech, rather than one according to the order of Aaron?" (Heb 7:11). Drawing on this, the council argued that perfection was not in fact attained through the levitical priesthood, so the need did arise for a different priest, who would be Jesus. Moreover, according to the prophecy of being a priest forever, according to the order of Melchisedech (Ps 110:4), the Council concluded that Jesus "through the power of an indestructible life" (Heb 7:16–17) must exercise his priesthood permanently. Hebrews was thus able to conclude its argument (7:25) that "consequently he is able for all time to save those who approach God through him," and from this observation the Council itself also concluded that Christ instituted himself "as a new Passover to be sacrificed [*immolandum*] by the church" regularly in the Mass.

It seems that a great amount of theological substance is being drawn by the Council of Trent from the traditional Old Testament proof text of Malachi 1:11, which required "a clean sacrifice" as can be seen in the final section of its decree, and even more from the verse of Psalm 110:4, taken to establish the sacrificing priesthood of Jesus, "you are a priest for ever according to the order of Melchisedech." This latter proclamation was originally an oracle concerning the Davidic king, but the verse became accepted in the Christian community as a prophecy referring to Jesus, and it was given greatly enhanced significance in the eyes of the church fathers and later of Trent by the fact that the original priest Melchisedech had actually offered bread and wine (Gen 14:18–20). The basic parallel was, as McGuckian notes, that "Melchizedek offered sacrifice in bread and wine, and so, in fulfilment of the figure, Christ our Lord offered sacrifice in bread and wine and commanded that the same be done in his memory."[88] It appears, then, that relying entirely on the prophetic foretelling read into the Melchisedech verse of the psalmist, the Council of Trent made the actually unproven assertion that at the Last Supper Jesus "declared" (*declarans*) himself appointed a Melchisedech-like sacrificing priest and that the Council further concluded that since the psalm was understood to prophesy that the one foretold would be "a priest for ever," then Christ will forever continue to exercise his sacrificial priesthood and do this through the church's Eucharist.

If the death of Jesus on Calvary is no longer, in an evolutionary perspective, seen as a sacrifice to God on behalf of the sinful and estranged human race, as I have earlier argued, it becomes difficult to sustain the view that the Eucharistic recalling of his death that he instituted for his followers to celebrate regularly can be considered as a sacrifice. And the proof provided by the Council of Trent that the Mass actually is "a truly propitiatory sacrifice" leaves much to be presumed, as I have indicated. Conversely, the evolutionary role of the Eucharist can then emerge as a regular community rite that commemorates and celebrates Christ's death as the supreme human instance of divine altruism, which also saves the human species from mortality and holds out the prospect of its increased communion in the risen Christ with a loving God.

THE EVOLUTIONARY COMMUNITY

The decree on the sacrifice of the Mass was not the only document on the Eucharist produced by the Council of Trent. In an earlier session, the thirteenth, it considered the sacramental characteristics of the Eucharist, being seriously concerned with the errors and schisms that it considered had arisen relating ironically to "what our Savior left in his church as a symbol of its unity and love, by which he wanted all Christians to be united and joined together" (DS 1635). Indeed, as the council teaches, the real presence of Christ in the Eucharist, which the council was at great pains to vindicate, enabled this sacrament "to be taken as the spiritual food of souls by which they would be nourished and strengthened, living with his life.... Moreover, he wanted it to be the pledge of our future glory and eternal happiness, and a symbol of the one body of which he is the head and we the members united to him in the closest bond of faith, hope and love" (DS 1636).

If, then, the teaching of the Council of Trent on the Eucharist as sacrifice is unproven and also inconsistent with the view that I am proposing—that the idea of sacrifice be replaced by the evolutionary purpose and achievement of the death of Jesus—the council's teaching on the sacramental purpose of the Eucharist as fostering our future life and happiness together in union with the risen Christ harmonizes well with the evolutionary role of the church that I explore here, as well as recalling the Eucharistic antiphon, *O sacrum convivium*, composed by Aquinas: "O sacred banquet, in which Christ is received, the memory of His Passion is renewed, the mind is filled with grace, and a pledge of future glory is given to us." Indeed, Vatican II's subsequent statement on the Eucharist, in addition to recalling the sacrificial character of the Eucharist, went on to stress its sacramental dimension in describing what Christ left his church as "a sacrament of love, a sign of unity, a bond of charity, a paschal banquet in which Christ is consumed, the mind is filled with grace and a pledge of future glory is given to us."[89] In doing so, it deliberately cites the Corpus Christi antiphon as referring to a paschal banquet entrusted by Christ to the church, and this official endorsement of the Eucharist as a meal, obviously based on the original farewell meal that Jesus shared with his disciples at the Last Supper, was developed considerably after the council, almost in preference to the sacrificial character of the Eucharist. Restoring the ancient practices of receiving the communion host in the hand and of the laity drinking from the chalice encouraged the meal dimension to be pursued, as did moves to deepen the theology of feasting, eating and drinking, in obvious anticipation of sharing in the messianic banquet at the end of history, as promised by Jesus (Mt 8:11).

One consequence was that in 2003 Pope John Paul II complained in an encyclical letter on the Eucharist that "at times one encounters an extremely reductive understanding of the Eucharistic mystery. Stripped of its sacrificial meaning, it is celebrated as if it were simply a fraternal banquet."[90] As he countered, "though the idea of a 'banquet' naturally suggests familiarity, the Church has never yielded to the temptation to trivialize this 'intimacy' with her Spouse by forgetting that he is also her Lord and that the 'banquet' always remains a sacrificial banquet marked by the blood shed on Golgotha."[91] As a consequence the pope strongly reasserted the sacrificial aspect of the Eucharist, as did his successor, Pope Benedict XVI in his 2005 postsynodal statement *Sacramentum caritatis*.[92]

In part 2 of his encyclical, Pope John Paul II also powerfully developed the idea that "the Eucharist builds the church" by creating community. Drawing the striking precedent of the covenant of Exodus, the pope observed that "by analogy with the Covenant of Mount Sinai, sealed by sacrifice and the sprinkling of blood (Ex 24:8), the actions and words of Jesus at the Last Supper laid the foundations of the new messianic community, the People of the New Covenant."[93] Indeed, the goal of the Eucharist, according to Pope John Paul II, is "the communion of mankind with Christ and in him with the Father and the Holy Spirit."[94] Again, then, as in the documents of Trent, the need is felt to reassert the sacrificial aspect of the Eucharist in a way that differs from the evolutionary purpose of the Eucharist that I am exploring; yet the ecclesial significance of the Eucharist is now brought out strongly, stressing more than previously the community dimension of communion with and in Christ and the universal goal of the Eucharist as to create an eschatological human community with Christ.

By way of conclusion, then, even if one discounts the sacrificial dimension of the Eucharist, a very rich theology remains that establishes the central significance of the Eucharist as building the church into the evolutionary community of Christ that is progressively sharing his risen life as humanity continues to evolve through death. In the church's fellowship meal, the risen Christ, in continuing to offer his body and blood to his disciples, shares with them the fruits of his altruism, his victory over death, achieved through his total self-dedication to his father and to his brothers and sisters, which he consummated on the cross. In offering his body to his disciples he unites them in communion with himself and with each other in an overall gift and command of altruism on their part, and in offering them his blood—it is "the blood of the covenant," not its shedding, that is in biblical terms the central uniting life force—he is uniting them with God as the origin of all altruism in the new covenant that he is instituting.

NOTES

1. Darwin, *Autobiography*, 87.
2. Kelly, *Early Christian Doctrines*, 472.
3. Ibid., 473–74, 483–84.
4. Augustine, *City of God*, XXI, 17, 995.
5. Chadwick, *Church in Ancient Society*, 139.
6. Augustine, *City of God*, XXI, 18, 998.
7. Rahner, "Hermeneutics of Eschatological Assertions," 339n15, 340.
8. Hanson, "Heaven and Hell," 152.
9. Hastings, "Hell," 291–92.
10. Mason, "Universalism," 733.
11. See also von Balthasar, *Dare We Hope*.
12. Viviano, "Gospel according to Matthew," 42:145.
13. Hastings, "Hell," 292.
14. See chapter 3, this volume.
15. See Aquinas, *Summa Theologiae* I, q. 75, a. 6.
16. Daly, *Creation and Redemption*, 51–52.
17. Rahner, "Hermeneutics of Eschatological Assertions," 341n16.
18. Rahner, "Christology within an Evolutionary View of the World," 160.
19. Ibid., 161.
20. Ibid., 164.
21. Ibid., 168.
22. Ibid., 164.
23. Rahner, *Hominization*, 45–93.
24. Rahner, "Christology within an Evolutionary View of the World," 165.
25. Ibid., 166.
26. Pope, *Human Evolution and Christian Ethics*, 172.
27. Darwin, *Descent of Man*, 143, 145.
28. Ibid., 143.
29. Ibid., 146.
30. Smart, *World's Religions*, 34–35.
31. Gerrish, "Schleiermacher," 644.
32. McGrath, *Christian Theology*, 206.
33. McGrath, *Justitia Dei*, 155 (emphasis added).

34. Macquarrie, *Principles of Christian Theology*, 323.

35. Mahoney, *Making of Moral Theology*, 193–202, 96–102.

36. Vatican Council II, Decree on the Church, no. 16.

37. Gerrish, "Schleiermacher," 645.

38. John Paul II, *On the Eucharist and the Church*.

39. Moule, *Sacrifice of Christ*, 12.

40. Jeremias, *Eucharistic Words of Jesus*, 205–6.

41. Ibid., 7.

42. Ibid., 133–36; Jungmann, *Mass of the Roman Rite*, 1:8.

43. Jeremias, *Eucharistic Words of Jesus*, 238.

44. Ibid., 87–88.

45. Ibid., 136.

46. Jungmann, *Mass of the Roman Rite*, 1:9–10.

47. Jeremias, *Eucharistic Words of Jesus*, 251–55.

48. Ibid., 251.

49. Ibid., 237.

50. Ibid., 252–53.

51. Ibid., 172.

52. Ibid., 171, 194.

53. Ibid., 195.

54. Wright, *Christian Origins and the Question of God*, vol. 2, *Jesus and the Victory of God*, 560–61.

55. Jeremias, *Eucharistic Words of Jesus*, 221–22.

56. Ibid., 222.

57. Ibid., 223.

58. Ibid., 225.

59. Ibid., 225.

60. Ibid., 224.

61. McGuckian, *Holy Sacrifice of the Mass*, 98.

62. O'Carroll, *Corpus Christi*, 58.

63. McGuckian, *Holy Sacrifice of the Mass*, 52.

64. Jeremias, *Eucharistic Words of Jesus*, 173.

65. Wright, *Christian Origins and the Question of God*, vol. 2, *Jesus and the Victory of God*, 561. Cf. 563, 577.

66. Meier, *Marginal Jew*, 1:424n87.

67. Ibid., 1:396.

68. Ibid., 1:399.

69. Wright, *Christian Origins and the Question of God*, vol. 2, *Jesus and the Victory of God*, 555.

70. Ibid., 556.

71. Ibid., 559.

72. Albright and Mann, *Matthew*, 320–21.

73. Meier, "Jesus," 78:51.

74. Ibid.

75. Malachi 1:11 Septuagint; *Didache* 14:1–3. Milavec, *Didache*, 530.

76. Brown, "Church in the Apostolic Period," 80:25.

77. Halliburton, "Patristic Theology of the Eucharist," 248.

78. Clark, *Eucharistic Sacrifice and the Reformation*, xviii; Vatican Council II, Decree on Liturgy, 47.

79. Clark, *Eucharistic Sacrifice and the Reformation*, 342.

80. Luther, "Pagan Servitude of the Church," 286.

81. Ibid.

82. Ibid., 289; Jungmann, *Mass of the Roman Rite*, 1:132.

83. Clark, *Eucharistic Sacrifice and the Reformation*, 112.

84. Jungmann, "Constitution on the Sacred Liturgy," 31.

85. Ibid., 32.

86. Clark, *Eucharistic Sacrifice and the Reformation*, 230–36, esp. 235.

87. Burke, "Epistle to the Hebrews," 60:5.

88. McGuckian, *Holy Sacrifice of the Mass*, 12.

89. Vatican Council II, Constitution on the Sacred Liturgy (*Sacrosanctum concilium*), 47.

90. John Paul II, *On the Eucharist and the Church*, 10.

91. Ibid., 48.

92. Ibid., 11–13; Pope Benedict XVI, Postsynodal statement, *Sacramentum caritatis*, October 2005.

93. John Paul II, *On the Eucharist and the Church*, 21.

94. Ibid., 22.

CHAPTER SEVEN

Theology in Evolution

HIS BOOK HAS aimed to explore a theology of evolution that will enable the Christian faith to take constructive and systematic note of the way in which the science of evolution has advanced our knowledge of human origins. Much of it will appear negative to many in terms of arguing to dispense with some traditional Christian beliefs, namely, the interconnected beliefs relating to original sin, the Fall, concupiscence, and the resulting need for human reconciliation and redemption and for a propitiatory sacrifice of atonement to an offended God. Yet my aim has been entirely positive. The work of constructing a theology of evolution entails a certain amount of rethinking and dismantling and of what could be called removing theological undergrowth, clearing the ground as a preparatory stage. Thus accepting scientific evolution and its implications, and looking to understand it in theological terms, means that we no longer need to believe that things went badly wrong for God's plans at the very start of his scheme of creation, with the gloomy consequence that all subsequent human beings start life as a miserable lot of sinners, what Augustine called a *massa damnata*, a "condemned lump."[1] Nor do we have to believe that for the divine plan to be rescued and got back on the road, this cosmic disaster needed to be made up for in some way and that this could only be achieved by offering a divine-human life in atoning sacrifice to God by way of compensation.

Much more positively, the developing of a theology of evolution entails uncovering and exploring new riches in God's ways of dealing with the human race. We have already invoked the view of Dionysius the Areopagite hat it is of the nature of goodness to communicate itself, a theme taken up by Aquinas and other theologians in the Latin maxim *bonum est diffusivum sui*, that is, "the good expands itself."[2] When this insight is applied to the divine work of creation it enables us to appreciate the unqualified reply that I offered earlier to the question in the *Catechism* of why God made us:

simply, to share his life generously with humanity. The unfolding of that project has entailed a very slow advance in what evolutionary science has come to term "deep time" on the part of nondivine, that is, created being through various stages of complexity up to and through the rise of human intelligence and its flourishing in morality and in religion. An intrinsic factor of this project, I have argued, is that God determined from the start to become one of us in the incarnation. This sharing our human lot was undertaken by Christ not for any remedial or reparative purpose, but basically with two positive aims: first, to teach and to show humans how to move out of, and beyond, any evolutionary self-centeredness and, as a species, to imitate the Creator's altruism or generosity, or agape in more biblical terms. Second, God became human to save humans from extinction, or death, the otherwise inevitable fate for individuals within the cosmic process of evolution. By leading the way through his own experience of death to usher the human species into a higher phase of living, the risen Jesus is now increasingly building up his church, his body of fellow humans, to share with them the divine communion and fellowship that God in his altruism has intended for them from the start.

Exploring such a momentous, but—thankfully—now very positive, theology has the consequence of dispensing with, or disposing of, traditional theological positions that are no longer considered necessary or helpful in light of accepting the facts of evolution, since they were created and developed in the first place for lack of any alternative explanation of the phenomenon of death.[3] Darwin's scientific advance has served to explain individual death as a regular evolutionary phenomenon affecting all living things in nature, long predating humanity, and in the process it has thrown in question the need for the whole Judeo-Christian intellectual construct of fall and redemption, whose purpose, I have argued, was to explain the origin of death as a penalty for human sin, with the corollary of continuing human sinfulness and debilitating moral frailty. It also has rendered unnecessary the need for that primordial sin, with the resulting fallen condition of human nature, to be atoned for in some way and to be redeemed by the sacrifice of an incarnate God who became human precisely for that purpose. Indeed, for practical purposes and in the interests of argumentative clarity, it may now be possible and useful to categorize the originally Israelite hypothesis of a primordial fall and the progression to a subsequent cosmic restitution as instances of speculative biblical theology, emerging from, and tied to, Israelite culture, rather than as instances of substantiated Christian belief.

EVOLUTIONARY IMPACT ON OTHER
TRADITIONAL BELIEFS

Going beyond what I have called the postevolutionary apologetics produced recently by several theologians to counter the attacks on religion and Christianity mounted by militant evolutionists, to take note of the major immediate modifications relating to the network of Catholic doctrines that I have proposed result from accepting the scientific doctrine of evolution, invites one to proceed further and consider what effect this change may have on other aspects and expressions of the Catholic faith. Thus the central belief in the existence and nature of God and of the Trinity of divine persons is essentially unaffected by accepting the scientific doctrine of evolution, although beliefs in the divine sustaining of creation and in divine providence in the governance of that creation can be enriched and given more immediacy by the deeper appreciation, as I have tried to show, that this loving God is continually at work undergirding the infinity of detail involved in the entire process of evolution. In addition, focusing evolutionary ethics as I have done on the central idea of altruism, a quality originating in God and witnessed by Jesus in his teaching and supremely in his death as well as being continuously invited from all human beings, serves to reinforce the belief that creation is entirely a drama of divine love and can be seen as enhancing the doctrine of humans created in God's image when this image is viewed, as I have suggested, as a derivation and shared reflection of the divine altruism.

It is important to realize that transferring one's acceptance from some of our traditional beliefs to a structure of beliefs more appropriate to the idea of evolution, as I have aimed to do, alerts us to both the importance and the risks of describing divine activities in human language, which is the only one we possess for that purpose. For instance, viewing God as a judge against the forensic backcloth of our human experience of trial procedures and often unrelenting justice, as appears more than hinted at in the creation and fall account in Genesis, later regularly in the Hebrew Bible, and as has recurred throughout the history of moral theology, appears on the whole to be more likely to lead to a false image of God than to an accurate one.[4] Again, considering God as a majestic deity that has to be appeased for being slighted and offended, and that must be placated by being given satisfaction by bloody sacrifice, is an approach dominated by an intransigent mentality that, as I have argued, Jewish culture found highly congenial but that can only with difficulty be exorcised out of early—and even later—Christian thought and belief.

Moreover, accepting that God cannot but respect the nature that is intrinsic to the nondivine being that he is in the process of creating, including humanity and human free choice, may throw light on the problems of natural catastrophes and moral enormities, as I have tried to elucidate. Yet, as I have also attempted to show, seeking to identify distinct stages in the divine creative activity and trying to make some sense of the idea of divine interventions appears to intensify the theological difficulties involved in trying to come to human terms with God's eternity and God's so-called foreknowledge. Pope expressed the matter well when he concluded that "as the primary cause, the Creator does not 'intrude' into natural processes for their proper operation, but works from within the inherent capacities, structures, and tendencies of creatures."[5]

So far as concerns our religious and theological approach to human creation itself, it appears that within a theology of evolution considerable reflection is now required on the traditional couplet of doctrinal ideas of nature and grace, and the question needs to be examined what meaning these terms can continue to convey within this new context. As contrasting ideas they were considered highly significant by Augustine as he confronted Pelagian moral optimism with what he considered the fact—and the experience—of human fallenness, and they later became central at the time of the Reformation to Luther's self-torturing reflections on human moral failure as well as to the magisterial decree of Trent on justification. In modern times Karl Rahner has done much to popularize the view that, as contrasted with the purely theoretical and systematic distinctions introduced between nature and grace and the historical controversies surrounding them, in actual experience (i.e., existentially) human nature has always been and remains forever conjoint with the influence of God's graceful invitations to share the divine life.[6] Perhaps with the acceptance of evolution and the discontinuing of belief in the Fall and in a sinful state of humankind, the need for this distinction between nature and grace ceases to exist, and the time has come to adopt a simpler view of human action and behavior under God rather than continuing to dissect it into different theoretical levels. This gives added attraction to the observation of Edwards that "we can think of our forebears as coming to self-consciousness in . . . a world in which God was already there in self-offering love as a constitutive dimension of human existence in the world."[7] For, Pope observes, "the theological story of the emergence of human awareness is the story of emergence into a gracious universe."[8]

When we turn to ask what light an evolutionary perspective sheds on Christology, which was one of the central questions explicitly identified by Pope John Paul II, then a central consideration focuses, I have suggested, not on the constitution of the incarnation, that is, the hypostatic union of humanity and divinity in the person of the Word, which can remain unquestioned, but on the divine purpose of the incarnation and the evolutionary role and significance of Jesus Christ.[9] This envisages Jesus as God becoming incarnate in order to challenge death and to share his victory over death with the rest of the human species, a purpose that can only strengthen belief in both the divinity and the humanity of Christ. The suffering and death of Jesus on Calvary out of love for his father and humanity remains of central significance in Christian evolutionary belief. He freely chose to submit to the hostility of his fellow humans rather than to surrender his witness to the true nature and wishes of his father, and in so doing he fought his way through human death and survived it. This achievement is now best viewed as his saving us from annihilating death rather than from sin and the Fall, far less from divine displeasure. In other words, the cross is no longer required to be identified in sacrificial terms as Jesus offering himself to an offended God in order to reconcile estranged humanity. It can be seen now as an inspiring instance and symbol of divine-human altruism that conducts the evolving human species through death to the possibility of an ever closer communion with the divine life.

The nexus of Catholic beliefs concerning the Virgin Mary cannot be entirely unaffected by the discontinuance of belief in original sin and in the Fall for which I have argued. What is clearly central to the church's Marian belief remains untouched by accepting the scientific doctrine of evolution, namely, the mystery of the divine motherhood as she contributed her Jewish genetic inheritance to the Word becoming flesh, as indeed can belief in the virgin birth, in Mary's sinlessness throughout her life, and in her bodily assumption to heaven on her life's completion. However, the idea that Mary was prepared for her divine vocation by being preserved from the stain of original sin and its consequences, that is, belief in the doctrine of the immaculate conception (what Wordsworth described as "our tainted nature's solitary boast"), is so intricately connected with the belief in original sin that with the demise of the latter there remains no purpose in continuing to maintain the former. Such a conclusion echoes the remark of Pelikan about the belief of the Eastern Church with regard to the defined doctrine of the immaculate conception of Mary, that "not having committed itself so unequivocally to the distinctively Augustinian doctrine of original sin, the East did not have the same obligation to define why Mary was an 'exception' to that universal rule."[10]

Belief in the sacramental system is modified in a number of ways within the theology of evolution that I am exploring. Our understanding of sacramental symbolism and causality remains unaffected, although the sacramental nature and potential of created reality appear enriched by the dynamic impetus with which this reality is now recognized as intrinsically endowed. However, the nature of three of the sacraments appears to be affected. Baptism remains the sacrament of initiation into God's people, the church, and the water symbolism continues to convey the ideas of life and of the power of the Spirit. The idea of being washed clean from the stain of original sin loses its relevance, although the theme of immersion and emergence, that is, of death and rebirth in Christ and in the womb of the church, can take on a new evolutionary and eschatological symbolism, that of our species being united with Christ in sharing his victory over death and his risen existence in the inner life of God. The sacrament of penance remains relevant as the recognition of personal sinfulness, which is in no way abolished by the process of evolution, and of the need for reconciliation with the community that may be required after any serious succumbing to aggression and self-centeredness that, as we have seen, are closely linked with the evolutionary process and that we are called to counter with the difficult moral call to altruism toward all our fellows. The nature of the Eucharist as a sacrifice is substantially affected by the theology of evolution, as I have considered at length in arguing that the idea of propitiatory sacrifice, to use the terminology of Trent, to atone for a human lapse from divine favor does not find a place within an evolutionary restructuring of faith. However, the sacramental recalling of the Last Supper in the Eucharistic transformation of bread and wine into the risen Lord's body and blood, and in the effective remembrance of his love-inspired death on the cross, remains a living source of inspiration and power to the new covenant community, as he intended it to be.

The only other sacrament that appears to require reevaluation as a result of accepting evolution is that of sacred orders, which in light of our earlier reflections would cease to be primarily what has been traditionally referred to as a "sacrificing priesthood." This is an evolution in this particular sacrament that may favor its further development adumbrated by Vatican II along the lines of preaching the Word in accordance with the new evolutionary appreciation of the gospel and of providing sacramental and spiritual leadership to the worshipping Christian community.[11] In addition, dispensing with the idea that Christian priesthood involves ordaining a man to act "in the person of Christ" by offering his atoning sacrifice to God removes whatever ground there was for restricting ordination to the priesthood to men and for excluding women.

So far as concerns beliefs connected with eschatology, or the traditional last things, I have suggested the possibility that belief in hell need not continue to be maintained within an evolutionary theology if those who are not destined to enter with Christ into the new phase of risen existence will not be condemned to everlasting suffering, but rather will be allowed to cease to exist at death, as may be considered more consonant with divine mercy. However, eschatological hope in the future can take on a stronger and more discernible appearance in the new evolutionary perspective of humanity as being part of a continuing dynamic process under divine guidance through history. This will perhaps be the more so as the human species becomes increasingly aware that, because in us non–divine being has reached the level of self-consciousness and the personal freedom to choose between different scenarios, the future of the universe now lies to a large extent in our hands and within our responsible decisions. This gives an entirely unexpected dimension to the statement of Aquinas that I have already noted, that every creature is subject to God's providence, but this applies to the human creature "in a more excellent manner, insofar as this is also made a sharer in providence, by taking foresight for itself and for others (*fit providentiae particeps, sibi ipsi et aliis providens*)."[12]

EVOLUTIONARY ETHICS

Christian evolutionary teaching on moral behavior, as Pope has shown, confirms what we have already noted with Huxley, that the idea involved in social Darwinism, of the alleged moral responsibility to favor only those most likely to survive, is basically fallacious.[13] In the circumstances it would be difficult to improve on Huxley's contrast that the purpose of morality "is directed, not so much to the survival of the fittest, as to the fitting of as many as possible to survive."[14] Moreover, our human moral past need not now be seen unhistorically as a paradisiacal state from which humanity chose to have itself expelled. And Pope's conclusion is as true, referring to the future as much as to the past: "Evolution undercuts any assumption that we ought to strive to return to an original moral order. There is no reason to think that there was ever a time when we were not conflictual, manipulative, selfish and prone to deceit and violence—as well as cooperative, generous, empathic, and altruistic."[15] In the circumstances, the deployment of altruism as the evolutionary expression of biblical agape, as I have argued, provides an all-embracing moral orientation of human behavior within an evolutionary context, while still leaving such behavior to be determined and specified in a multitude of ways adapted according to circumstances, as Pope has argued.[16]

Perhaps one major modification that results from switching one's moral perspective to that of evolutionary development relates to what has traditionally been referred to in terms of the doctrine of natural law, based as this is on how one understands human nature, that is, now in an evolutionary perspective. As Bröker noted, "If the idea of 'nature' has changed from the conception of a static and hierarchical succession of stages to that of a dynamic continuum to which ever fresh opportunities are opened up, then we are faced with the question—and this question does not already assume the answer—of whether we must not also attempt a new derivation of the idea of natural law."[17] Exploring the connection between natural law and evolution, van Melsen observes that in the past natural law was based on a preevolutionary notion of nature, with the logical consequence that if man evolves so also should natural law, particularly insofar as "the process of hominization continues for ever."[18] Moreover, the complexity of the evolutionary present as well as the richness of the evolutionary future are also brought out by Rahner's expansion of the idea of human nature to include that of human culture, so that the variability and malleability of culture have to be transported into our full understanding of human nature, that is, of what it is to be human at any given time and what this morally entails.[19]

Haught makes an excellent point concerning moral motivation in an evolutionary context when he writes of the morality entailed by evolution: "I would propose that an evolutionary ethic would pursue essentially the same virtues as those prescribed almost universally by the world's religious traditions. However, this pursuit of virtue would now be fired by a much stronger sense that our moral lives are contributing to the ongoing creation of a universe." In fact, as he notes, with obvious reference to environmental and ecological considerations, "an awareness that our own conduct can contribute at least something to the ongoing creation and expansion of cosmic beauty can give our moral lives what they have often lacked, a sense of being connected meaningfully and creatively to what is going on in the universe at large."[20]

This idea of humans being connected meaningfully opens another possible natural law theme or insight implied by evolution. Aquinas wrote of a precept of natural law resulting from the human being's unique rational nature that involves "knowing the truth about God and living in society."[21] The connection between reason and knowing the truth is obvious enough, but it is interesting to note that for Aquinas the shared possession of rationality entails and involves humans living together and pursuing their purposes in concert, confirming Aristotle's dictum that human beings are by nature political, that is, social, animals.[22] The dynamic unity and synergy of the evolving human species contributes to human beings as a whole a new dimension of human solidarity in a shared origin and destiny and gives added moral significance to the value of the common weal, in the attractive old English phrase, or of shared human well-being. From this it is no great step to accept the importance of the common good and global justice as a basic ethical criterion in all human matters, especially when this is theologically enriched by the human vocation to mutual altruism originating in Trinitarian love, which we have considered, and to pursue the unity of humanity as a single moral family even as far as aspiring to the global expression of cosmopolitanism, without necessarily being committed to any specific political form of this.[23]

Another dimension of being human that lies at the very center of the evolutionary process must be the human capacity to reproduce itself, that is, human sexuality, which has in recent years received progressive ethical appreciation and which could well now call for further ethical reflection. What began in our animal forebears as the instinctive drive to reproduce themselves evidently became adapted to the needs of their offspring for continued parental care and protection during the comparatively long process of maturation. With the progress to hominization, this sustained mutual support of parents for each other, which initially helped them cooperate to provide a caring environment for their offspring, came to be appreciated as human values in their own right, expanding beyond the physical process of reproduction to become a medium of interpersonal communication and sharing within a wide variety of personal and social contexts. Human, no longer simply animal, sexuality thus came to contribute to the personal and social enhancement and development of the individual persons involved in what had evolved into human sexual companionship. This interpersonal relationship based on human sexual differentiation is now capable of being exercised in numerous ways in society, most evidently in sharing the capacity for loving reproduction and upbringing of offspring but now also finding expression in a variety of personal and social contexts through other forms of relationships between the sexes that express and are influenced by their mutual interest and attraction. Reflection along this line confirms Pope's suggestion that knowledge of evolution supports a greater sensitivity to concrete particularities in sexual ethics "because it does not draw such an intimate connection between the Creator's will and the natural reproductive end of sex."[24]

"DEVELOPMENT OF DOCTRINE"?

Of the questions that Pope John Paul II put to evolutionary studies, two were considered earlier in our examination of the doctrine of humans created in the image of God and in the area of Christology. The pope's final question—and a startling one—was whether an evolutionary perspective sheds any light "even upon the development of doctrine itself?"—a papal question that appears to open up the entire subject of Christian theology and that seems prepared to consider the prospect of deep and perhaps widespread change for the future, resulting not only in a theology of evolution but also in an evolution of theology.[25]

My conclusions in previous chapters have included proposing that the death of Christ on Calvary be viewed in a new evolutionary light, not as saving us from sin, but as breaking through death to a new form of communion with God that is shared by Christ with his fellow humans. As a result, this has dispensed with the traditional doctrines of original sin, the Fall, human concupiscence, and the views of the Last Supper and Calvary as propitiatory sacrifice to God to atone for the fall. Can the suggestions made about these doctrines be considered as a development of doctrine in the sense meant by Pope John Paul II?

The idea of doctrines or beliefs developing or progressing has existed since the Christian community's earliest days, and basically it is viewed as the community's awareness, understanding, and appreciation of how one aspect or another of divine revelation and faith can become in time more explicit or more articulated or expanded. The classic historical instances of such doctrinal development occurred in the early church in relation to beliefs in both the divinity and the humanity of Christ and in the triune nature of God.[26] The claim to continuity or discontinuity in beliefs and practices ("faith and morals") in the past life of the Christian community was a central issue raised by Protestants during the Reformation.[27] In the nineteenth century, advances in biblical and other scholarship focused fresh critical historical and theological interest on the church's beliefs, with the consequence that Pope Pius X felt it necessary to condemn the so-called modernist movement for what he considered its defective views on the relative character of doctrines. In the 1907 Decree of the Holy Office, *Lamentabili*, the pope inveighed against theologians and philosophers who wanted to accommodate Catholic doctrine to modern scholarship and science, and he condemned the view ascribed to them that "scientific progress demands that the concepts of Christian doctrine concerning God, creation, revelation, the Person of the Incarnate Word, and Redemption be re-formed."²⁸ Subsequently, in the encyclical letter *Pascendi*, which has acquired the reputation of having helpfully formulated the disparate elements of Catholic modernism into a recognizable system before condemning it, the pope blamed modernists for requiring

> the intrinsic *evolution* of dogma ... [claiming that] dogma is not only able, but ought, to evolve and to be changed (*Evolvi tamen ac mutari dogma non posse solum sed oportere*). . . . For amongst the chief points of their teaching is this which they deduce from the principle of *vital imma-nence*; that religious formulas, to be really religious and not merely theological speculations, ought to be living and to live the life of the religious sentiment. . . . Hence it comes that these formulas, to be living, should be, and should remain, adapted to the faith and to him who believes. Wherefore if for any reason this adaptation should cease to exist, they lose their first meaning and accordingly must be changed.²⁹

The classic study of the development of doctrine was the essay produced in 1845 by the then Anglican John Henry Newman in which he argued that the issue centered on a real continuity of doctrine between the beliefs of the early church and those of later generations.³⁰ Newman provided a list of what he considered tests of fidelity to authenticate legitimate developments, which come down basically to the criteria of preservation, or identity, and continuity. As Pelikan notes, "The concepts of identity and continuity were a way of protecting the idea of development of doctrine against the charge of innovation," and for Newman such development could take the form of making explicit the implicit content of the doctrine, or its enlargement from within like the flowering of a shrub, or through the addition of new matter from outside that does not affect the substance of the doctrine.³¹

The question arises whether the suggestions that I have considered in earlier chapters of this study can be judged as offering a genuine development of the church's beliefs in those appropriate areas. The proposal in chapter 2 that the doctrine of humans created in the image of God can be interpreted as their imaging the divine altruism and the inner Trinitarian life seems entirely consonant with the substance of the basic doctrine while adding a new facet to it. The Christological proposals that the purpose of the incarnation was to teach and exemplify God's altruism and to conduct the human species through death to a fuller participation in the inner life of God appear to harmonize positively with the whole idea of

God becoming incarnate. In fact, evolutionary Christological development could also be recognized, I suggest, as a continuation of the advance in viewing Christ's actions made by the early Christian community from the national Israelite context to an international context, which N. T. Wright explains convincingly. He shows how Jesus was seen by himself and by his contemporaries as continuing the tradition of the itinerant prophets of Israel, bringing his people a message from their covenanting God and leading a group of followers in a movement of urgent renewal.[32] His repeated message that the kingship of God was at last approaching was "a warning of imminent catastrophe, a summons to an immediate change of heart and direction of life, an invitation to a new way of being Israel." In other words, Jesus was offering to the Jewish people the welcome news "that Israel was about to be vindicated against her enemies, that her god was returning at last to deal with evil, to right wrongs, to bring justice to those who were thirsting for it like dying people in the desert."[33] In expansion and development of this mission of Jesus, the early community that he founded expanded the vision from Israel to a universal theater of action, from a national to a world view, in what Wright calls "a major redefinition." This "self-consciously sees itself as the time when the covenant purpose of the creator, which always envisaged the redemption of the whole world, moves beyond the narrow confines of a single race . . . , and calls into being a transnational and trans-cultural community. Further, it sees itself as the time when the creator, the covenant god himself, has returned to dwell with his people, but not in a Temple made with hands."[34]

If we accept that doctrinal progression offered by Wright and then move the focus of attention now beyond the Israelite and even the universal setting to the cosmic evolutionary context, this enables us to appreciate more fully the entire divine drama of God's all-encompassing initiative of creative love and to experience a progression in our appreciation of Jesus Christ as first the messiah of Israel, then the firstborn of all creation (Col 1:15), and now most fully the agent of human evolution as, in a sense far beyond what Paul could have had in mind, "the firstborn from the dead" (Col 1:18).

When we consider our other, more negative, conclusions proposed, of abandoning the doctrines of original sin, the Fall, concupiscence, and the sacrificial redemption of fallen humanity through propitiatory sacrifice to an offended God, any idea of identity and continuity with the tradition becomes more than difficult to maintain. At the most, these traditional doctrines appear so connected that they stem as a logical series of beliefs from one basic consideration, as I have argued, namely, the Israelite preoccupation with finding an acceptable explanation of human death. The basic common feature between that idea and the modern understanding of God's activity within a context of cosmic evolution that I have explored appears to be the aim of exonerating God from any appearance of inflicting extinction on innocent human creatures, which appears a far cry from the circumstantial contents of the traditional doctrines.

Rahner has some interesting, if somewhat lengthy, observations that may be of help here, leading us beyond the parameters of the idea of doctrinal development. As he wrote,

> The changes which have appeared during the last hundred years up until the most recent time cannot all be included under the heading of "the transition from the implicit to the explicit," from the less to the more precise, or as the simple addition of new supplementary insights. There has also been the transition from error to true insight, not without struggle, pain and bitter personal sacrifice. Much of what is and must be taught today—this applies even to Vatican II—with regard to questions of biblical studies, questions of the nature of marriage, freedom of conscience, sociological questions, questions on the borderland between science and theology, problems in the history of dogma—much of this was at an earlier time, fought over and highly suspect in theology; opposed to it was the *sententia communis* [common opinion] protected and propagated by the *magisterium*, even though not of course, in a definitive and obligatory form. The generally accepted academic theory that there are *sententiae per se reformabiles* [views in principle reformable] in the theology and in official teaching as well, is not merely a theory but also—if we are honest—a theory confirmed by fact.... The facts and the Church's doctrine oblige the theologian to be modest and self-critical, taking the possibility of error into account even when presenting a traditional doctrine and one which is favored by the Church's teaching office. Theology must be aware of this since it does not only *live* its historicity, as it did almost exclusively in the past, but nowadays is also consciously *aware* of it. It must ponder the matter, and always seriously include it anew in its calculations. In one respect, therefore, it will move more slowly and hesitantly ..., but on the other hand it will often more easily find the courage to give up an obsolete position without each time having to apply too much skill in interpreting traditional formulas.... This courage is a better act of faith than the anxious conservatism which only gives up such a position when development has far outrun the mental framework

of the thesis in question, so that the latter can only be found haunting text-books [and—one might add—catechisms]; and the damage done by this time is very great as regards the readiness to believe and the confidence in the Church's teaching authority on the part of intellectuals and also on the part of ordinary people.[35]

In addition to drawing attention to the possibility of simple previous theological error or ignorance, Rahner also usefully draws attention to the influence that can be exercised by particular cultures in formulating popular religious beliefs, as may be the case in the origin of the doctrines of the Fall and concupiscence that I have considered here. Thus he observed about the so-called revelation about angels that "the remarks about angels in the Old Testament (upon which the New Testament depends) do not give the impression of having been communicated from heaven, but of having drifted into the minds of the Old Testament theologians from their cultural and religious environment."[36]

Along similar lines, Maurice Wiles has a salutary warning about the reformability of doctrines, especially in light of new knowledge. He reminds us, for one thing, that a doctrine once arrived at continues to depend on the arguments that originally produced it for its validity. "If one believes that the result of successful doctrinal discussion is the attainment of an objective knowledge of clearly defined religious entities, then that knowledge will be thought of as a secure and permanent possession for all time. It will be regarded as the assured result of theological endeavor and as valid in all situations and in all contexts. It will be natural to assert the truth of such doctrinal conclusions absolutely without reference to the arguments by which they were established and to look upon them as a secure foundation upon which further theological work of theological construction can be built."[37] Further, he alerts us to the need for continued care in perusing the historical grounds claimed for some doctrines. As he writes,

> We must not too quickly impose alien criteria of judgment from the comparative detachment of our modern world. Nevertheless, in the long run something very like that is just what we have to do. If we are concerned not merely with the history of doctrinal development but with evaluating that doctrine for ourselves in the light of its historical process of development, we must raise questions about the truth and falsity of the arguments used in that process and the results achieved by it. And this we can only do from one position and with one set of criteria: that is,

from the position of our contemporary world and with the criteria that seem to us appropriate to the subject-matter under review. We need, therefore, to be on the look-out for features in the story of development which, by virtue of their logical form, might tend to throw doubt upon the validity of the conclusions that stem from them."[38]

From such observations by Rahner and Wiles it seems to follow that my negative verdict on the arguments that have been adduced in the past justifies my conclusions regarding the reformability and dispensability of the doctrines of original sin, the Fall, and the continuing existence of concupiscence, as well as of the doctrines of the redemption and sacrificial character of Christ's death on Calvary and of the Eucharist. The urgent question then arises as to what further value these beliefs may continue to possess in Christian life and whether, in fact, they may be held onto in some modified or adapted modern version, or be abandoned altogether.

DEMYTHOLOGIZING DEATH

As I have attempted to demonstrate, there is no biblical warrant for considering that a first sin had a cataclysmic effect on the whole of human nature, far less that such an effect was inherited by every subsequent instance of human nature by being transmitted from generation to generation through sexual intercourse. Nor is there any scriptural ground for maintaining that even when the collective guilt of such sin is dispelled by baptism there remains in all the baptized an inherent weakness, or concupiscence, that regularly incites everyone to succumb to their unruly feelings. With the development of modern evolutionary science, that particular myth and all the accretions that it gathered in the course of theological history are no longer necessary, death being now recognized as an essential biological process that applied to all living entities well before the advent of humanity and that has naturally encompassed all human beings since their first arrival on the cosmic scene. As I have mentioned before, it may well be true that at some stage in human evolution something went badly wrong, morally speaking. But there are no grounds for claiming that it was a single moral catastrophe that implicated all subsequent human beings and still reverberates through the whole of humanity. What went wrong was that men and women began to sin and have kept on sinning, making moral choices affecting each other that were out of harmony with the cosmic design and destiny that their creator had in mind.

In his most famous contribution to modern theology, the process of demythologization, Rudolf Bultmann highlighted the need to eliminate outdated mythology from the proclaiming of the gospel.[39] In many cases this involved removing from the biblical description of events the traces of a primitive worldview within which the revelation was first presented (such as the "three-decker universe" and the prevalence of miraculous interventions), and their replacement where necessary by expressions more consonant with modern science. As I have noted, ancient Israel was deeply concerned with the phenomenon of human death and extinction and with accounting for it alongside a belief in a provident Creator. It contrived to do this by mythologizing death, turning it from a physical puzzle that they were at a loss to explain into a religious myth that explained it in terms of a primordial narrative of divine command and human disobedience that led to divine punishment: "In the day that you eat of it, you shall die" (Gn 2:17).

Today, however, we are in a better scientific position to account for the phenomenon of death, seeing it as an essential stage in biological development and a step in the process of natural selection among all living entities, not just humans. We thus have no further need for a mythical explanation of human dying. We can demythologize death, dispensing with the need to keep postulating a divinely inflicted punishment for an initial act of human disobedience. As a consequence we can also dismantle the massive theological structure that has resulted from the mythologizing of death, including original justice, or the exploring of the primordial state of pre-fallen human existence; the nature of the original sin; and the consequent, permanent fallen state of human nature into which all humans are thought to have been born as a result, not to mention the succession of theological attempts devised to explain how the mythological sinful predicament of fallen humanity was to be remedied.

Any proposal to dispense with the traditional doctrines of original sin and the fallen state of humanity as no longer required or justified will inevitably be greeted with deep dismay by many Christian believers who will feel that this move fails to do justice to the pervasiveness and universality of sin throughout human history and everyday existence. According to P. Henrici, for instance, there is a persuasion among many Christians that the spread and extent of human sinful behavior can be explained "only by the hypothesis of original sin," which resulted in a powerful and intrinsic component in all human individuals predisposing them to behave sinfully.[40] However, S. Wiedenhofer was not alone in acknowledging that a problem emerged in the 1950s and 1960s as dissatisfaction arose from the realization that "the apparently timeless affirmations of neo-scholastic theology were simply not confirmed by tradition as rediscovered in historical terms or by Scripture as read in the light of the historical-critical method."[41] Accordingly, he went on to examine various attempts to restore theological credibility to the doctrines of original sin and the Fall, although he commented, rather too readily, that the subject "is not easily surveyed."[42]

In fact, in recent years, as our awareness of the Bible and its contents has become more sophisticated and as our scientific knowledge of how humanity originated has increased, various Catholic theologians have sought to retain the traditional doctrines of the Fall, original sin, and concupiscence out of respect for past church teaching and for the authority of the *magisterium*, while on occasion reinterpreting such doctrines in various ways in an attempt to make them more intellectually acceptable to modern times.[43] Such attempts include the idea that the original sin was a collective turning against God by the first generation of humans, not the first couple, or that its effects spread through influence and social accumulation rather than through procreation.[44] Karl Rahner offers a loyal but labored explanation that Adam represents a sinful, small, original group of humans.[45] Piet Schoonenberg's *Man and Sin* and its introduction of the theme of "the sin of the world" won much popularity in its day for attempting to present a credible theology of sin in terms of the origin, extent, and contagion of human sinfulness in history.[46] Other writers such as Mark O'Keefe explored the idea of social sin, including a Lonerganian perspective on the subject.[47] Gaffney, in his *Sin Reconsidered*, drew attention to an attempt to explain sin as the predicament from which Christ saves us, or the sheer need for salvation. Rather than start from sin as a problem that requires Christ's intervention, this view chose to start from the idea that sin is basically our need for Christ. As Gaffney observed, "What sin represents is, from this point of view, not the forfeiture of life's original quality, but the unaccomplishment of its ultimate destiny: not paradise lost, but, as it were, paradise ungained."[48] As I have earlier noted, Gaffney also points to a more psychological reinterpretation of sin that would view it not as a lapse from a primordial state of innocence and human perfection but as a striving of the individual to attain to a state where moral exertion is seen as "part of the normal and natural development of maturing human personalities, rather than as the legacy of a primordially wounded nature."[49] A similar approach can be found in Daly's suggestion of interpreting original sin as the evolutionary development of humanity inevitably involving moral vulnerability, on which Kevin Kelly commented that, as the species reached self-awareness, "with this self-consciousness, bringing freedom of choice with it, sin becomes part of the story of evolving humanity."[50]

Denis Edwards, in *The God of Evolution*, surveys various ways that have been developed to understand how original sin and concupiscence can be thought of in light of human evolution.[51] He balks at placing at sin's door all the discrepancy and infallibility that humans experience and then has his own detailed proposal to make, following Rahner and others, to distinguish between the disorder that springs from sin and the disorder "that is intrinsic to being a *limited* and *finite* human being."[52] Celia Deane-Drummond writes, "While the idea of a 'fall upwards' posits humanity in continuum with the created order, it does not seem to do justice to the radical depth of evil found in human history, including the evil effects of human actions on nonhuman species." Yet her further comment that "in evolutionary terms the fall could be thought of as that sharper awareness of the capacity for negative choice that is present in the human community, with its enhanced capacity for moral action" seems to refer simply to the evolved human capacity for sinning that emerged with hominization.[53]

Haught rejects the biblical account of original sin (and the means undertaken to remedy it): "Evolutionary science . . . has rendered the original cosmic perfection, one allegedly debauched by a temporally 'original' sin, obsolete and unbelievable. Simultaneously it has also abolished, at least in principle, the whole cosmological framework in which motifs of reparation and expiation have become so deeply entrenched in our cultures and our classical spiritualities."[54] Strangely, however, after such strong words Haught is unwilling to abandon the idea of original sin, asking, "What, then, might original sin mean?" In reply he suggests that being born into an unfinished universe, each of us is subject to strong pressures to express indifference to God's cosmic aim.[55] He is surely correct in observing that "it is theologically inappropriate to identify original sin simply with the instincts of aggression or selfishness that we may have inherited from our nonhuman evolutionary ancestry." Where he is less than correct, however, is when he goes on to comment that "even though these tendencies are part of our evolutionary legacy, the substance of 'original sin' is the culturally and environmentally inherited deposit of humanity's violence and injustice that burdens and threatens to corrupt each of us born into this world."[56] This, and his reference to "our flawed condition," is no more than an eloquent statement of the traditional understanding of what the doctrine of original sin came to mean for many Christians.[57]

On all of this the 1994 *Catechism of the Catholic Church* is content to reiterate the traditional Catholic doctrines concerning original sin and the Fall, as we have seen, and adds simply (387), "without the knowledge Revelation gives of God we cannot recognise sin clearly and are tempted to explain it as merely a developmental flaw, a psychological weakness, a mistake, or the necessary consequences of an inadequate social structure, etc." Yet what we have concluded about the doctrines of original sin and the Fall cannot be ignored, and the question must be seriously asked what is to be gained by attempting—even, or especially, in these attenuated ways— to preserve a church doctrine if it is no longer needed and whose original purpose, which is to provide an explanation of the phenomenon of death, has now been fulfilled by evolutionary science rather than by theological imagination.

Perhaps, however, a further question remains. Why has sin become so central for many people in the life of faith? One thinks of extreme instances such as Augustine, Calvin, Pascal, and even in modern times, Reinhold Niebuhr, not to mention the countless nameless individuals who have placed, and who place, such emphasis on the prevalence of sin and the corruption of human nature. Why does a profound sense and aware- ness of original sin appear so central to the beliefs of many, though by no means all, Christians, appearing at times as almost tantamount to a deep distaste for ordinary human nature? As I mentioned earlier, Illingworth challenged his fellow Anglicans for making it the center of their religion, or at least introducing a major imbalance into their religious concerns.[58] He seemed to ascribe the near-exclusive practical obsession with sin and redemption on the part of some believers to a deeply evangelical, not to say fundamentalist, personal conviction, born of a profoundly intimate expe- rience of having been forgiven and saved from damnation in the blood of the sacrificed and redeeming Christ. It appears that still today in some quarters there is evidence for the charge that Illingworth brought against the Reformers, that they "were so occupied with what is now called Soteri- ology, or the scheme of salvation, that they paid but scant attention to the other aspects of the Gospel," and that "the religion of the Incarnation was narrowed into the religion of the Atonement."[59] Yet, as the process of this exploration has revealed, the reality seems to be that original sin and the fall of the human race have no revelationary, far less historical, warrant. The obvious conclusion appears to be that it would now be more theologically appropriate to drop these beliefs as unnecessary and cumbersome theo- logical baggage.

It cannot be stressed sufficiently that the proposal to dismantle the traditional doctrines of original sin and the fall of humanity that is pro- posed here does not for a moment mean that in adopting an evolutionary perspective to reality one is going easy, or soft, on sin. On the contrary, the evolutionary interpretation provides a deeper and more satisfying understanding of what sin is, rather than just behavior involving the disobeying of a deity, as Genesis depicted it. Traditionally, sin is expressed basically as a failure, in the Greek *hamartia*. As observed earlier, it is a refusal to love (as Daly summed it up),[60] and it can be seen in the context of evolution as an unwillingness to accept the divine plan for human development and solidarity, as a preference for self and one's interests over those of others, and as a refusal to accept the image of God's own altruism that is sown in our human nature at creation and that continually urges us to share our personal and social resources generously with others. All of this wrongdoing has been accompanying humanity since its arrival on the evolutionary scene. It is impossible, of course, to calculate the volume of sin, as it were, produced in a world subject to original sin and the fall of humanity and compare this with the volume of sin produced in a world without these features and to draw from any difference conclusions about a better or worse world. The total amount of moral evil delivered in every conceivable human scenario is simply unimaginable, so it makes no sense to argue that human history will contain less or more sin depending on whether original sin and the Fall are human realities rather than theological constructs. Perhaps, ultimately, what the new evolutionary approach to the doctrines of original sin and the Fall contributes to theology and to the Christian life of faith is to cut sin down to size, real though it is, and to stop being obsessed with it. And this can be no bad thing.

SAVING SACRIFICE?

As in the cases of the doctrines of original sin and the fall of the human race, there have also been in modern times various attempts to adapt the traditional doctrine of the expiatory sacrifice of Jesus on Calvary, which is envisaged as atoning for and remedying original sin and the Fall and which I have attempted to show is inadequate within the new context of evolution as providing a theological explanation of the death of Jesus. R. J. Daly's study of the origins of the Christian doctrine of sacrifice opens with the bold claim that "basic to the understanding of Christianity is the concept of Christian sacrifice."[61] That may be the case as currently understood at least by some believers, but surely far more basic to the understanding of Christianity is the incarnation, not sacrifice, and if our understanding of the purpose of the incarnation changes, as I have argued it should, then our acceptance of the idea of Christian sacrifice will have to change accordingly and lose whatever centrality it may have had in the perception of Christian belief.

It may be worth recalling the observation of Macquarrie noted earlier that "the Church has never formulated a doctrine of the atonement with the same precision with which it has tried to define the person of Christ. Instead, we find several explanatory models that have developed side by side. Even in the New Testament, a considerable variety of ways of understanding the atoning work of Christ is to be found."[62] To which we can add again the comment of J. N. D. Kelly that "modern students are sometimes surprised at the diversity of treatment accorded by even the late fathers to such a mystery as the Atonement."[63] In the circumstances it is not surprising that today more theologians have become aware of how unsatisfactory the theology of sacrifice appears, even apart from the acceptance of evolution, and have sought some way of reinterpreting or reexpressing the whole idea of atonement, with its satellite ideas of sacrifice and justification. In 1930 an attempt was made by the Swedish Lutheran scholar Gustaf Aulén, as part of the reaction to the humanism of Liberal Protestantism, to go back before Anselm and reinstate the early patristic view, which he called the classic idea of the atonement, a doctrine that he viewed as "absolutely essential in Christian theology" and as "the completion of the Incarnation."[64] For Aulén, as (he claimed) for Luther, the atonement involved a dramatic divine conflict with "the power of sin," which resulted in a victory achieved by God in Christ over sin, death, and the devil.[65] He seemed to see no need to question the source, the presuppositions, or the implications of the basic primitive conviction that underlay his whole work, what he called "the conflict of God with the dark, hostile forces of evil, and His victory over them by the Divine self-sacrifice."[66]

By contrast, in chapter 4 McGrath observed that in the twentieth century the concept of justification "was seen to be in urgent need of translation out of the legal and forensic language of the sixteenth century into the *lingua franca* of modern western culture," as instanced in the work of Heidegger, Bultmann, Tillich, and others.[67] Celia Deane-Drummond observed that "Even contemporary scholars who have welcomed an understanding of God as primarily a God of love find difficulties in expressing an adequate portrait of the atonement." She went on to ask "in what sense does atonement need to be revisited . . . what elements can be retained . . . and in what sense can atonement be broadened to include *all creatures*, not just those with moral capacities?"[68] In fact, her study has much material covering theories of the atonement, yet it does not show much evidence of a necessity to establish the need for atonement or to identify what historical reason there might be for such a need.

As we also saw in chapter 4, Kirwan examined attempts of various modern authors to express the idea of sacrifice, and he did so under three headings: first, views that "insist that what is valuable or authentic in Christianity is incompatible with sacrifice," including views derived from feminist theology; second, views that insist on maintaining the continuing centrality of Christ as High Priest; and the third and "arguably mainstream position" allowing for "a Christian usage of sacrifice, but with severe qualification, namely with a recognition that the notion has undergone a process of radical 'spiritualization,' or interiorization."[69] Perhaps typical of this last is the attempt made by Rowan Williams to show "why it is still useful to use the language of sacrifice at all in the speaking of worship and eucharist."[70]

My own comment on the whole body of largely modernizing literature aimed at making the doctrines of original sin and sacrifice still acceptable in some form or other is to recall how in the field of science much is written of the ingenuity and complexity of attempts that have been made regularly in history to "save the phenomena," or the way things appeared, in the face of developments that actually called for radical reappraisals of contemporary explanations and theories. So here one cannot help wondering at all the modern attempts to "save the data" of the biblical text concerning the origin of sin and of the sacrificial and atoning interpretation of the death of Jesus, in the apparent conviction that the scriptural text must continue to be saved and made intelligible and acceptable, rather than accepting, as I have argued, that starting from the Hebrew Bible it is the expression and inheritance of a particular and now outmoded sin-centered culture. It is reminiscent of all the energy expended in accounting by means of ingenious cycles and epicycles for the movements of the planets within a geocentric cosmology rather than accepting the much simpler and more intellectually satisfying heliocentric system of Copernicus.

In a culturally wide-ranging study of various ways of understanding the meaning and application of the idea of atonement as a context within which to explore its Christian significance, Dillistone tried to get to the heart of the matter when he concluded that "the very *idea* of atonement only becomes possible within a situation where an original design has been damaged or an expressed purpose disrupted. Within a specifically religious context, atonement means to deal with man's alienation in such a way that a general restoration of harmony becomes possible."[71] What this captures and expresses well is the traditional understanding of the state to which humanity reduced itself in damaging God's original design and disrupting the divine purpose, and what would therefore be looked for from atonement by Christ, namely, the removal of alienation and the restoration of harmony and design. However, to what extent that conceptual core would commend itself to modern evolutionary thinking remains doubtful, at the very least. In the face of all the attempts to save the traditional beliefs in the Fall and the redemption, the basic question is surely why we cannot just strip away all the theological growth that has multiplied through the history and literature of original sin and concupiscence and sacrifice and that is still being, sometimes unthinkingly, produced.

As I stressed in urging the evolutionary demythologizing of death that this in no way dispels the occurrence of sin in human living, similarly here in urging that we discontinue professing that the death of Jesus was an expiatory sacrifice to God to win God's forgiveness of sinful human beings, I am not for a moment aiming to diminish the reality and central significance in Christian belief of the death of Jesus on the cross, but only to remove the notion of its being an expiatory sacrifice aimed at appeasing God. As I have maintained regularly, Jesus freely accepted death at the hands of his fellow humans to manifest his totally faithful love of God and his concern for his fellows, thus expressing and exemplifying in human terms the mutual altruism, or generous love, of the Trinity of Father, Son, and Holy Spirit for one another and summoning his fellow humans to display a similar altruism toward each other. In addition, in his death and resurrection Jesus took on human death as an evolutionary fate, and defeating it, won through to a new phase of human life and ushered his human fellows into a closer union and destiny within the rich life of God.

It is important to be clear that the original description of the death of Jesus on the cross as a sacrifice, as we find this in the New Testament, did not view it as a metaphor but as a bloody reality. As Trent expressed it, since "in this divine sacrifice which is performed in the mass that same Christ is contained and sacrificed unbloodily who 'offered himself once on the cross bloodily' [Heb 9:14, 27], the holy council teaches that it is a truly propitiatory sacrifice" (DS 1743). The idea of sacrifice might well remain in the Christian spiritual vocabulary and continue to be applied in a metaphorical sense, expressing the idea of giving up something one treasures or values for the sake of others, as in sacrificing one's comfort or time or even one's life. However, to continue using such a metaphorical use of sacrifice could easily result in still connecting it with the Crucifixion and continuing to regard the death of Jesus as the original Christian sacrifice, contrary to what I propose.

STRAINING FAITH

If attempts are made to continue to hold loyally even in some adapted or accommodated form to the traditional beliefs that this discussion has considered as outmoded in an evolutionary context, one consequence can easily be to create a strain on the faith of believers and a strain on the credulity of nonbelievers. The intellectual difficulties raised by these traditional beliefs, and a reluctance on the part of church authorities to acknowledge or to face these difficulties, especially in the new evolutionary context, can all too easily create "no-go" areas in the minds of believers and can contribute to a general sapping of confidence in the teaching authority of the church or, indeed, in the credibility of religion. Rahner's warning is ever relevant, especially in postmodern times: "If modern man finds the *content* of revelation unworthy of belief through the fault of theology, he will think himself justified, not illogically, in further doubting the *fact* of revelation."[72]

Rahner's reference to "the fault of theology" as possibly leading to an abandonment of revelation raises the issue of the nature and purpose of theology. Saint Anselm of Canterbury provided a famous definition of theology as "faith seeking understanding" (*fides quaerens intellectum*), but as I have written elsewhere, it might be more intellectually satisfying to view theology as providing a dialectic between our belief and our experience.[73] As I commented,

> It is, if we may so express it, a matter of trying to make faith-sense of experience, and at the same time of making experience-sense of faith; of finding an overall context of a meaning and purpose to life within which to locate all our ordinary experiences and interrelate them, and at the same time of continually checking such a vision of life against each new experience as it arises. This dialectical activity of submitting experience to the bar of belief and of submitting belief to the bar of experience is today a requirement of every believer, on pain of leaving their experience unanchored and their belief unsubstantiated.[74]

Of course, the point of such a view of theology is not to remove all strain from religious belief. Strain and tension are inevitable whenever the creaturely human mind attempts to come to some comprehension and appreciation of the very existence of God and of God's activity in the world, perhaps especially today in an evolutionary context. One need not go so far as Sir Thomas Browne did in the seventeenth century in opining in his *Religio Medici*, "Methinks there be not impossibilities enough in Religion for an active faith," and who loved "to lose my self in a mystery, to pursue my Reason to an O *altitudo* (Rom 11:33)."[75] The whole of theodicy, that is, trying to reconcile the existence of a loving and powerful God with the pain and suffering that are encountered by many people in their lives, is one striking witness to the legitimate strain that belief can regularly bring with it. Yet it is part of the pride of Christianity, especially in its Catholic tradition, to hold out for some place for human and God-given reasoning in our reflecting upon God and God's ways. Otherwise we give way defeatedly to fideism and its arbitrary ways. Hence it appears to be the case that undue strain can be caused for believers in a particular doctrinal or religious or moral position maintained by the church authorities when the evidence does not appear to warrant it, or when the reasons for maintaining it, especially in spite of persistent difficulties, do not, or no longer, obtain. Such now appears to be the case for the doctrines of original sin, the Fall, concupiscence, and sacrificial atonement.

Particularly in a postmodern age that is disposed to question everything there is an urgent need for the church to get its teaching right, that is, not to make unwarranted demands on believers and as a result put undue strain on their faith, as can be argued with regard to explanations about human origins. Such teaching is not conducive to encouraging religious faith if it has nothing to offer to the growing advance of evolutionary science, nor is it conducive to respecting the powers of human reason if traditional beliefs about original sin, the Fall, and atonement are uncritically reiterated, even when they are found to lack historical foundation or reasonable justification. Paul Ricoeur had sharp comments to make on this sort of situation:

> The harm that has been done to souls, during the centuries of Christianity, first by the literal interpretation of the story of Adam, and then by the confusion of this myth, treated as history, with later speculations, principally Augustinian, about original sin, will never be adequately told. In asking the faithful to confess belief in this mythic-speculative mass and to accept it as a self-sufficient explanation, the theologians have unduly required a *sacrificium intellectus* [sacrifice of the mind] where what was needed was to awaken believers to a symbolic superintelligence of their actual condition.[76]

To pursue critical questioning of Christian beliefs with intellectual and unflinching honesty is to offer another meaning to the phrase "straining the faith." It is worth recalling here Rahner's observation of the need for "the courage to give up an obsolete position without each time having to apply too much skill in interpreting traditional formulas," as has been regularly attempted—such courage, in Rahner's view, being "a better act of faith than . . . anxious conservatism."[77] It is now not a matter of putting one's faith under undue and unjustified stress by declining to subject it to an honest critique or by evading hard questions; it is the challenge of aiming to purify one's faith by straining out those elements for which it is recognized there is no longer any warrant and thus making it possible to present Christian faith in a manner that enlightens much more than contradicts modern human experience. In this manner of proceeding, some response would be forthcoming to the expressed wish of Pope John Paul II for an intense dialogue with contemporary science "that has, on the whole, been lacking among those engaged in theological research and teaching," as well as providing "a much-needed ministry to others struggling to integrate the worlds of science and religion in their own intellectual and spiritual lives."[78]

SUMMING UP

At the beginning of this work I quote two sentences that may be considered to sum up my whole enterprise of exploring Christianity in evolution: a line from a prayer ascribed to Saint Ignatius Loyola and a verse from Saint John's gospel. Ignatius's petition, "Lord, teach me to be generous," can be seen as seeking to learn how to act from Jesus, who put a human face on the divine creative generosity, who offered his fellows a program of moral altruism to counter the sinful self-centeredness associated with the evolutionary process, and who in his suffering and death gave an unforgettable example and inspiration of generosity by identifying himself with his father's will and with the good of his fellow humans. The verse of Saint John's gospel with which I have also prefaced this work, "I have come that they may have life" (Jn 10:10), can be recognized within an evolutionary context to possess a degree of richness that could not have been hitherto appreciated in identifying the ultimate aim of Jesus's coming to earth in the incarnation as being to defeat death and to lead humanity to an enhanced new stage of living within the divine Trinity.

These two ideas, generosity and life, form the basis of my answer to the questions raised by Pope John Paul II of what enlightenment might be looked for from an evolutionary perspective upon the whole vista of Christian belief. They point to our belief's potentiality to develop and be enriched in new terms with the discovery and acceptance of human evolution through natural selection. I have sketched a theology of evolution within the context of modern science and against the background of what appears reluctance to take evolution ungrudgingly into effective account in the Catholic Church's theological reflection and teaching. This project will inevitably have involved mistakes, misunderstandings, and errors. My hope, however, is that the broad lines that I have developed here may prove basically acceptable and may encourage others to respond to the pope's challenge, to consider how the Christian religion can provide a welcome to the scientific advance of human understanding, and find generous room for it, making the Christian gospel appealing, attractive, and life-giving to modern generations.

NOTES

1. "Hinc est universa generis humani massa damnata." Augustine, *City of God*, XXI, 12 (Migne, *PL* 41, 726), 989.

2. Dionysius, *De divinis nominibus*, 4. 20 (Migne, *PG* 3, 720); Aquinas, *Summa Theologiae*, I. 5. 4 ad 2; chapter 2, this volume.

3. See chapter 3, this volume.

4. See Mahoney, *Making of Moral Theology*, 247–58.

5. Pope, *Human Evolution and Christian Ethics*, 107.

6. Rahner, "Order of Redemption within the Order of Creation."

7. Edwards, *The God of Evolution*, 127.

8. Pope., *Human Evolution and Christian Ethics*, 72.

9. See chapter 3, this volume.

10. Pelikan, *Christian Tradition*, 5:280.

11. Vatican Council II, Decree on the Ministry and Life of Priests, esp. nos. 6 and 9.

12. Aquinas, *Summa Theologiae*, Ia IIae, q. 92, a. 2.

13. See chapter 1, this volume.

14. Huxley, *Collected Essays*, 9:82.

15. Pope, *Human Evolution and Christian Ethics*, 313.

16. See chapter 1, this volume.

17. Bröker, "Aspects of Evolution," 12.

18. Van Melsen, "Natural Law and Evolution," 24.

19. Rahner, "Evolution and Original Sin," 33.

20. Haught, *God after Darwin*, 141–42.

21. Aquinas, *Summa Theologiae*, I-II, q. 94, a. 1.

22. Aristotle, *Politics*, I, 1253a, 2–3.

23. See Mahoney, *Challenge of Human Rights*, 95, 178–86.

24. Pope, *Human Evolution and Christian Ethics*, 313.

25. Letter of His Holiness John Paul II to Reverend George V. Coyne, June 1, 1988.

26. See Kelly, *Early Christian Doctrines*.

27. See Mahoney, *Making of Moral Theology*, 120–35.

28. DS 3464.

29. Pius X, *Pascendi dominici gregis*, no. 13.

30. Newman, *Essay on the Development of Christian Doctrine*, 70. On the development of Newman's thought, see Pelikan, *Christian Tradition*, 273–78.

31. Pelikan, *Christian Tradition*, 277.

32. Wright, *Christian Origins and the Question of God*, vol. 2, *Jesus and the Victory of God*, 167–68. See 163–97.

33. Ibid., 172.

34. Ibid., 219.

35. Rahner, "Historicity of Theology," 78–79.

36. Ibid., 30–31.

37. Wiles, *Making of Christian Doctrine*, 123.

38. Ibid., 16–17.

39. Bultmann, *New Testament and Mythology and Other Basic Writings*.

40. Henrici, "Philosophers and Original Sin," 489–501, at 490.

41. Wiedenhofer, "Main Forms of Contemporary Theology of Original Sin," 514–29, at 515.

42. Ibid., 514.

43. See Pope, *Human Evolution and Christian Ethics*, 154–57; Kapusta, "Darwinism from *Humani generis* to the Present," 31–32.

44. Korsmeyer, *Evolution and Eden*, 96–97.

45. Rahner, "Evolution and Original Sin," 30–35.

46. Schoonenberg, *Man and Sin*.

47. O'Keefe, *What Are They Saying about Social Sin?*

48. Gaffney, *Sin Reconsidered*, 48.

49. Ibid., 41. See chapter 3, this volume.

50. Daly, *Creation and Redemption*; Kelly, *New Directions in Moral Theology*, 124.

51. Edwards, *God of Evolution*, 60–64.

52. Ibid., 64–70, at 65.

53. Deane-Drummond, *Christ and Evolution*, 169.

54. Haught, *God after Darwin*, 149.

55. Ibid., 146.

56. Ibid., 147.

57. Ibid., 148.

58. See chapter 1, this volume. Illingworth, "Incarnation in Relation to Development," 210–12.

59. Illingworth, "Incarnation in Relation to Development," 183.

60. Daly, *Creation and Redemption*, 1. See chapter 1, this volume.

61. Daly, *Origins of the Christian Doctrine of Sacrifice*, v.

62. Macquarrie, *Principles of Christian Theology*, 314–15.

63. Kelly, *Early Christian Doctrines*, 4.

64. Aulén, *Christus Victor*, 151, 12. See chapter 4, this volume.

65. Aulén, *Christus Victor*, 148n2, 105, 147.

66. Ibid., 159.

67. McGrath, *Justitia Dei*, 409.

68. Deane-Drummond, *Christ and Evolution*, 175. On her exploration of what kind of atonement theory might be most useful in consideration of the nonhuman world, see 178–79.

69. See chapter 4, this volume; Kirwan, "Eucharist and Sacrifice," 214–15.

70. Williams, *Eucharistic Sacrifice*, 27.

71. Dillistone, *Christian Understanding of Atonement*, 236–37.

72. Rahner, "Historicity of Theology," 41.

73. Anselm, *Anselm of Canterbury* (Migne, *PL* 158, 225). On the following, see Mahoney, "Testing Faith."

74. Mahoney, *Bioethics and Belief*, 112.

75. Browne, *Religio Medici*, pt. 1, sec. 9.

76. Ricoeur, *Symbolism of Evil*, 239.

77. Rahner, "Historicity of Theology," 78–79.

78. Letter of His Holiness John Paul II to Reverend George V. Coyne, June 1, 1988.

Bibliography

A NOTE ABOUT SOURCES

DS = Denzinger-Schönmetzer, *Enchiridion Symbolorum Definitionum et Declarationum de rebus fidei et morum*, ed. 33. Freiburg: Herder, 1965.

Migne, *PG* = Migne, J. P., ed. *Patrologia Cursus Completus*, series Graeca. 166 vols. Paris: Lethielleux, 1857–66.

Migne, *PL* = Migne, J. P., ed. *Patrologia Cursus Completus*, series Latina. 221 vols. Paris: Lethielleux, 1844–64.

WORKS CITED

Abelard. *Comm. super Pauli Epistolam ad Romanos*. Migne, *PL* 178.

Ackelén, J. "Science and Theology." In *Christianity: The Complete Guide*, ed. J. Bowden, 1098–99. London: Continuum, 2005.

Acker, J. "Creationism and the *Catechism*." *America*, December 16, 2000.

Albright, W. F., and C. S. Mann. *Matthew: Introduction, Translation and Notes*, in *The Anchor Bible*. New York: Doubleday, 1971.

Alszeghi, Z. "Development in the Doctrinal Formulations of the Church concerning the Theory of Evolution." *Concilium* 6 (June 1967): 14–18.

Anselm. *Anselm of Canterbury: The Major Works*. Oxford: Oxford University Press, 1988. Migne, *PL* 158.

Aquinas, Saint Thomas. *Scriptum super libros Sententiarum P. Lombardi*. Paris: Lethielleux, 1929–47.

———. *Summa Theologiae*. Roma: Editiones Paulinae, 1962.

Aristotle. *Politics*. Oxford: Clarenden Press, 1959.

Augustine. *City of God*. Trans. H. Bettenson. Harmondsworth: Penguin Classic, 1980.

———. *Confessions*. Trans. H. Chadwick. Oxford: Oxford University Press, 1991.

———. *Contra duas epistolas Pelagianorum*. Migne, *PL* 44, 549–638.

———. *Contra Iulianum opus imperfectum*. Migne, *PL* 44, 641–874.

———. *De Genesi ad litteram*. Migne, *PL* 34, 245–486.

———. *De nupt et conc*. Migne, *PL* 44, 413–74.

———. *De Trinitate*. Migne, *PL* 42, 819–1098.

———. *Sermones*. Migne, *PL* 38, 23–484.

Aulén, G. *Christus Victor: An Historical Study of the Three Main Types of the Idea of the Atonement*. London: SPCK, 1978.

Batson, C. D., and Shaw, L. L. "Evidence for Altruism: Towards a Pluralism of Prosocial Motives." *Psychological Inquiry* 2, no. 2 (1991): 107–22.

Benedict XVI, Pope. Postsynodal statement. *Sacramentum caritatis*, Vatican, 2005.

Binmore, K. *Natural Justice*. Oxford: Oxford University Press, 2005.

Boehm, C. "Explaining the Prosocial Side of Moral Communities." In *Evolution and Ethics: Human Morality in Biological and Religious Perspective*, ed. P. Clayton and J. Schloss, 78–100. Cambridge: Eerdmans, 2004.

Boethius. *De Consolatione Philosophiae*. Ed. A. Fortescue. London: Burns, Oates & Washbourne, 1929.

Brodrick, J. *Robert Bellarmine: Saint and Scholar*. 2nd ed. London: Burns & Oates, 1961.

Bröker, W. "Aspects of Evolution." *Concilium* 6 (June 1967): 5–13.

Brown, A. *The Darwin Wars: The Scientific Battle for the Soul of Man*. London: Touchstone, Simon & Schuster, 1999.

Brown, R. E. "Church in the Apostolic Period." In *The New Jerome Biblical Commentary*. London: Chapman, 1989.

Browne, Sir T. *Religio Medici*. London: J. M. Dent, Everymans Library, 1952.

Browning, R. *Poetical Works*. London: Smith, Elder and Co., 1908.

Bultmann, R. *The New Testament and Mythology and Other Basic Writings*. Augsburg: Fortress, 1984.

Burke, M. M. "The Epistle to the Hebrews." In *The New Jerome Biblical Commentary*. London: Chapman, 1989.

Byrne, J. *Glory, Jest and Riddle: Religious Thought in the Enlightenment*. London: SCM, 1996.

Callan, C. J., ed. *Catechism of the Council of Trent*. Trans. J. A. McHugh. 2nd revised ed. London: Herder, 1923.

Calvin. *Institutes of the Christian Religion*. Trans. Beveridge. Edinburgh, 1845.

Carmichael, C. M. *The Origins of Biblical Law*. London: Cornell University Press, 1992.

Cassirer, E. *The Philosophy of the Enlightenment*. Princeton, NJ: Princeton University Press, 1968.

Catechism of the Catholic Church. London: Geoffrey Chapman, 1994.

Catholic International Theological Commission (ITC). *Communion and Stewardship: Human Persons Created in the Image of God*, Vatican, 2004. San Francisco: Ignatius Press, 2009.

Chadwick, H. *The Church in Ancient Society: From Galilee to Gregory the Great*. Oxford: Oxford University Press, 2001.

Clark, F. *The Eucharistic Sacrifice and the Reformation*. 2nd ed. Oxford: Basil Blackwell, 1967.

Clifford, R. J. "Genesis." In *The New Jerome Biblical Commentary*. London: Chapman, 1989.

Cobb, J., and Griffin, D. *Process Theology: An Introductory Exposition*. Louisville, KY: Westminster Press, 1999.

Copleston, F. C. *A History of Philosophy*. Vol. 8. London: Burns, Oates & Washbourne, 1966.

Cornwell, J. *Newman's Unquiet Grave: The Reluctant Saint*. London: Continuum, 2010.

Cotter, J. F. *Inscape: The Christology and Poetry of Gerard Manley Hopkins*. Pittsburgh, PA: University of Pittsburgh Press, 1972.

Coyne, G. "God's Chance Creation." *Tablet*, August 6, 2005, 6–7.

Cragg, G. R. *The Church and the Age of Reason, 1648–1789*. New York: Atheneum, 1961.

Daly, G. "Creation and Original Sin." In *Commentary on the Catechism of the Catholic Church*, ed. Michael J. Walsh, 82–111. London: Geoffrey Chapman, 1994.

———. *Creation and Redemption*. Dublin: Gill and Macmillan, 1988.

Daly, R. J. *The Origins of the Christian Doctrine of Sacrifice*. London: Darton, Longman and Todd, 1978.

Darwin, C. *The Autobiography of Charles Darwin*. London: Collins, 1958.

———. *The Descent of Man and Selection in Relation to Sex*. London: John Murray, 1901 (1st ed. published 1871).

Dawkins, R. *The Selfish Gene*. Oxford: Oxford University Press, 1976.

———. *The Selfish Gene*. Oxford: Oxford University Press, 1989.

Deane-Drummond, C. *Christ and Evolution: Wonder and Wisdom*. London, SCM Press, 2009.

Delio, I. *Christ in Evolution*. Maryknoll, NY: Orbis, 2008.

Denzinger-Schönmetzer [=DS] *Enchiridion Symbolorum Definitionum et Declarationum de rebus fidei et morum*, ed. 33. Freiburg: Herder, 1965.

Desmond, A., Moore, J., and Browne, J. *Charles Darwin*. Oxford: Oxford University Press, 2007.

Devlin, C., ed. *The Sermons and Devotional Writings of Gerard Manley Hopkins*. London: Oxford University Press, 1959.

De Waal, F. *The Age of Empathy: Nature's Lessons for a Kinder Society*. New York: Crown, 2009.

Dillistone, F. W. *The Christian Understanding of Atonement*. London: SCM Press, 1984.

Dixon, T. *The Invention of Altruism*. Oxford: Oxford University Press, 2008.

Dodd, C. H. *The Founder of Christianity*. London: Collins, Fontana, 1973.

Domning, D. P. "Evolution, Evil and Original Sin." *America*, November 12, 2001.

Donahue, J. R., and D. J. Harrington. *Gospel of Mark*. Collegeville, MN: Liturgical Press, 2002.

Dupré, L. *The Enlightenment and the Intellectual Foundations of Modern Culture*. New Haven, CT: Yale University Press, 2004.

———. "Intelligent Design: Science or Faith?" In *Darwin and Catholicism: The Past and Present Dynamics of a Cultural Encounter*, ed. L. Caruana, 169–80. London: T&T Clark, 2009.

Durant, J., ed. *Darwinism and Divinity: Essays on Evolution and Religious Belief.* Oxford: Basil Blackwell, 1985.

Edwards, D. *The God of Evolution: A Trinitarian Theology.* New York, Paulist Press, 1999.

Fitzmeyer, J. A. "Romans." *The Anchor Bible.* Vol. 33. London: Geoffrey Chapman, 1993.

Flew, A. G. N. *Evolutionary Ethics.* London: Macmillan, 1976.

Gaffney, J. *Sin Reconsidered.* New York: Paulist Press, 1983.

Gensler, H. J. "Darwin, Ethics and Evolution." In *Darwin and Catholicism: The Past and Present Dynamics of a Cultural Encounter,* ed. L. Caruana, 121–33. London: T&T Clark, 2009.

Gerrish, B. A. "Schleiermacher." In *The Oxford Companion to Christian Thought,* ed. A. Hastings, A. Mason, and H. Pyper, 644–46. Oxford: Oxford University Press, 2000.

Gore, C., ed. *Lux Mundi: A Series of Studies in the Religion of the Incarnation.* 7th ed. London: John Murray, 1890.

Grant, C. *Altruism and Christian Ethics.* Cambridge, Cambridge University Press, 2001.

Grenz, Stanley J. *The Social God and the Relational Self: A Trinitarian Theology of the Imago Dei.* Louisville, KY: John Knox Press, 2001.

Haight, R. "Jesus and Salvation: An Essay in Interpretation." *Theological Studies* 55 (June 1994): 225–51.

Halliburton, R. J. "The Patristic Theology of the Eucharist." In *The Study of Liturgy,* ed. C. Jones, G. Wainwright, E. Yarnold, and P. Bradshaw, revised ed., 245–57. London, SPCK, 1992.

Hampson, N. *The Enlightenment: An Evaluation of Its Assumptions, Attitudes and Values.* Harmondsworth: Penguin, 1984.

Hanson, A. T. "Heaven and Hell." In *A Dictionary of Christian Theology,* ed. A. Richardson, 151–52. London: SCM, 1974.

Hastings, A. "Hell." In *The Oxford Companion to Christian Thought,* ed. A. Hastings, A. Mason, and H. Pyper, 291–92. Oxford: Oxford University Press, 2000.

Haught, J. F. *God after Darwin: A Theology of Evolution.* 2nd ed. Boulder, CO: Westview Press, 2008.

———. *Making Sense of Evolution: Darwin, God, and the Drama of Life.* Louisville, KY: Westminster John Knox Press, 2010.

Hebblethwaite, B. *The Incarnation: Collected Essays in Christology.* Cambridge: Cambridge University Press, 1987.

Henrici, P. "The Philosophers and Original Sin." *Communio* 18 (Winter 1991): 489–501.

Heron, A. "The Person of Christ." In *Keeping the Faith: Essays to Mark the Centenary of Lux Mundi,* ed. G. Wainright, 99–123. London, SPCK, 1989.

Hick, J. "Evil and Incarnation." In *Incarnation and Myth: The Debate Continued,* ed. Michael Goulder, 77–84. London: SCM, 1979.

Hughes, G. J. *Is God to Blame?* Dublin: Veritas, 2007.

Huxley, T. H. *Collected Essays.* Vol. 9, *Evolution and Ethics and Other Essays.* London: Macmillan and Co., 1901.

Illingworth, J. R. "The Incarnation in Relation to Development." In *Lux Mundi: A Series of Studies in the Religion of the Incarnation,* ed. C. Gore. 7th ed., 181–214. London: John Murray, 1890.

Iraenaeus. *Adversus haereses.* Migne, *PG* 7.

Jeremias, J. *The Eucharistic Words of Jesus.* London: SCM, 1966.

John Paul II, Pope. *Keeping the Lord's Day Holy.* Dublin: Veritas, 1998.

———. Letter of His Holiness John Paul II to Reverend George V. Coyne, SJ, Director of the Vatican Observatory, June 1, 1988. www.vatican.va/holy_father/john_paul_ii/letters/1988/. Accessed October 30, 2009.

———. *Message to the Pontifical Academy of Sciences on Evolution,* November 14, 1996.

———. *On the Eucharist and the Church.* London. CTS, 2003.

Jungmann, J. A. "Constitution on the Sacred Liturgy." In *Commentary on the Documents of Vatican II,* vol. 1, ed. Herbert Vorgrimler, 1–87. London: Burns Oates, 1967.

———. *The Mass of the Roman Rite: Its Origins and Development (Missarum Sollemnia).* Vol. 1. New York: Benziger Brothers, 1950.

Kant, I. "Beantwortung der Frage: Was ist *Aufklärung?*" *Werke* 4 (1913): 169–76.

Kapusta, P. "Darwinism from *Humani generis* to the Present." In *Darwin and Catholicism: The Past and Present Dynamics of a Cultural Encounter,* ed. L. Caruana, 27–42. London: T&T Clark, 2009.

Kelly, J. N. D. *Early Christian Doctrines.* Revised 5th ed. San Francisco: Harper, 1978.

Kelly, K. T. *New Directions in Moral Theology: The Challenge of Being Human.* London: Geoffrey Chapman, 1992.

King, U. *Spirit of Fire: The Life and Vision of Teilhard de Chardin.* New York: Orbis, 1996.

Kirwan, M. "Eucharist and Sacrifice." *New Blackfriars* 88 (March 2007): 213–27.

Kitcher, P. *Living with Darwin.* Oxford: Oxford University Press, 2007.

Korsmeyer, J. D. *Evolution and Eden: Balancing Original Sin and Contemporary Science.* New York: Paulist Press, 1998.

Küng, H. *The Beginning of All Things: Science and Religion.* Cambridge: Eerdmans, 2007.

Locke, J. *The Reasonableness of Christianity.* Oxford: Clarendon, 1998.

Luther, M. *Lutherswerke.* Vol. 2. Weimar, 1883.

———. "The Pagan Servitude of the Church." In *Martin Luther: Selections from His Writings,* ed. John Dillenberger, 249–359. New York, Doubleday, 1962.

Lyttelton, A. "The Atonement." In *Lux Mundi: A Series of Studies in the Religion of the Incarnation,* ed. C. Gore. 7th ed., 275–312. London: John Murray, 1890.

Mackey, J. P. *The Scientist and the Theologian on the Origin and Ends of Creation.* Dublin: Columba Press, 2007.

Macquarrie, J. *In Search of Deity: An Essay in Dialectical Theism.* London: SCM, 1984.

———. *Principles of Christian Theology.* Revised ed. London: SCM, 1977.

Mahoney, J. *Bioethics and Belief: Religion and Medicine in Dialogue*. London: Sheed and Ward, 1984.

———. *The Challenge of Human Rights: Origin, Developments and Significance*. Oxford: Blackwell, 2007.

———. *The Making of Moral Theology: A Study of the Roman Catholic Tradition*. Oxford, Clarendon, 1987.

———. "The Sin of Pride." In *Tradition and Unity: Sermons Published in Honour of Robert Runcie*, ed. Dan Cohn-Sherbok, 282–89. London: Bellew, 1991.

———. "Testing Faith: Thoughts for St. Anselm's Day." *Thinking Faith*, 2008. www.thinkingfaith.org (accessed April 21, 2008).

———. *The Ways of Wisdom*. An inaugural lecture in the F. D. Maurice Chair of Moral and Social Theology. London: King's College, 1987.

Manning, Henry Edward Cardinal. *Sermons on Ecclesiastical Subjects*. 3 vols. London: Burns, Oates & Co., 1870–73.

Mason, A. "Universalism." In *The Oxford Companion to Christian Thought*, ed. A. Hastings, A. Mason, and H. Pyper, 733–34. Oxford: Oxford University Press, 2000.

McBrien, R. P. *Catholicism*. London: Geoffrey Chapman, 1980.

McGrath, A. *Christian Theology: An Introduction*. 3rd ed. Oxford: Blackwell, 2001.

———. *Dawkins' God: Genes, Memes, and the Meaning of Life*. Oxford: Blackwell, 2005.

McGrath, A. E. *Justitia Dei: A History of the Christian Doctrine of Justification*. 3rd ed. Cambridge: Cambridge University Press, 2005.

McGuckian, M. *The Holy Sacrifice of the Mass: A Search for an Acceptable Notion of Sacrifice*. Leominster: Gracewing, 2005.

McKenzie, J. L. "Aspects of Old Testament Thought." In *The New Jerome Biblical Commentary*, 77:1–178. London: Chapman, 1989.

Meier, J. P. "Jesus." In *The New Jerome Biblical Commentary*, ed. R. E. Brown, J. A. Fitzmeyer, and R. E. Murphy, 1316–28. London: Geoffrey Chapman, 1990.

———. *A Marginal Jew: Rethinking the Historical Jesus*. New York: Doubleday, 1991.

Michel, A. "Incarnation." In *Dictionnaire de Théologie catholique*. Vol. 7, cols. 1445–1539. Paris: Letouzey et Ané, 1922.

Midgley, M. *Beast and Man: The Roots of Human Nature*. Sussex: Harvester Press, 1978.

———. *The Ethical Primate: Humans, Freedom and Morality*. London, Routledge, 1994.

———. *Evolution as a Religion: Strange Hopes and Stranger Fears*. Revised ed. London: Routledge, 2002.

Milavec, A. *The Didache: Faith, Hope and Life of the Earliest Christian Communities, 50–70 C.E.* New York: Newman Press, 2003.

Minges, P. *Joannis Duns Scoti Doctrina Philosophica et Theologica quoad res praecipuas proposita et exposita*, ad Claras Aquas [Quaracchi]. Vol. 2. Florence: St. Bonaventure's College, 1930.

Mivart, St. George Jackson. "Difficulties of the Theory of Natural Selection." *Month* 11 (July 1869): 35–53; (August 1869): 134–53; (September 1869): 274–89.

Mooney, C. F. *Teilhard de Chardin and the Mystery of Christ*. London: Collins, 1966.

Moule, F. D. *The Sacrifice of Christ*. London: Hodder & Stoughton, 1956.

Muddiman, J. "The New Testament: The Tradition of Interpretation." In *Companion Encyclopedia of Theology*, ed. P. Byrne and L. Houlden, 102–21. London, Routledge, 1995.

Newman, J. H. *Apologia*. Oxford: Clarendon, 1967.

———. *An Essay on the Development of Christian Doctrine* (1845 ed.), ed. J. M. Cameron. London: Penguin, 1974.

O'Carroll, M. *Corpus Christi: An Encyclopedia of the Eucharist*. Wilmington, DE: Michael Glazier, 1988.

O'Keefe, M. *What Are They Saying about Social Sin?* New York: Paulist Press, 1990.

O'Malley, J. W. *What Happened at Vatican II?* Cambridge, MA: Harvard University Press, 2008.

Oman, J. *Grace and Personality*. London: Collins, Fontana, 1964.

The Oxford Companion to the Bible. Oxford: Oxford University Press, 1993.

Peacocke, A. "Biological Evolution and Christian Theology—Yesterday and Today." In *Darwinism and Divinity: Essays on Evolution and Religious Belief*, ed. J. Durant, 101–30. Oxford: Basil Blackwell, 1985.

———. *Theology for a Scientific Age: Being and Becoming—Natural, Divine and Human*. Enlarged ed. Minneapolis: Fortress Press, 1993.

Pelikan, J. *The Christian Tradition: A History of the Development of Doctrine*. Vol. 5. Chicago: University of Chicago Press, 1989.

Pittenger, N. *Catholic Faith in a Process Perspective*. New York: Orbis, 1981.

Pius X, Pope. Encyclical letter. *Pascendi dominici gregis* (1907). www.papalencyclicals.net.

Pius XII, Pope. Encyclical letter. *Humani generis* (1950). www.papalencyclicals.net.

Polkinghorne, J. *Exploring Reality: The Intertwining of Science and Religion*. London: SPCK, 2005.

———. *Theology in the Context of Science*. London: SPCK, 2008.

Pope, S. J. *The Evolution of Altruism and the Ordering of Love*. Washington, DC: Georgetown University Press, 1994.

———. *Human Evolution and Christian Ethics*. Cambridge: Cambridge University Press, 2007.

Poulshock, J. "The Leverage of Language on Altruism and Morality." In *Evolution and Ethics: Human Morality in Biological and Religious Perspective*, ed. P. Clayton and J. Schloss, 114–31. Cambridge: Eerdmans, 2004.

Pseudo-Dionysius. *De divinis nominibus*. Migne, PG 3.

Rahner, K. "Christology within an Evolutionary View of the World." *Theological Investigations*, vol. 5, 157–92. London: Darton, Longman & Todd, 1966.

———. "Evolution and Original Sin." *Concilium* 6 (June 1967): 30–35.

———. "The Hermeneutics of Eschatological Assertions." In *Theological Investigations*, vol. 4, 323–46. London: Darton, Longman & Todd, 1966.

————. "The Historicity of Theology." *Theological Investigations*. Vol. 9, 64–82. London: Darton, Longman & Todd, 1972.

————. *Hominization: The Evolutionary Origin of Man as a Theological Problem*. London: Burns and Oates, 1965.

————. "Intellectual Honesty and Christian Faith." In *Theological Investigations*, vol. 7, 47–71. London: Darton, Longman and Todd, 1971.

————. "The Order of Redemption within the Order of Creation." In *Mission and Grace*. London: Sheed and Ward, 1963.

————. "The Theological Concept of Concupiscentia." In *Theological Investigations*, vol. 1, 347–82. London: Darton, Longman & Todd, 1961.

Räisänen, H. "The New Testament in Theology." In *Companion Encyclopedia of Theology*, ed. P. Byrne and L. Houlden, 122–41. London, Routledge, 1995.

Ratzinger, J. *"In the Beginning ...": A Catholic Understanding of the Story of Creation and the Fall*. Grand Rapids, MI: Eerdmans, 1995 [German original 1986 based on 1981 Lenten homilies delivered in Munich as "A Creation Catechism for Adults" (p. ix)].

Ricoeur, P. *The Symbolism of Evil*. Boston: Beacon Press, 1969.

Rideau, E. *The Thought of Teilhard de Chardin*. New York: Harper & Rowe, 1967.

Ridley, M. *The Origins of Virtue: Human Instincts and the Evolution of Cooperation*. London: Penguin, 1996.

Rolnick, P. A. "Darwin's Problems, Neo-Darwinian Solutions, and Jesus' Love Commands." In *Evolution and Ethics: Human Morality in Biological and Religious Perspective*, ed. P. Clayton and J. Schloss, 302–17. Cambridge: Eerdmans, 2004.

Ruse, M. "Evolutionary Ethics Past and Present." In *Evolution and Ethics: Human Morality in Biological and Religious Perspective*, ed. P. Clayton and J. Schloss, 27–49. Cambridge: Eerdmans, 2004.

————. "The Significance of Evolution." In *A Companion to Ethics*, ed. P. Singer, 500–510. Oxford: Blackwell, 1993.

Schloss, J. P. "Evolutionary Ethics and Christian Morality: Surveying the Issues." In *Evolution and Ethics: Human Morality in Biological and Religious Perspective*, ed. P. Clayton and J. Schloss, 1–24. Cambridge: Eerdmans, 2004.

Schönborn, C. "Short Introduction to the Four Parts of the *Catechism*." In *Introduction to the Catechism of the Catholic Church*, by Josef Ratzinger and Christoph Schönborn, 70–71. San Francisco: Ignatius Press, 1994.

Schoonenberg, P. *Man and Sin*. Notre Dame, IN: Notre Dame Press, 1965.

Scullion, J. P. "Creation-Incarnation: God's Affirmation of Human Worth." In *Made in God's Image: The Catholic Vision of Human Dignity*, ed. R. Duffy and A. Gambatese, 7–28. New York, Paulist Press, 1999.

Sewell, D. *The Political Gene: How Darwin's Ideas Changed Politics*. London: Picador, 2009.

Smart, N. *The World's Religions: Old Traditions and Modern Transformations*. Cambridge: Cambridge University Press, 1993.

Southern, R. W. *Saint Anselm: A Portrait in a Landscape.* Cambridge: Cambridge University Press, 1991.

Speaight, R. *Teilhard de Chardin: A Biography.* London: Collins, 1967.

Spencer, N. *Darwin and God.* London: SPCK, 2009.

Tanner, N. ed. *Decrees of the Ecumenical Councils.* Washington, DC: Georgetown University Press, 1990.

Teilhard de Chardin, P. *Activation of Energy.* London: Collins, 1970.

———. *Christianity and Evolution.* London: Collins, 1971.

———. *The Heart of the Matter.* London: Collins, 1978.

———. *Le milieu divin.* London: Collins, 1960.

———. *The Phenomenon of Man.* London: Collins, 1965.

Tennant, F. R. *The Origin and Propagation of Sin.* Cambridge: Cambridge University Press, 1902.

Theissen, G. "Evolution." In *Christianity: The Complete Guide,* ed. J. Bowden, 448–52. London: Continuum, 2005.

Trent, Council of. Decrees, DS 1500–1835. In *Decrees of the Ecumenical Councils,* ed. N. Tanner, vol. 2, 660–799. Washington, DC: Georgetown University Press, 1990.

Trigg, R. "Theological Anthropology." In *Companion Encyclopedia of Theology,* ed. P. Byrne and L. Houlden, 453–71. London, Routledge, 1995.

Vandervelde, G. *Original Sin: Two Major Trends in Contemporary Roman Catholic Reinterpretation.* Washington, DC: University Press of America, 1981.

Van Melsen, A. "Natural Law and Evolution." *Concilium* 6 (June 1967): 24–29.

Vatican Council II, Constitutions and Decrees. In *Decrees of the Ecumenical Councils,* ed. N. Tanner, vol. 2, 820–1135. Washington, DC: Georgetown University Press, 1990; W. M. Abbott, *The Documents of Vatican II.* London: Geoffrey Chapman, 1965.

Viviano, B. T. "The Gospel according to Matthew." In *The New Jerome Biblical Commentary,* 630–74. London: Chapman, 1989.

Von Balthasar, Hans Urs. *Dare We Hope "That All Men Be Saved"?* San Francisco, CA: Ignatius Press, 1988.

Von Rad, G. *Genesis: A Commentary.* 2nd revised ed. London, SCM, 1963.

Ward, K. "Christian Ethics," In *Keeping the Faith: Essays to Mark the Centenary of Lux Mundi,* ed. G. Wainright, 224–49. London: SPCK, 1989.

———. *God, Chance and Necessity.* Oxford: Oneworld, 1996.

Weld, A. "The Philosopher among the Apes." *Month* 15 (July 1871): 71–101.

Wendel, F. *Calvin: The Origins and Development of His Religious Thought.* London: Collins, Fontana, 1974.

Westermann, C. *Genesis.* Edinburgh: T. & T. Clark, 1988.

Whitehead, A. N. *Process and Reality: An Essay in Cosmology.* Cambridge: University Press, 1929.

Wiedenhofer, S. "The Main Forms of Contemporary Theology of Original Sin." *Communio* 18 (Winter 1991): 514–29.

Wiles, M. *The Making of Christian Doctrine: A Study of the Principles of Early Doctrinal Development.* Cambridge: Cambridge University Press, 1967.

Williams, P. A. *Doing without Adam and Eve: Sociobiology and Original Sin.* Minneapolis, MN: Fortress Press, 2001.

Williams, R. "Eucharistic Sacrifice: The Roots of a Metaphor." Grove Liturgical Studies no. 31. Bramcote: Notts, 1982.

Wilson, E. O. *Sociobiology: The New Synthesis.* Cambridge, MA: Harvard University Press, 1976.

Wright, N. T. *Christian Origins and the Question of God.* Vol. 2, *Jesus and the Victory of God.* London: SPCK, 1996.

Yarnold, E. *The Theology of Original Sin.* Cork: Mercier, 1971.

General Index

Scriptural Index